EARLY CHILDHOOD EDUCATION SERIES
Leslie R. Williams, Editor

ADVISORY BOARD: Barbara T. Bowman, Harriet K. Cuffaro, Stephanie Feeney, Doris Pronin Fromberg, Celia Genishi, Stacie G. Goffin, Dominic F. Gullo, Alice Sterling Honig, Elizabeth Jones, Gwen Morgan

(continued)

Educating and Caring for Very Young Children

THE INFANT/TODDLER CURRICULUM

Second Edition

DORIS BERGEN, REBECCA REID, AND LOUIS TORELLI

Foreword by Bettye Caldwell

Teachers College, Columbia University
New York and London

Published by Teachers College Press, 1234 Amsterdam Avenue, New York, NY 10027

Excerpts from NAEYC Accreditation Standards in Part II are from NAEYC (2005), *NAEYC Early Childhood Program Standards and Accreditation Criteria: The Mark of Quality in Early Childhood Education*, Washington, DC: Author. Reprinted with permission from the National Association for the Education of Young Children.

Library of Congress Cataloging-in-Publication Data

Bergen, Doris.
    Educating and caring for very young children : the infant/toddler curriculum / Doris Bergen, Rebecca Reid, and Louis Torelli ; foreword by Bettye Caldwell.—2nd ed.
      p. cm.
    Includes bibliographical references and index.
    ISBN 978-0-8077-4920-3 (pbk.)
1. Early childhood education—Curricula—United States. 2. Child care—United States. 3. Play—United States. 4. Child development—United States. 5. Individualized instruction—United States—Case studies. I. Reid, Rebecca. II. Torelli, Louis. III. Title.
    LB1139.4.B47 2009
    372.19—dc22   2008024048

ISBN 978-0-8077-4920-3 (paperback)

Printed on acid-free paper

Manufactured in the United States of America

16 15 14 13 12 11 10 09   8 7 6 5 4 3 2 1

The second edition of our book is dedicated to Professor Leslie Williams, who was a member of the department of Curriculum and Teaching at Teachers College Columbia for the past 33 years. Dr. Williams cofounded the Rita Gold Center on that campus, which provides excellent educare for children 3 months to 5 years. As coeditor of the Early Childhood Education series for Teachers College Press, she was an early supporter of our first edition. She also provided 6 years of leadership for the Journal of Early Childhood Teacher Education. *She will be remembered for her teaching and scholarship, leadership in early childhood education, and advocacy for excellence in educare for all young children.*

Contents

Foreword

In the first edition of this volume, I wrote that for those who have looked for a book that helps to bring the development of infants and toddlers into the conceptual architecture of education generally assumed to be applicable only to older children, the wait was over. I am pleased that this second edition remains true to its original concept of "A Curriculum for Infants and Toddlers," while fully aware that such terminology continues to wave a red flag in front of many people. It does so without in any way endorsing a strategy that would jeopardize the needs of very young children for supportive and nurturant care by parents and persons outside the family. It continues to be a seminal text purporting to help train adults—educarers—to design environments capable of melding education and care into a unified process: educare. As one who has urged these terms on the field for over a quarter of a century, I am delighted that this creative group of authors has continued to advocate for the concepts that underlie the terms and, by using them freely in this excellent book, helped them come trippingly off the tongue and not sound merely like a catchy dot-com–like phrase used to identify an avant-garde website.

In a number of papers (see Caldwell, 1991) and countless talks given to early childhood groups across the country, I have urged adoption of these terms—not because I especially like neologisms, but because the old terms we have in this field are barnacled with negative connotations and literally retard progress in the field. Although this is primarily true of the *care* side of the new term ("It's just baby-sitting, isn't it?"), the *edu* side is not exempt ("Hey, the schools are ruining our big kids; let's not let them do that to our little kids also"). Because of the persistence of these negative ideas, it continues to be difficult to develop the kind of social policy that would guarantee adequate financial support for a comprehensive network of high-quality programs integrating education and care into a cohesive and unified service.

So it is now even more important to use this new terminology based on new concepts; of the two, the latter are more important. A new concept—now widely accepted even by people who cling to the old terminology—is that the service we see, use, or provide, is never either education or care: It is always both. When we are dealing with very young children, we cannot educate them without simultaneously providing nurturant care. To proclaim or advertise otherwise is simply to mislead.

Not only does the term *educare* make good sense linguistically, but it also offers another advantage—that is, a new name for a field offers a promise that a new service has been created. This service is not only different from, but better than, previous services. And that is the message we want to embrace for our infants in this new century. The educare they receive will be more helpful to them than the old either-or pattern of service that was available to their forbears.

And in its second edition, this book will continue to help. It is a splendid book in every way. The rationale given for using the term *curriculum* when writing about infant-toddler programs—anathema to many people—is logical and persuasive. The curriculum areas chosen as anchor points—knowledge construction, social and emotional relationships, and play development—are wise and well-grounded in empirical child development research. For those who want to skip the details of some of the research, this is possible; for those who want citations, they are there. This separation makes for much smoother reading than is currently possible for much of our professional writing, which tends to interrupt the semantic flow of many of the sentences with multiple parentheses listing authors and dates.

The authors recognize that the development of programs for infants and toddlers (or for children of any age, for that matter) is really a matter of environmental design. By introducing the reader to real children of different developmental stages who live in families that have different values and resources, the authors reveal the infrastructure upon which the educare environment can build. And for this building process suggestions, not prescriptions, are offered. Such an approach is developmentally appropriate and intellectually sound. And it shows respect for the people who will provide the recommended pattern of service. Educarers of all levels of experience and training will respond favorably to this show of respect, a manifestation of public support not always available to them.

The field of educare, and the countless numbers of children who use its services, will continue to benefit from the efforts of Bergen, Reid, and Torelli to help guide us all through the 21st century with new concepts, new terminology, and new optimism.

—*Bettye Caldwell*

Acknowledgments

The authors wish to thank the 24 families who shared stories about their young children's development, permitted videotaping, and provided photographs. Without their cooperation and interest, this book would not have been possible. Because of their assistance, prospective educarers will understand that every child is unique and worthy of their special attention. We also wish to thank all the readers of our first edition who have made it possible for a second edition to be published.

The Meaning of Curriculum for Infants and Toddlers

JASON IS A 7½-month-old with fine blond hair and alert blue eyes. His mother can tell by his expressions and body language where he wants to go and what he wants to touch. Jason enjoys rattles and other sounds, especially those he makes himself. He seeks different textures to explore, such as bricks and other surfaces. He has become more adventurous since he began scooting around on his stomach. He loves repetitive social games when he can predict what will happen next. A favorite pastime with his father is "roughhouse." His mother's only concern is that he is just beginning to sit alone, something she expected would come sooner, given his early signs of muscular strength.

Jason's mother says he needs a secure base in her arms from which to warm up to people he doesn't know. It took him a week to feel comfortable with his home educarer, but he is now open and friendly with her and her family. Mom wants his educarer to be aware of her son's unique personality and needs. He doesn't like sudden, loud noises and is a light sleeper. Motion calms him so that he can fall asleep. When he cries, it means he needs something, so if the need cannot be met right away, he should be comforted until it can be met. His mother wants his educarer to respond to his social needs, understand his tendency to be cautious, and know that he loves social interactions with familiar people. She wants his name used frequently and would like him to have interesting toys and stimulating experiences.

Given Jason's temperament and developmental level, what should the curriculum be in his educare program? Is there supposed to be a curriculum for infants of Jason's age?

1

W HEN WE WROTE the first edition of this book, which focuses on developmentally and culturally appropriate infant and toddler curriculum, we believed it filled a distinctive need: to demonstrate what curriculum should be for very young children. The traditional definition of curriculum—"the aggregate of courses of study given by a school" (Random House Living Dictionary, 2000)—has never been appropriate for young children. Although programs for 3- to 5-year-olds often define *curriculum* as the sum of all experiences provided in the preschool, this definition was not used for infant and toddler programs because they were not considered "school" (i.e., "educative") experiences.

This perspective has changed greatly as early learning, brain development, and the No Child Left Behind Act have emphasized the importance of experiences during the first 3 years of life. Developmentally and culturally appropriate early learning experiences were also supported in the 1998 legislation for Early Head Start, making it the largest single provider of group programs for infants and toddlers nationally. The four components of Early Head Start—(1) child development, (2) family development, (3) community development, and (4) staff development—broaden the scope of infant and toddler curriculum (Fenichel, Lurie-Hurvitz, & Griffin, 1999). More recently, learning standards for infants and toddlers (e.g., NAEYC, 2007), books with "curriculum" in the title (e.g., Dodge, Rudick, & Berke, 2006; Gonzalez-Mena & Widmeryer, 2003), and funding for infant/toddler programs that emphasize early learning are evident (e.g., see http://www.buffettearlychildhoodfund.org/educare.html).

It is necessary to include both education and care perspectives in the definition of *infant/toddler curriculum*. Past wisdom and professional practice emphasized that very young children require care by warm, nurturing adults who meet their basic needs in a relatively spontaneous and intuitive manner, without focus on planned learning experiences. That is why the terms *caregiver* and *child care* have been prevalent in programs for children under age 3. However, meeting both care and education goals for infants and toddlers is now a societal as well as family responsibility. Both planned and spontaneous educational experiences should begin at the earliest ages.

In our first edition, we embraced the term *educarer* as the appropriate designation for staff members who work in infant/toddler programs. The term, initially coined by Betty Caldwell (see the Foreword), makes clear the combined goals: both care (the long-standing goal) and education (the more recently identified goal). Educarers are concerned equally with both goals, providing curriculum experiences that are developmentally and culturally appropriate for very young children. We have been pleased to see that the term *educare* has now been embraced by a number of foundations, state agencies, and other promoters of programs for infants and toddlers (e.g., http://www.dss.mo.gov/cd/early/educare.htm; http://www.nextdoormil.org/Educare/index.cfm). Thus, people who work in infant and toddler programs are appropriately designated as *educarers*.

REVISING THE DEFINITION OF *CURRICULUM*

When educators of older children develop a curriculum, they identify "learning standards" that are appropriate for age or grade. Recently, learning standards have been identified for infants and toddlers; they use similar terminology but are more broadly stated to meet the needs of very young children. Infant/toddler curricula now address this broader focus, requiring educarers to relate curriculum activities to learning standards.

Curriculum for this age level differs from that of later age levels. For example, Dodge, Rudnick, and Berke (2006) defined *curriculum* as a "framework for pulling all of the pieces of developmentally appropriate practice together" (p. 6). Gonzales-Mena (1997) stressed that curriculum is "a plan for learning . . . [that is] really everything that happens in the program" (p. 43). Lally et al. (2003) described a responsive curriculum that emphasizes, first, careful observation of individual children's interests and needs, and second, planning learning environments that support child-initiated learning. Gerber (1991) called this approach "relationship-building and respectful" of young children, while Surbeck and Kelley (1991) termed it "personalized" care. Sexton, Snyder, Sharpton, and Stricklin (1993) emphasized that this curriculum must include young children with special needs and their families.

Our definition of *curriculum* is congruent with the views of these authors. We believe that infant and toddler curriculum should be a dynamic, interactive experience that builds on respect for and responsiveness to young children's interests, curiosity, and motives, and to their families' goals and concerns. Young children are motivated to learn; their curriculum must address physical, social-emotional, and cognitive needs, and be inclusive of children with special needs and varied cultural backgrounds. That is why we use a case approach, emphasizing observing and responding to the curriculum needs of individual children, considering goals and concerns of their families, and promoting learning standards that are identified as important for very young children to achieve.

OVERVIEW OF THE BOOK

This book has three major parts. Part I discusses basic principles of good infant and toddler curriculum in relation to children's early developmental needs. It focuses on play as the basis for curriculum at this age level, while stressing how educarers can meet learning standards within a responsive and play-based environment. Factors in the physical and social environment necessary to foster play-based development and learning are also described. In Part II, case descriptions of actual infants and toddlers, drawn from observations and parent interviews, are provided. These cases foster discussion of how curriculum addresses universal and unique aspects of children's development, as well as learning standards. Part III looks at broader family, community, and societal influences that affect infant and toddler development and learning. It explores ways to enhance curriculum quality for very young children, given conditions that exist in the 21st century.

Part I

BASIC PRINCIPLES OF INFANT AND TODDLER CURRICULUM

SAVANAH IS A sociable baby with a round face; soft, curly brown hair; a wide-eyed expression; and an ever-ready smile. At 31 inches and almost 25 pounds, she is one of the larger 1-year-olds in her educare group.

Savanah is alert to the emotional atmosphere around her and her feelings are hurt easily. When she has discomforting experiences such as getting an immunization shot, she is difficult to console and is not able to calm herself. Her mother says she cries even when her older brother is reprimanded. Savanah demands much adult time and attention, and likes to be held often. At educare, she calls out to potential playmates and approaches them by grabbing their legs and flashing her winning smile.

She is standing on her own and cruising around independently, venturing farther afield. She likes to climb the staircase at home, and despite her sensitivity, she rarely cries when she takes a tumble. Walking and climbing consume much of her attention, but she is beginning to babble actively. She is experimenting with using a spoon, but prefers eating with her fingers. When Savanah engages in unacceptable behavior, her mother tells her "no" first, then removes her from the area after a second warning. Mom worries about whether Savanah's speech is progressing as it should, since Savanah has had persistent ear infections for over 2 months.

Savanah's mother wants her daughter's educarers to be loving and responsive to her needs, to teach Savanah to adjust to others and learn to interact well with them, and to be aware of the skills she is currently mastering. She wants educarers to "do more for Savanah than I am able to do at home."

How can educarers meet the expectations of Savanah's mother? Given Savanah's present cognitive, social-emotional, and play skills, what are appropriate curriculum activities and what should her educare environment be like?

PART I discusses essential elements of curriculum for young children and environmental design factors that implement that curriculum. The infant and toddler curriculum is not framed within traditional content fields, but rather is based on the developmental needs and strengths of very young children. Therefore, we define *curriculum* as the provision of the optimum learning environment. While we make clear how this curriculum relates to traditional content fields and early learning standards, we stress that there should be no formal teaching of standards. Citing knowledge gained from early brain research, Thompson (2006) confirms that for infants and toddlers, "Learning is not primarily a matter of imparting knowledge, but rather of the child's active construction of understanding from experience" (p. 49).

Because infant/toddler professionals must be both educators and caregivers, we use the term *educarers* to refer to those who plan and implement responsive curriculum for young children (see Mangione, 2006). It is imperative that you see yourself as an educarer, not only a caregiver, because you must consider that both education and care are vitally important. In reading this book, you will learn to reflect upon your present practices and expand, revise, and add new behaviors to your repertoire; gain further knowledge about young children's development and learning; and understand why the responsive play-based curriculum supports such learning.

In Chapters 1 and 2, we describe infant and toddler educare within a curriculum framework that is theoretically sound, responsively based, highly practical, and thoughtfully individualized. It is grounded in the rich research base amassed in the past 25 years, drawing especially on research from the last 10 years. (Studies are described in the Research Notes accompanying Chapter 1.) The research is also connected to present learning standards. Our goal is to prepare educarers who can provide the optimum in environments for very young children and articulate the importance of such environments to families, other professionals, and society as a whole.

Play as the Medium
for Curriculum

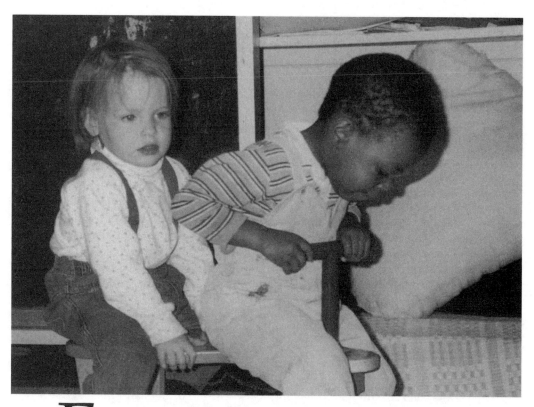

For almost 20 years, policy rhetoric in the United States has had a stated goal that all children should be "ready to learn" by kindergarten age (Task Force on Education, 1990). More recently, promoted by federal legislation (the No Child Left Behind Act of 2001), the emphasis initially focused on elementary and high school student learning of specifically identified skills has extended downward into early childhood. As a result, articulated learning standards and "evidence-based" approaches have greatly affected traditional preschool (age 3–5) curriculum and teaching methods. Identification of such standards for children ages 0–3 has now been achieved as well (NAEYC, 2007). Although these standards try to preserve a developmentally sound focus, voices have expressed concern that time for play is being threatened (e.g., Ginsburg, 2007). The author of this document states that "Play is integral to the academic environment" (p. 182). Thus, it is imperative that the case for play as the medium for the infant/toddler curriculum must be reemphasized. Every adult who has spent time with infants knows that they come into the world already demonstrating an eagerness for learning. They are "ready to learn" even before they are born! Newborn infants have learned to recognize their mothers' voices while they are still in the womb (Spence & DeCasper, 1987). Brain research makes clear how vital the early years are in forming neural pathways between brain cells (neurons) and their connecting links (synapses):

> At birth, an infant brain has about 100 billion neurons—nearly enough to last a lifetime. Each one can produce up to 15,000 synapses. The first three years of life are when the vast majority of synapses is produced.The number of synapses increases with astonishing rapidity until about age three. . . the child's brain becomes super-dense, with twice as many synapses as it will eventually need. In the second decade of life, most of these excess synapses are eliminated. Brain development is, then, a process of pruning. This is why early experience is so crucial: those synapses that have been activated frequently by repeated early experience tend to become permanent. (Shore, 1996, pp. 11–12)

Thus, the types, varieties, and intensities of experiences that young children encounter are very important for brain development.

Positron emission tomography (PET) scan images of the brains of newborns show that although the neurons are present in the neonate brain, many of those in the higher brain centers (e.g., the cortex) are not densely connected and active. The "lower brain," which regulates sleeping, breathing, and other vital functions, and the sensory areas (e.g., vision) show the most activity. By the end of the first year, in terms of activity centers, 1-year-old infants' brains look almost like the brains of adults, with all areas functioning (Chugani, 1995, 1997). Brain weight doubles, from 1 pound at birth to 2 pounds by age 2, because of the expansion of glia cells, which encase the neurons in fatty sheaths (myelin) that enable electrical and chemical messages to travel quickly through the neural networks. By age 2, the brain has 70% of its adult weight (and 90% by age 6).

Human infants are not physically mature at birth, so they spend much of their first few months of life learning how to adapt their basic survival behaviors to caregiving routines. They develop internal regulation of processes that govern behaviors such as eating and sleeping. They learn to understand the external world through visual, auditory, and other senses. They observe faces and objects intently, locate sounds in space, react to and recognize odors, respond to touch, and discriminate tastes. These rudimentary skills are combined in sensory modes (e.g., both sight and sound). They respond to social-emotional cues and examine object properties through physical actions. They exhibit intense and extended interest in novel stimuli.

As synaptic connections expand during the toddler years, toddlers' early language gives clues to how they organize thinking and try to understand their experiences and "construct knowledge." The knowledge they construct during the first 3 years of life forms the basis for later learning of "academic" subjects such as mathematical reasoning and literacy skills. Infants and toddlers are active designers of their own curriculum as they explore their environment. Their playful interactions with that environment are the medium through which they make sense of their world. Although all children share universal developmental achievements, they also have temperament differences that influence their style of exploration and interaction with objects and people, and, thus, their reactions to curriculum experiences.

In a classic longitudinal study, Chess and Thomas (1989) identified temperament characteristics on which children may differ:

1. Level and extent of motor activity
2. Regularity of basic functions (sleeping, eating)
3. Withdrawal from or acceptance of new stimuli
4. Adaptability to environmental changes
5. Sensitivity level to stimuli
6. Energy intensity of responses
7. General mood or disposition
8. Distractibility potential
9. Attention span and persistence in activity

They combined these characteristics into three temperament types:

- "Easy" children (40%) were positive in mood, regular in functions, adaptable, and only moderately intense in reactions, with an approachable response to new situations.
- "Difficult" children (10%) were negative in mood, irregular in sleeping and eating patterns, slow to adapt, very intense in reactions, and tended to withdraw in new situations.
- "Slow to warm up" children (15%) had low activity levels and low intensity of reactions, but were slow to adapt and likely to withdraw in new situations.

The other 35% of infants combined temperament qualities. Thomas and Chess learned which child-rearing and educational practices were effective with each temperament type. They found that some temperaments changed as children grew older, and suggested that development is influenced by both the environment and the child's characteristics. They state, "If the two influences are harmonized, one can expect healthy development of the child; if they are dissonant, behavioral problems are almost sure to ensue" (Thomas, Chess, & Birch, 1997, p. 93).

As an educarer, you will have many opportunities to observe child temperament/environment interactions and to vary the curriculum to provide the best environments for children of all temperaments. Many temperament factors can be observed in different styles of children's play.

WHY PLAY SERVES AS THE MEDIUM FOR CURRICULUM

In recent years, the role of play in some programs for young children has been diminished, as adults embraced direct teaching of learning standards. Sometimes a curriculum labeled "play-based" now involves adults teaching specific skills through structured "funlike" activities or requiring all children to perform the same learning tasks. That type of "work disguised as play" is not developmentally appropriate for an infant/toddler curriculum (Bergen, 1998, 2006). Rather, young children's freely chosen play should be the medium through which their development and learning occur. If the environment provides sufficient variety of experiences through the play, young children's learning will be greatly enhanced. A medium can be defined as "the natural habitat of an organism" (Bergen, 1998, p. 8), and play is the "natural habitat" of young children. Play also serves as a communications channel between adults and children, provides the creative material through which they organize and understand their experiences (i.e., "construct knowledge"), and determines the context for their social-emotional development. In order to articulate the learning standards being advanced through play, educarers must understand how play serves as young children's medium for constructing knowledge.

CONSTRUCTING KNOWLEDGE THROUGH PLAY

Although the first years of life were once thought to be empty of educational value, brain research has uncovered a wealth of information on early cognitive processes. For example, Epstein (1978) found that spurts in brain growth correspond to stages of cognitive development identified by Piaget (1952). The first spurt occurs at 18 to 24 months (the beginning of the preoperational stage), when representational thought and language begin. Other researchers have found that early learning processes are similar to those human beings use to construct knowledge throughout life: attention; motivation; imitation and elaboration; habituation; discrimination, categorization, and concept development; memorization; and intermodal coordination. These basic learning modes must be well developed to foster later learning of content knowledge and skills.

Attention

From the first months of life, young children attend to the sights, sounds, and other sensory stimuli that they experience. A common behavior that adults often remark upon is the intensity of infants' gaze upon human faces when they are being held. Infants also attend to moving objects, simple geometric shapes, contrasting colors, and, of course, to sounds, tastes, smells, and touches (see Research Note 1.1). This early ability to attend to such stimuli blossoms into actions that create stimuli; for example, infants produce and watch movements of their own hands and feet. Infants also increase their attention span through their playful manipulation of objects and people in their world. Play extends their attention span by enabling them to increase the novelty of their environment through their own actions. Toddlers show great ability to attend to self-chosen activities, and by age 3, many spend long periods of time in play alone or with others. They attend well to activities that they have chosen, however, rather than activities chosen by

Research Note 1.1. Infants of 4 months can categorize colors and fixate on color even if the background is in the same color category. They fixate more quickly on colors with contrasting backgrounds, implying that infant color recognition is a perceptual process (Franklin, Pilling, & Davies, 2004). Children from two language groups whose language terms segment color differently both perceived color categories similarly (Franklin et al., 2005).

adults. Because the ability to attend and to sustain attention is important for all types of learning, a curriculum that supports young children in learning to attend, lengthen, and control attention helps them meet all types of learning standards.

Educarers can play an important role in helping young children increase their attention spans by being good observers of their natural interests and providing accessible and responsive materials that engage them in exploring their interests. To encourage concentrated periods of play, you can vary the environment to keep it interesting, call attention to novel stimuli in the environment, and play with children who need encouragement to attend for longer periods.

You should avoid frequent interruptions when children are attentively engaged in self-directed play because allowing enough time for in-depth play experiences will increase their attention spans. Your scaffolding of peer and adult interaction will also increase their attention span.

Motivation

Discussions of how to enhance school learning often focus on self-motivation and strategies to increase the motivation of learners. With infants and toddlers, motivation for learning does not need to be externally induced. Unless young children have an illness or disability that impairs their opportunities to act on their environment, they constantly exhibit a motivation for learning. They are motivated to sit, stand, and walk; to make sounds and communicate through gestures and words; to learn the properties of objects; to interact with animals and people; and to solve self-defined problems. Some researchers call this "mastery motivation" and suggest that there may be individual differences in how much motivation is directed to object mastery or to social mastery (see Research Note 1.2). Because young children's motivation for learning is so great, sometimes adults become "worn out" answering their questions, responding to their interests, and facilitat-

Research Note 1.2. Wachs (1993) found that 55% of 12-month-olds had social mastery motivation and 45% had object mastery motivation. Twenty-four-month-olds whose mothers positively evaluated their attempts at mastery of a challenging task were more persistent at challenges at 36 months (Kelley, Brownell, & Campbell, 2000). Typically developing infants increased mastery behavior between 6 and 12 months and again between 18 and 24 months, while infants with Down syndrome increased mastery behavior during the 12 to 18 month period (Dayus, Glenn, & Cunningham, 2000).

Research Note 1.3. Eighteen- to 24-month-olds who were given novel objects and shown either pretense or instrumental actions with the objects used similar imitative patterns, suggesting that both involve cultural learning; they looked longer during demonstrated pretense actions, indicating that pretense is a more social, intersubjective activity (Rakoczy, Tomasello, & Strianer, 2005) Two-year-old twins' imitative ability was related to their vocabulary, pretend play, and social behavior, but there were both genetic and environmental individual differences (McEwen et al., 2007).

ing ways for them to investigate problems they identify. Because later learning of educational content requires a high level of internal motivation, all efforts should be made to encourage motivational strengths.

An educarer needs to be responsive to children's motivational signals when planning curriculum activities. With children who have difficulty expressing their motivational intent (e.g., a physically disabled child who cannot show a desire to touch or play with a toy), your ability to read more subtle motivational signals such as eye contact or body tension is crucial. Because play, by its very nature, is an internally motivated activity, learning through play is highly motivating for all children. Play contributes to children's "learning set"; that is, children see learning as an enjoyable activity and, thus, want to learn more and more. When young children are motivated to try difficult tasks (e.g., dressing themselves), you can provide encouragement and assistance rather than "taking over" the task, and you can acknowledge their efforts, even when the result is only partially successful.

Imitation and Elaboration

Research demonstrates that even young infants imitate behaviors if they are within the infants' range of skills. For example, they will thrust out their tongue after seeing an adult perform this behavior. Infants practice imitation skills frequently, and they are quite adept at imitation, even delayed imitation, by the toddler age period. After they have performed an imitated behavior a number of times, they do not continue to repeat it exactly. Instead, they add variations, elaborating upon the behavior they practiced through imitation and individualizing their style of response. For example, they laugh at sound or language patterns, repeating them over and over with increasing variations. Piaget (1952) described imitation as accommodation, a behavior through which infants attempt to reproduce what they have observed. He called the playful elaborative behaviors that result after initial imitation assimilation, the process of shaping new experiences into existing cognitive schemes (see Research Note 1.3). Both imitation and play are essential for constructing knowledge; imitation is an initial catalyst for learning, and elaboration through play is the means by which that learning is mastered. Skills that are needed to meet learning standards are often imitated by young children before they focus on specific learning tasks.

When you as an educarer observe the kinds of behaviors young children are imitating and the ones they elaborate in play, you learn much about their thinking

---

Research Note 1.4. Habituated 4- to 5-month-old infants looked longer at novel direct gaze faces than at averted gaze faces, indicating that the direction of the gaze modulates face recognition in young infants (Farroni, Massaccesir, Menon, & Johnson, 2007). Infants of 2, 4, and 6 months who were habituated to faces and voices of same gender adults and to mismatched face/voices discriminated the two conditions at 4 and 6 months but not at 2 months (Bahrick, Hernandez-Reif, & Flom, 2005). Infants with slower thresholds of auditory processing at 6-9 months (measured by habituation) predicted language impairments at age 3 (Benasick & Tallal, 2002).

---

processes. One of the best ways for you to know what children have mastered is to watch their elaborations. The more varied ways they perform actions or verbal patterns, the more likely it is that they are mastering them. Because children are such good imitators, you also must remember that they learn ways to express their behaviors and feelings from their adult models. For example, if you look at picture books with infants, by the time they reach toddler age, they will already have mastered the print awareness skills of page turning, picture looking, and story narrative, all of which are essential for later reading skill.

Habituation

When infants are initially exposed to a sensory stimulus, they attend to that stimulus intently. If it is an abrupt stimulus, such as a loud noise, or an aversive stimulus, such as a pinprick, they may cry and actively withdraw. They stare at many types of visual stimuli. It seems as though they are trying to absorb the information in that stimulus. If the same stimulus is repeated often, however, they respond less strongly, and over time their response becomes minimal. They have learned what that stimulus signifies, and no longer respond to it as a novelty. The ability to habituate to a stimulus—that is, to become familiar with it and thus to minimize response to it, is an important human ability that is a root aspect of learning. Human beings are constantly bombarded by sights, sounds, and other sensory information. If they could not "tune out," (i.e., habituate) to stimuli, they would be in a constant state of turmoil. Infants are so good at habituating that their ability to do so is a measure used in one of the earliest tests of typical development (Brazelton, Nugent, & Lester, 1987). Measures of habituation are often used to discern what infants can discriminate, what they have learned, and what they remember (see Research Note 1.4). During play, young children interact with many types of stimuli and learn when to give attention and when to ignore stimuli. Habituation is really an example of learning because it means that the child has already understood the meaning of that particular stimulus. It is a signal that the child is ready for a higher learning skill.

An educarer should note that when infants or toddlers no longer pay attention to particular "favorite" toys, it is an indication that they have already learned what they needed to know from that toy and need to have the educarer provide more novelty, either by demonstrating another use for the toy or combining that

Research Note 1.5. Newborns are able to demonstrate discrimination of unfamiliar and familiar voices, using sucking responses (Floccia, Nazzi, & Bertoncini, 2000). Infants of 6 months begin to form abstract categorical representations of spatial relationships independent of specific objects, but as infants acquire spatial language, it aids them in forming categories (Casasola, 2008). Six- to 9-month infants who had difficulty discriminating auditory cues were more likely to have language impairments at age 3 (Benasick & Tallal, 2002).

toy with others, perhaps using the toy in a pretend sequence. In a responsive environment, all educarers are attuned to the habituation signals that children give and know that they should vary the environment to maintain moderate levels of novelty, because that is when the most elaborated play and learning occur.

Discrimination, Categorization, and Concept Development

A basic characteristic of humans is the ability to make sense out of the continuous flow of stimuli that they receive. Infants observe which sensory experiences are different and similar, and cluster their experiences with objects and actions into categories, thus attempting to organize those experiences meaningfully. According to Greenspan (1989), categorization is shown first in infants' differential emotional responses to family members. He views emotions and cognition as intertwined in learning, and brain research confirms this view (Perry, 1994; Perry, Pollard, Blakley, Baker, & Vigilante, 1995). Studies observing infants' action schemes show the impressive development of early discrimination and categorization ability (see Research Note 1.5). The ease with which young children learn to discriminate and categorize suggests that these are naturally occurring cognitive processes. By observing children's "mistakes" (e.g., calling all furry animals "dog"), adults can monitor young children's concept development and provide help in linking individual discriminations into categories or broader concepts. Vygotsky (1962) described the "zone of proximal development" (ZPD) as the space between what children can do without assistance and what they can learn to do with a small amount of assistance. Adults can provide "scaffolding" (Wood, Bruner, & Ross, 1976) in which they help children learn within their zone of proximal development. Scaffolding helps children move from assisted to independent performance (see Research Note 1.6). These skills are exceptionally important for learning in

Research Note 1.6. By 14 to 18 months, children remembered three-step behavior sequences modeled by adults and peers both immediately and 1 week later, but those imitating peers remembered better (Ryalls, Gul, & Ryalls, 2000). Mothers actively scaffold social conversations with 2- and 3-year-olds (Ensor & Hughes, 2008). English mothers' gestures accounted for 29% of total communication behaviors in free play and a counting task with their 20-month-old children; thus, gestures as well as speech are used in scaffolding child communication (O'Neill, Bard, Linnell, & Fluck, 2005).

Research Note 1.7. Rovee-Collier (1997) reported that 4-month-old infants placed in a special crib remembered to kick to move a object; however, if the setting differed, they did not remember. When deferred imitation was investigated (Barr, Rovee-Collier, & Campanella, 2005), 6-month-old infants could remember and imitate modeled actions (either active replication or passive watching actions) both 1 day and 10 days afterward. If they repeatedly retrieved the memory, they could imitate the action after 1½ months and generalize the action, supporting the role of repeated events in increasing infant knowledge.

---

content fields such as mathematics, literacy, science, and social studies.

As an educarer, you can closely observe what children already know and what they still have trouble doing, and decide what help they need from you to discriminate between categories and broaden concepts. For example, when a child can identify pictures of a cat and dog, you might say, "Cats and dogs are both animals. Can we find some more animals?" You can give children opportunities for active manipulation of a wide range of objects; talk about the features of objects and actions; use categorical names for groups of objects; and point out similarities and differences in actions, spatial locations, and people. Such scaffolding techniques will assist early concept development, which is essential for later content learning.

Memorization

Early theorists did not think infants had much memory capability; however, recent research shows that infants can demonstrate long-term memories in some situations. Infants can remember to perform an action when they are in an environment where they have performed that action before, can remember where objects have been placed at an earlier time, and can do "delayed" imitation, performing an action they saw after a period of time has past. Research on infant memory has expanded adults' understanding of the importance of early experiences and the long-term learning stored in memory during the first years. Repetition that occurs during children's play with objects may contribute to memory ability (see Research Note 1.7). When young children acquire language, they can demonstrate their memory capability more easily, often recalling things with a photographic-like memory. Toddlers remember labels of objects, repeat the language of stories read to them, recite poems, and sing songs. By late toddler age, these types of memory displays are common occurrences, and children show in pretend play that they have memorized sequences and styles of certain social scripts, such as "going to bed" and "talking on the telephone." Memory skill development provides children with excellent learning skills because much learning requires the use of memory strategies.

As an educarer, you can encourage children to enact pretend sequences and give them opportunities to respond to and repeat stories, poems, and songs. Because emotional and cognitive development are closely tied at this age, children are likely to remember events and concepts that have highly charged emotional content. Not all memories are good; children's fears may be traced to events that

Research Note 1.8. Infants show initial intermodal coordination at 6 months. Five- to 7-month-olds could match videotaped faces and voices by looking longer at the correct face (Bahrick, Nettor, & Hernandez-Reif, 1998). They preferred children's faces. Infants at this age showed intermodal perception, preferentially looking longer at points of light connected to other infants' leg movements, which indicated that they recognize their own leg movements and can coordinate movement and vision (Schmuckler & Fairhall, 2001). They cannot match inverted faces (Bahrick et al., 1998) or their own movements if inverted (Schmuckler & Fairhall, 2001).

have a high charge of negative emotions. To build children's positive memory ability, you can provide warm, playful, and positive emotional interactions when you want children to remember specific types of learning. This creates strong relationship bonds with you and also promotes enhanced memory abilities.

Intermodal Coordination

Although all infant sensory systems function quite well at birth or soon after, infants' ability to coordinate more than one sensory modality (e.g., vision and hearing) develops during the first year. Infants learn to interface vision and touch, recognize movement and speed of objects, and reach for and grasp objects, all of which require intermodal coordination (see Research Note 1.8). Much early infant play provides intermodal coordination experiences. In object exploration, young children may touch, taste, look at, and hear the object. Toddlers learn to coordinate their own bodies in space and to combine a number of sensory modalities in play. Coordination of visual and auditory experiences are particularly important for many types of learning. Because kinesthetic actions are prominent in young children, these can be combined with other sensory experiences to establish firm links with learning content.

You can give young children a wide variety of objects that have differing sensory characteristics, thus allowing them to experience more than one sensory modality at the same time. You can have toys that require them both to look and listen, observe and reach to touch, or touch and listen. By providing a play-rich environment that has many opportunities to practice intermodal coordination skills, you can greatly assist children's development. The higher the level of coordination among sensory modes of learning, the more strongly these associations are made.

Communication and Emerging Literacy

One phenomenal achievement that occurs during these years is the development of a fully functioning communication system. Because most children develop language without specific teaching, some theorists say there may be an innate predisposition for language (Chomsky, 1976). Although actual production of meaningful language usually starts sometime between 9 months and 20 months, even young infants communicate through cries, gestures, and vocalization, and

---

Research Note 1.9. Infants from 4 to 24 weeks produced more speechlike syllabic sounds when their mothers were smiling and they were looking at the mothers' faces (Hsu, Fogel, & Messinger, 2001). Hearing infants exposed to either speech or signs from 6 to 12 months showed specific rhythmic patterns, either in babbling (speech-exposed) or in hand motions (sign-exposed) (Petitio, Molowka, Sergio, Levy, & Ostry, 2003). Infants of 21 months recognized partial words as quickly and reliably as whole words, but were more accurate if they had more than a 100-word vocabulary (Fernald, Swingley, & Pinto, 2001). Eighteen to 23-month-olds had longer eye fixations to pictures with correctly pronounced verbal labels rather than mispronounced labels, demonstrating that familiar words are phonetically well specified before children have large vocabularies (Swingley & Aslin, 2000).

---

parents treat them as "communication partners," involving them in turn-taking verbal and nonverbal interactions. Infants also begin to show understanding of the meaning of language in the latter half of the first year, and indeed, by 12 months they are adept at following simple directions. By 13 months, they typically understand about 50 words. Comprehension ability at 13 to 15 months seems to predict language production ability at 2 to 2½ years. (Nelson, 1973).

Toddlers typically go through a period of one-word or holophrastic speech, in which the word conveys the entire meaning of a thought. For example, "Car" may mean "I want to go in the car," or "I see a car." Adult interpretation of the child's meaning relies on the context in which it is spoken. Telegraphic speech, which leaves out the modifiers ("Go car" might mean "I want to go in the car"), is a common pattern in toddlers. Young children's communication is individual, with some children focusing on object references (e.g., labeling toys) while others are expressive (e.g., naming people and feelings) (Shore, 1997).

As children gain experience with the language symbol system, they make connections between spoken language and the pictures and marks (print) in books. At first, they use physical and visual cues to gain meaning from these symbols; then they connect the sounds of language to symbolic materials. They begin to make their own "marks" in early scribbles, which are precursors of both drawing and writing. In literacy development, there is first a stage of exploration (ages 1–2) and then a stage of emerging literacy (beginning about age 3). The scribble writing of 2-year-olds begins to be prephonemic (making marks that look like letters), and early phonemic writing (making letter marks and labeling their sounds) begins at ages 2½ to 4. Reading requires three "senses" to develop: a sense of story, a sense of print and word, and a sense of letter and sound (Roskos, 1999). Research suggests that children whose emerging literacy develops well have had playful and informal adult interaction around literacy materials from infancy on (IRA/NAEYC, 1998; see Research Note 1.9).

Language and literacy are culturally transmitted and are greatly affected by social interactions. Piaget (1952) says this type of knowledge is "arbitrary"; it is learned by social transmission rather than by action on the physical environment (i.e., it is "social" rather than "physical" knowledge). Therefore, the environment that is provided in the earliest years will influence literacy development at later ages.

As an educarer, you can influence literacy development by serving as a language model, being responsive to young children's communication attempts, and engaging children in playful interaction with literacy materials. When you participate in language-rich play routines, you teach children appropriate communication patterns. When you provide narrative comments on play activities (e.g., "I see you are making a big block tower"), you help children understand the meanings of their actions and the words that explain them. When you look at pictures or books, use rhyming chants, point out letters and names, read and talk about stories, and encourage drawing and scribbling, you further the development of literacy skills identified in learning standards. Ideally, there should be an educarer who speaks the child's native language, but if you do not, you can still engage in warm, responsive communication during these types of activities; value and respond to the child's communication attempts; and work with the family to promote such activities with adults who do speak the native language (Pearson & Mangione, 2006).

DEVELOPING SOCIAL-EMOTIONAL RELATIONSHIPS THROUGH PLAY

Play is also a major factor in infant/toddler development of social and emotional relationships. Much of what children learn in adult-child care and play routines is how to regulate emotions and act in socially appropriate ways. Brain research provides evidence that social-emotional experiences are involved in cognitive processes in an elemental way. For example, the neurotransmitter (a chemical that sends messages through the neurons) cortisol is increased when young children are in stressful situations. A chronically high level of cortisol is related to the destruction of neurons in the hippocampus (a brain area involved in learning and memory). Young children who have stable, nurturing environments are less likely to exhibit cortisol elevation when they encounter stressful situations, while those exposed to abuse and neglect are more likely to have a strong physiological response even to minimal stress (Gunnar & Nelson, 1994; Perry, 1994). Because the brain consists of an interconnected network of neurons, something that affects one area of the brain (e.g., the emotions) also affects other areas (e.g., language, cognition). Theorists and researchers have studied other aspects of social-emotional development, such as how children learn to express emotions, develop trust and attachment, and gain self-confidence in independent and social actions. In recent years, because of increased knowledge about how stress affects brain development, more attention has been paid to the consequences of environmental trauma, such as abuse or neglect, on infant mental health.

Emotional Expression

Researchers have learned much about the range of emotions evident even in the early months of life. Emotional expression seems to have an innate base; it enhances the survival of infants by gaining adult attention and responsive care (Izard, 1980). Neonates show a smilelike expression (not a true social smile), distress, and disgust. By 4 to 6 weeks, the social smile appears. Anger, surprise, joy,

Research Note 1.10. Four-month-old infants' facial expressions showed joy at tickling, sadness at sour taste, and surprise at a jack-in-the-box and masked stranger. Predicted fear to a masked stranger and anger to arm restraint was not demonstrated, raising questions about Izard's differential emotions theory. Individual differences suggest that temperament may influence emotional expression (Bennett, Bendersky, & Lewis, 2002). Dominant emotional expressions may develop over time, explaining why fear is not exhibited until about 7 months (Ackerman, Aber, & Izard, 1998).

and sadness can be seen in infants by the age of 4 months, and fear and shame by 6 to 9 months (see Research Note 1.10). During the second year, contempt and guilt appear, giving young children the same range of major emotional responses that adults show. Greenspan and Greenspan (1985) have identified six stages of emotional development that occur during the first 3 years:

1. Self-regulation of basic emotions
2. Falling in love (e.g., forming an attachment to a caregiver)
3. Developing interactional communication with others
4. Gaining an organized sense of self
5. Creating emotional ideas
6. Using emotional thinking (fantasy)

As an educarer, you need to be aware of the range of young children's emotions and respect the expression of those emotions. Your interactional play with children helps them to increase their emotional range and learn to monitor their own arousal level. You can help children understand emotions by labeling them (e.g., "You are feeling angry [sad, happy] right now"). By understanding early emotional development, you can assist young children in moving positively through these developmental stages. If you observe children whose emotional tone seems depressed, overly tense, or disassociated from environmental conditions, it is important to note this and discuss it with a mental health professional who can investigate potential causes of this emotional disregulation.

Psychosocial and Attachment Development

Early social and emotional development has also been described by Erikson (1963) and Bowlby (1969). Erikson identified two psychosocial developmental crises that occur during the birth to age 3 period: developing trust versus mistrust and developing autonomy versus shame and doubt. According to Erikson, if infants are in relatively predictable, caring environments where their needs are met, they develop the ability to give and receive love and to trust caregivers to be there for them. They show this trust/mistrust dimension both by engaging in positive interactions with family members and educarers and by showing suspicion of unfamiliar adults (e.g., stranger and separation anxiety by 7–10 months). According to Bowlby and his colleague Ainsworth (1979), a secure attachment is formed with primary caregivers during this same age period. The stages of attachment formation are:

1. Preattachment (birth to 6 weeks)
2. Attachment in the making (6 weeks to 6–8 months)
3. Clear-cut attachment (6–8 months to 18–24 months)
4. Reciprocal relationships (after 18–24 months)

Separation anxiety is highest during clear-cut attachment, but by stage 4, children can understand that their relationships are stable and ongoing, and anxiety diminishes. Conditions that produce a strong attachment bond with a primary caregiver are similar to those that produce a trusting infant. If infants have developed trust (Erikson's term) and secure attachment (Bowlby's term) by 12 months, they can enjoy their new mobility by exploring their environment with the knowledge that their "secure base" will remain. When toddlers' trust and attachment are well established, they can then expand their sense of self as autonomous beings (Erikson's autonomy stage) who explore confidently, express their needs clearly, and attempt to control not only their own bodies but also the actions of adults and peers. Through pretend play, they begin to express and master emotional needs.

Although attachment research has focused on child attachment to mothers, fathers and siblings are also important attachment figures, and if there is an extended caregiving family, attachments to those individuals are also made. If children are securely attached in infancy, they are more likely to appear cognitively and socially competent at later ages (see Research Note 1.11). Children who have not achieved a secure attachment may exhibit severe withdrawal, aggressive behaviors, or disorganized emotional control. They may appear consistently anxious in the educare environment and may not be able to risk or try experiences that foster learning because of high anxiety. These behaviors may indicate that there are mental health issues within the child's family or in other life settings,

As an educarer, you facilitate attachment and trust when you provide warm and consistent nurturing and engage in social play routines. Turn-taking play such as "peekaboo" provides good opportunities for strengthening trust and attachment because children can learn to control the emotional interaction. They can form strong attachment bonds to their educarers, and these child-educarer attachments do not interfere with the strength of family-child attachments. Instead, they

---

Research Note 1.11. Synchrony (temporal coordination of micro-level social behavior) with mother and father at 3 months was related to optimal attachment behaviors at 1 year and lower levels of behavior problems at 2 years (Feldman, 2007a, 2007b). Mothers' greater sensitivity to distress of infants at 6 months was associated with increased odds of secure attachment at 15 months (McElwain & Booth-Laforce, 2006). A meta-analysis of parental behaviors in 66 studies found parent/child turn-taking responsive interactions and parental efforts to assure infants of support and reassurance were most associated with infant attachment security (Kassow & Dunst, 2005).

Research Note 1.12. Children of parents who used a mutually responsive relationship style and low-power assertiveness during the first 2 years were more compliant to parent requests and had strong self-regulatory capacities at 52 months (Kochanska, Akan, Prisco, & Adams, 2008). Mothers' and 2-year-olds' talk that had connected turns and references to mental states predicted children's social understanding at age 4 (Ensor & Hughes, 2008).

broaden children's secure base, permitting them to play confidently within the educare environment. You can also facilitate the autonomy needs of toddlers by providing a safe and interesting environment that encourages choices, self-regulation, self-care skills, independent play, and interactions with peers. You can help parents understand how to provide a safe, trusting, and responsive environment at home that allows their children to develop autonomy.

Prosocial and Social Cognitive Development

Through social interactions with adults and peers, young children gain a sense of themselves as separate beings and an understanding of social rules of behavior, such as turn-taking and sharing. By the age of 4 to 8 months, infants begin differentiating themselves from parents as a "separate self" (and differentiating familiar people from strangers). They have a firm self-identity by age 1. Their sense of self continues to develop from 12 to 18 months, enabling them to show early prosocial behavior such as compliance to adult requests, cooperation in play, and empathy for others. By age 2, they enjoy helping adults with small tasks and like to imitate adult activity (Allen & Marotz, 1999). Motivations for compliance and cooperation are often in conflict with motivations regarding the sense of self (i.e., autonomy), however, as an experience with 2-year-old Connor illustrates. When he resisted complying with his mother's request, she said, "Connor, you need to obey Mommy." He replied, "But Mommy, I need to obey me!" (see Research Note 1.12).

Empathy development begins in infancy with what Feinman (1991) calls "social referencing," which is the ability to perceive the feelings of others and use cues for expressing one's own feelings and interpretations of events. It is demonstrated when infants react with an emotional response similar to one that is being expressed by a family member (e.g., being fussy when Mother is upset). Empathy has both a cognitive and an emotional component (Damon, 1988). Before age 1, infants have only a global sense of empathy; by that age, they have genuine concern but don't know what action to take. You see this empathy when a young toddler is distressed over seeing a peer hurt, but the toddler does not act to help the peer. Between age 2 and 3, children begin to respond effectively when they feel empathy because they see each person as "unique" and can decide what that specific person needs to feel better (e.g., a hug, giving the person an object). By age 3, they show signs of race, gender, and age awareness, and they may show protectiveness to younger children. In pretend play social scripts (e.g., dinnertime), toddlers' developing social cognition is shown in role-taking as play partners with older siblings and peers. Performing a role requires the social cognition skill of perspective-tak-

Research Note 1.13. Mothers who were victims of violence as children were more likely to show psychological aggression toward their 6- and 18-month-old children, and by age 4 the children showed more behavior problems (Thompson, 2007). A meta-analysis of 15 studies of interventions to improve disorganized infant attachment showed that direct sensitivity-focused interventions initiated at about 6 months of infant age were more effective than those focused on parent support and mental representations (Bakerman, Kranenburg, Van Lizendoom, & Juffer, 2005).

ing. Gaining empathy and the ability to know how to act to help another person is also dependent on having "theory of mind," which is the cognitive process of understanding that other people have different thoughts from one's own. The ability to take the perspective of other people is an essential skill that is needed for content learning; this ability develops during the preschool years.

As an educarer, you can best facilitate social cognition and prosocial behavior through involving children in social games (e.g., turn-taking) and pretend play. You should give young children many opportunities to interact with adults and peers in these types of play. For toddlers, you should provide a few social rules of conduct, such as sharing toys, helping to clean up, and lunchtime manners. You can help children understand the meaning of others' social behaviors by providing explanatory comments (e.g., "Jim is crying because you took all of the blocks, and he doesn't have any to play with"), and by modeling prosocial behavior yourself (e.g., saying "Thank you" when a toddler gives you something, or "I'm sorry" if you accidentally bump into her).

Mental Health Development

The previous discussion of methods that educarers can use to enhance infants' social-emotional development is related to the issue of fostering infant mental health. According to Pawl (2006), "Infant mental health is many things. Its essence lies in the child's inner well-being, which has many aspects and comes from many sources" (pp. 74–75). As more becomes known about the risks to infant mental health that may come from parental depression or abusive practices, violent neighborhoods, negligent out-of-home care, and societal traumatic events, mental health development receives increasing attention (see Research Note 1.13).

One major area identified as problematic is "relational trauma," which can harm right brain development, affect regulation, and general mental health (Schore, 2001). Such trauma is believed to result from insecure or disordered attachment development, and it is exhibited in poor regulatory functioning (e.g., disruptive behaviors) by toddler age (Thomas & Clark, 1998). Other trauma-related behaviors include reenactment of the acts in play, using related words or phrases repeatedly, having nightmares or severe emotional distress that disrupts routine activities, anxiety, aggression, impulsivity, extreme or multiple fears, and a loss of developmental gains (Lieberman, 2006). The number of explusions of 3- to 4-year-olds from prekindergarten programs is increasing due to behavior problems (Gilliam, 2006; Perry, Dunne, McFadden, & Campbell, 2008), giving increased attention to mental health issues in infants and toddlers.

As an educarer, you can ameliorate mental health issues through your own consistent, playful, and caring interaction with the children in your care. However, you also need to recognize child behaviors that are associated with mental health issues, suggest to families practices that will promote infant mental health, and learn where and how to refer children to mental health services when their mental health becomes a grave problem. Because children are often with you for many hours during the day, your role in helping them learn how to express their feelings appropriately, gain a trusting and secure attachment to you and to peers, and begin to control their feelings and actions in prosocial ways is extremely important. Thus, you can foster infant mental health through your role as an educarer.

PLAY'S ROLE IN LEARNING

The increased emphasis on learning standards (as well as assessment practices being used in settings for older children) has diminished educarers' understanding of play's role in learning and the importance of play development. Every educare setting should be designed to foster children's play skills. To be good facilitators of a play-based curriculum, educarers need to understand the stages of play development during the infant and toddler years and be knowledgeable about developmentally appropriate ways to facilitate playful learning.

Stages of Play Development

Early Practice Play with Objects

Because play grows out of infants' sensorimotor exploration of their environment, exploration and practice play alternate frequently at this age and are often difficult to distinguish from one another. Infants begin sensorimotor exploration by consistently using a few action schemata (e.g., movement patterns such as mouthing) and using them indiscriminantly with every object they explore. They gradually develop differentiated schemes appropriate to the characteristics of objects (Uzguris & Hunt, 1974). For example, young infants will put a ball, a set of toy keys, and a cup into their mouths, or they will shake both a rattle and a stuffed doll. By 12 months, however, infants' discrimination is shown in their use of a variety of differentiated action schemes. That is, they shake keys, throw balls, and rock dolls. Understandings of successful ways to interact with objects come from models that adults provide, but many are elicited by the "affordances" of the objects themselves (Wachs, 1985). Affordances are combinations of variety, number, and characteristics of objects that invite interaction and signal what types of actions children can do. Objects may have "responsive" elements such as bells or squeaks, pop-up parts, or various-shaped holes that invite children to take certain actions (i.e., shake, hit, pat, or put other objects in them). Children initially explore what

Research Note 1.14. Fathers' sensitive and challenging play during the toddler age predicted adolescents' internal working model of attachment (Grossmann et al., 2002). Mothers' speech and play behavior with 6-, 9-, and 14-month-old males and females showed no difference in the infants' play behavior, but mothers of daughters engaged in conversation and made more interpretations of the play, while mothers of sons gave more instructions and drew attention more. The researchers concluded that different messages are transmitted to sons and daughters (Nelson & Clearfield, 2006).

the objects can do, then repeat these action schema with increasing elaboration. Piaget (1962) called this type of play "practice play." Practice play begins at about 4 months, as soon as infants can act to make an effect such as pressing a lever to hear a resulting noise. During the learning phases of crawling and walking, children often spend most practice play time on those motor skills, engaging in practice play with their own bodies. Practice play is at its height during the period from 9 months to 36 months; thus, it is the major type of self-initiated play for infants and toddlers (see Research Note 1.14).

As an educarer, you can foster young children's mastery of physical, cognitive, and social-emotional skills by giving them many opportunities for practice play. You can provide toys and other objects that can be manipulated in various ways. By carefully planning what the affordances of objects in the environment will be, you provide cues for playful learning. When the curriculum is embedded in the physical environment, it promotes development of "physical and relational knowledge." One concern that has been expressed by observers in some educare environments is that the use of technology-enhanced toys and devices (e.g., swings or mobiles with computer chips that are activated for long periods without adult involvement; toys that sing, talk, or react in other ways) may cut down on adult/child interaction time. Although practice play with objects is important, that play should be interspersed with adult/child interaction. Children should also have access to toys without technology-enhanced affordances, such as blocks, books, puzzles, and baby dolls, because more elaborative play often occurs with these toys.

Early Play with Social Routines/Games

When infants are about 2 months old, they begin to learn through play interactions with parents and educarers. Infants respond to playful turn-taking social routines initiated by adults at about the same time as their social smile appears. When parents and educarers interact using animated facial expressions, close facial contact, open eyes and mouth, and high-pitched and strongly emphasized vocalizations, they communicate to infants the idea that play is a nonliteral activity that occurs within a "playframe" (Sutton-Smith, 1979). These actions that signal "this is play" (Bateson, 1956) seem to be surprisingly easy for infants to understand. Infants show their understanding by exhibiting smiles and laughter, excitement, and interest in repeating the actions. Humor development is also enhanced because the play frame is also a "humor frame" that communicates the joy of play.

Research Note 1.15. Play of resident biological fathers and mothers of diverse cultures who showed sensitive cognitive stimulation, positive regard, and high interaction with toddlers predicted higher scores on cognitive tests at 36 months (Tamis-LeMonda, Shannon, Cabrera, & Lamb, 2004). African American fathers showing nurturance during play, financial support, and positive parenting attitudes had 3-year-olds with cognitive and language competence (Black, Dubowitz, & Starr, 1999). In interactive play with a technology-enhanced toy, child laughter and parent communication was most evident in social game play with the toy's features (Bergen, 2006).

The brief and sporadic play interactions of adult and 3-month-old become highly scripted social routines or "games" by 6 months. Fathers and infants especially enjoy physical games in which the trusted adult carefully moves the child through space. Infants usually laugh delightedly when they are raised higher or lower or pulled up from a lying position to a sitting position. Their anticipation of the adults' actions can be seen in their expectant faces and body preparedness.

By 7 to 9 months, infants give invitational signals themselves and become genuine turn-taking players. A favorite interactive play activity for 9-month-olds is peekaboo, and although this "game" is initiated by adults, by 9 months, the child controls the pace and number of times it is repeated (often too long for the adult's interest span!). Interactive sound play is also enjoyed by infants under age 1, usually in response to adults making strange noises while moving their faces close to the child's face or body.

Bruner and Sherwood (1976) suggest that infants learn a rule pattern of contact-withdrawal-recontact during early social play that is a prototype for later games with rules. Also, young children learn not only about interactive play but also about the general rules for effective social interaction (see Research Note 1.15). Parents typically engage in social games without having had any training, although the extent and quality of playful interactions varies among family members.

Educarers should routinely engage children in such play interactions because they are as important as basic caregiving interactions. You can combine social games with basic care; for example, you can play peekaboo or a mild tickling game while diapering or dressing a child. When educarers have a number of children to care for, they may feel that they do not have time during routine caregiving to take some playful moments. However, the tasks are usually accomplished more easily when play is incorporated in the task. Most important, you should be sure that every child, not just those who are most responsive or appealing, has the enjoyable experience of social game play. Because curriculum is embedded in the social environment, it promotes the development of social knowledge, which is especially important for many later school activities.

Early Evidences of Pretend Play

A fascinating development during the second year is the emergence of pretend play, in which objects, actions, and social roles are transformed from literal to nonliteral states. The earliest glimpses of pretend are often child-imitative actions

Research Note 1.16. When mothers played with 11- to 12-month-old infants, they used pitch height and pitch range to signal play and nonplay; with 15- to 16-month-olds, their variations in pitch engaged children in pretense (Reisland & Snow, 1997). Although children between 19 and 30 months showed a significant increase in pretend play level and meaningful sequences of play, their exploratory style was inconsistent. The researchers concluded that exploration and play measure unique aspects of toddler competence (Rusher, Cross, & Ware, 2002).

fostered by mother, father, or sibling actions, but they soon become child-initiated pretend actions. For example, Mother may pretend to drink from an empty cup, calling its imaginary contents "milk," and the young child then "drinks milk" or pours Mother some "milk" from an empty pitcher. Later, the child replicates these pretend actions spontaneously and elaborates on them.

Simple pretending schemes can be seen in 1-year-olds, especially those who already have a repertoire of "label" words, but they are prevalent in most children by 18 months. Because both language and pretend play are evidence of representational thought, speech production and pretend play usually appear at similar times. Children whose language comprehension is developing well, even if they are not yet producing speech, will respond to adult suggestions to "rock the baby" or "drive the car" (often while making enginelike sounds).

Although the ability to pretend seems to be a naturally occurring development, researchers have found great variation in the amount and depth of pretend that different children exhibit during the toddler age period. Some of that difference may be due to personality characteristics, but it is also influenced by the objects that are available for play and by parental and sibling modeling and facilitating of pretend. Wolf and Grollman (1982) identified two personality types—"patterners" and "dramatists"—whose early play differed in terms of preference for object play or social and pretend play, respectively.

Toddlers can use ambiguous objects in pretend. For example, they may pretend to "eat cake" with a block being the cake instead of needing a realistic cake-like object (Bretherton & Beeghly, 1989). Older toddlers may also use counterconventional objects, such as treating a pan as a baseball bat, and some begin to use imaginary objects.

Mothers, fathers, older siblings, and peers facilitate pretend play in many ways. For example, Miller and Garvey (1984) noted that mothers provide contexts and props, respond positively to child pretend actions, model pretend actions, and interact as play partners. There are cultural differences in the models provided, however (see Research Note 1.16).

As an educarer, you will expect to see only simple types of pretend play in toddlers. However, you should make the facilitation of pretend play a goal and provide replica objects that are likely to elicit early pretend play. You can also encourage elaboration by suggesting pretend actions and modeling such actions. For example, if a child is feeding a doll, you might suggest and demonstrate washing its face, rocking it, and putting it to bed. With your assistance, toddlers can play out simple pretend scripts. They often need your involvement to keep the pretense going, however, especially if a peer is involved in the play.

Facilitating Playful Learning

Educarers can do much to assist young children's play development by setting up a physical and social environment that helps them move from exploration to practice play, provides scaffolding to encourage social games and pretend play, and helps them gain self-efficacy as players. You should promote children's exploration of the object world by having responsive, varied, and novel objects, and by providing time for children to engage in practice play with such objects. Practice play fosters development of complex practice play skills, as well as physical and relational knowledge. By using vocal and visual signals to help infants learn "this is play," modeling play that is slightly advanced for the child's play level (i.e., scaffolding), and transforming objects in interactive pretense, you support children's social and pretend play development. Adults of both genders should engage in social games so that young children learn style differences. As social play increases, you should provide scaffolding for such play with peers. Social play increases children's social knowledge, and it also strengthens their attachment bonds with you. Especially during the toddler years, when children's autonomy develops, play promotes self-efficacy (i.e., the belief that they can achieve desired ends and affect their world), which Bandura (1997) says is important for learning and performance throughout life. When you facilitate children's choices, control, and mastery during play, their self-efficacy is enhanced, forming a base for effective later learning.

USING EARLY LEARNING STANDARDS IN INFANT/TODDLER CURRICULUM

As noted earlier, professional organizations and state education departments have developed early learning guidelines for children from birth to age 3 According to the National Child Care Information Center (2007), 22 states and three territories have adopted and are implementing standards or guidelines for learning outcomes in language, literacy, and math as well as other developmental domains. The National Association for the Education of Young Children (2007) provides specific early learning standards for children from birth through age 8 as part of their early childhood program accreditation. About half of the 63 curriculum standards apply to infants and toddlers/twos. The standards cover social-emotional development, early literacy, language development, physical development, social studies, health and safety, creative expression and appreciation for the arts, science, early mathematics, and technology.

Although the content language of standards (e.g., math, science, social studies) are not usually applied to curriculum for young children, each standard builds on emergent skills that are consistent with infant/toddler development. These can be incorporated easily into educarers' curriculum planning because they are described in broad terms that can fit into various curricular or developmental areas. For instance, a 2-year-old helping to make pudding is developing emergent skills related to health and safety (hand washing, small/large muscle exercise, nutrition), language development (listening to and using words describing the color, flavor, texture, and temperature of pudding), early mathematics ("let's put more milk in the pudding"), and science (discovering that the pudding can be changed from a powder to a liquid state). Some commercial curricula loosely incorporate early learning standards in their design (e.g., Dodge, Rudick, Berke, 2006) and others suggest ways to connect other curricula to specific state guidelines (Gronlund, 2006).

Educarers must use caution, however, when following curriculum guides to ensure that they focus on processes rather than outcomes because these emergent skills develop over time and build on one another. Most important, such experiences must be provided in the context of a playful, respectful, nurturing environment that addresses children's psychosocial needs while building on their interests and curiosity. Educarers need to "consider the source" and be knowledgeable about standards to ensure that they are indeed appropriate for the children with whom they work. They should plan methods to enhance learning and assessment procedures that are consistent with very young children's developmental and cultural needs. In Part II of this book, we include suggested relationships between the NAEYC standards and curriculum ideas.

EVALUATING CHILDREN'S PROGRESS THROUGH THE PLAY-BASED CURRICULUM

A responsive play-based curriculum has always required educarers to be systematic and careful observers of individual children's ability to develop skills, integrate experiences, and construct knowledge. With the present emphasis on achievement of early learning standards, educarers' ability to be competent at assessing the progress of young children has become even more important. The word *curriculum* implies that educarers will try to further goals of learning and development for all children in educare, whatever their age, skills, or temperament. Thus, careful observation of individual children's actions and skills and systematic recording of evidence of their learning progress is essential. (See Chapter 11 in Cohen, Stern, & Balaban, 1997, for detailed information on observation skills.)

Educarers can keep track of the abilities that each child demonstrates independently, those performed with just a little assistance (ZPD range), and those for which great assistance is needed. Abilities in the ZPD range are most likely to improve with educarer facilitation (Bordrova & Leong, 1998). This requires you to engage in consistently "intentional" behavior to meet the needs of very young children. By keeping daily charts of children's independent and assisted play activities, the basic needs you have met, and the learning achievements they exhibit, you will have good information to share with families. You can discuss how the children's home experiences, both basic (e.g., sleeping patterns) and unusual (e.g., Grandma's visit) are related to their learning progress. You should assemble charted information, observational records, and artifacts (e.g., block-building photos; scribbled pictures) into portfolios that show each child's development over time (Apple, Enders, & Wortham, 1998). These records will assist you in individualizing the curriculum to meet the needs of every child while documenting learning. A method of monitoring child progress using an individualized planning profile is shown in Figure 1.1 (adapted from Apple et al., 1998).

FIGURE 1.1 Individualized Planning Profile: Infants and Toddlers

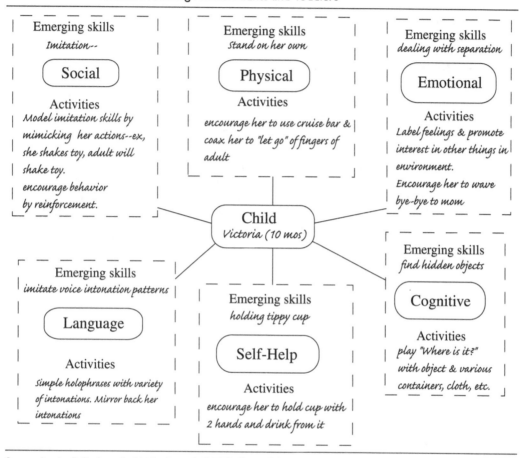

Source: Apple, P., Enders, S., & Wortham, S. (1998). Figure 3.8 from Portfolio assessment for infants, toddlers, and preschoolers: Bridging the gap between data collection and individualized planning (p. 43). In S. C. Wortham, A. Barbour, B. B. Desjean-Perrotta, P. Apple, & S. Enders (Eds.), Portfolio assessment: A handbook for preschool and elementary educators. Olney, MD: Association for Childhood Education International. Reprinted by permission of the authors and the Association for Childhood Education International, 17904 Georgia Avenue, Suite 215, Olney, MD 20832. Copyright © 1998 by the Association.

SUMMARY

The curriculum for infants and toddlers is based on opportunities for active learning through play with objects in the physical environment and with family members, educarers, and peers in the social environment. Infant and toddler development proceeds rapidly through a number of stages, and the learning that is facilitated within a play-based curriculum is extensive and significant. Although there is no one way that play-based curriculum should be structured, examples of curriculum activities that educarers can use to meet the needs of individual children are described in the chapters in Part II, and examples of how they are related to learning standards are given. Further resources for curriculum are listed in Appendix A.

QUESTIONS FOR DISCUSSION

1. What do you think are the most surprising things researchers have uncovered about infant and toddler capabilities, and how does this knowledge affect your thinking about infant and toddler curriculum needs?
2. Why should you tell families that it is important to play with their children, and what kinds of play would you suggest?
3. How would you explain to families that their children are meeting learning standards through the development of their cognitive and social-emotional abilities?

Chapter 2

Designing Play-Based Curriculum Environments

The curriculum for infants and toddlers is especially tied to the physical environment (e.g., arrangement of space, built equipment, objects and materials) and social environment (e.g., number and types of people who are present, their methods of social-emotional interaction) because environmental exploration and play are major educational activities for young children (Torelli & Durrett, 1998). Their environmental exploration (e.g., touching, climbing, crawling, walking) provides not only opportunities for physical skill development, but also cognitive and social-emotional competence. Educarers must plan environments that build upon young children's primary learning modes, evaluate the effectiveness of existing environments, and make changes to enhance environmental quality, by drawing on a basic principle of environmental design.

A PRINCIPLE OF ENVIRONMENTAL DESIGN

In planning appropriate environments, you must consider how that environment may affect the behavior and emotions of children and adults who will spend long periods of time there. Often, much thought goes into the design of business and

home environments, but that attention has not always been paid to environments for young children, partly because they are often located in "found spaces" rather than in spaces built specifically for them. Inappropriately designed environments for young children may range from ones that are garish, overbright, crowded, and noisy to ones that are bland, dull, sparse, and quiet. A good principle for educarers to use in evaluating the appropriate level of environmental stimulation is that it should have a moderate load (Mehrabian, 1976).

Environmental load refers to the rate of information flow and the quantity and intensity of stimuli in particular environments. Very high-load environments include huge, busy airports and megasize shopping malls. These are large-scale, complex, dense, and crowded, and have intermittent and random stimuli. Improbable and surprising events may happen that provide highly novel experiences. Conversely, extremely low-load environments include physicians' individual examining/waiting rooms, prison solitary confinement cells, and private spaces such as bedrooms. The qualities of low-load environments include familiarity, redundance, small scale, simplicity, sparseness, uncrowdedness, and certainty. They typically have continuous, still, or patterned (routine) stimuli.

Environmental load is judged by the balance of novelty and complexity in an environment. Although people vary on the level of each that they desire, in general, most people prefer environments that provide a balance. Environments for children that have a preponderance of very high- or low-load features can induce behaviors that educarers prefer not to see. Environments at either end of the continuum may cause child anxiety and frantic behaviors, over- or underexcitability, passiveness and withdrawal, or extremes of emotional expression. Because stressful environments can actually harm young children's brain development, the educare environment should not add to stresses that children may experience in other settings in their lives. That is why a moderate load is ideal for infant and toddler programs.

Educarers work in a variety of environments, including the children's own homes, family day-care homes, nonprofit and for-profit child-care centers of varying sizes, Early Head Start programs, and specially funded family projects. The moderate load principle of environmental design is an evaluation yardstick for all of them. In a home setting, the load may be high due to the presence of many children and/or adults, blaring televisions, cluttered rooms, and objects of great variety, or it may be low due to a lack of objects to manipulate, little sound (either music or voice), few wall decorations, and the presence of only one child and the educarer. Similarly, an educare center program may have spaces that are too large or too small for children to feel comfortable, too much or too little adult or peer interaction, and either continual changes or unrelieved sameness. If you are in such a setting, you may notice that children have a low quality of exploration and play, and you should determine how to increase or decrease the load appropriately.

This principle of environmental design can help you plan an educare environment that has some high- and some low-load features. Temperament differences may determine the level of load that is optimal for certain children; thus, a child with an "easy" temperament could tolerate a higher load than one who is "slow to warm up." However, because most young children explore space comfortably in moderate-load settings and play attentively with slightly novel toys, a moderate-load environment is preferable. You should have varied and complex materials as well as redundant and simple ones, and you should balance adult interaction time with time alone. Both familiarity and novelty should be present. For infants, the moderate-load environment should create a homelike atmosphere, with familiar qualities of softness combined with some varied novel objects. For young toddlers, a construction area that consistently has large wooden hollow blocks (familiarity), with a variety of accessories such as vehicles, people, animal figures, and signs that can be added and removed (novelty), is a good combination.

In addition to monitoring environmental load, you must also be aware of a number of specific guidelines that have been recommended for high-quality physical and social environments.

QUALITY GUIDELINES FOR PHYSICAL ENVIRONMENTS

The physical environment includes a range of components, including types of materials and equipment available, quantity and arrangement of space, length and sequencing of time blocks, quality of sensory materials, and setting constraints or challenges. All physical environments for young children should be aesthetically pleasing, safe, health-promoting, comfortable, convenient, flexible, spacious enough for free movement, and stocked with a variety of accessible objects and materials to allow choices (Torelli & Durrett, 1998).

An Aesthetically Pleasing Environment

Although aesthetics are often considered last rather than first in planning environments, it is our view that it is essential that children's physical environments be aesthetically pleasing (Greenman, 2005; Torelli & Durrett, 1998). Olds (1998) explains why this should be the case:

It is both illusory and possibly harmful to assume that an environment is suitable merely because it is lacking egregious faults of design and safety and can pass rudimentary safety and cleanliness standards. Environments, like all aspects of life, are potent purveyors of stimulation, information, and affect, and their effects are always felt and incorporated in some way. Children live according to the information provided by their senses, and feast upon the nuances of color, light, sound, touch, texture, volume, movement, visual and kinesthetic vibration, form, and rhythm, by which they come to know the world. Their play is largely a response to variations in the environment. As the Hindus claim, "Sarvam annam," everything is food. Environments must be consciously and lovingly created to uplift the spirit and honor children's heightened sensibility. It is not sufficient that a setting be adequate. It must, instead, be beautiful. (pp. 123–124)

Beautiful environments for infants, toddlers, and educarers are not more expensive environments. Rather, they are ones in which you have considered and chosen aesthetically pleasing colors, furniture, pictures, materials, and objects to buy or to make. Your environment should not be cluttered and should have simple lines and contrasts, containing both interesting and soothing elements for children and adults. Preferably, the built environment (e.g., cabinets, floors) should be made of natural materials, and should include generous amounts of natural light. Aesthetically pleasing environments are usually ones with moderate load, providing a range of sensory experiences that foster a balanced level of stimulation.

A Safe and Health-Promoting Environment

It may seem obvious that the environment must be safe, with no physical dangers such as uncovered electrical plugs, unstable furniture and cabinets, unenclosed steps, or other hazards. But standards for a safe environment also change as children progress from infancy to toddlerhood. As children begin to sit, crawl, walk, run, and climb, increasing the range of their exploration and play, the environment must be periodically reviewed for potentially unsafe elements.

At every age, a safe environment is one that has a challenge level that meets and stretches children's developing abilities. It should have many more features that invite safe child-environment interaction than features that require rigorous and continual adult monitoring. When children begin to climb, there need to be safe ways for them to climb, not adult prohibitions on climbing because of risky structures in the environment. The best balance is a "yes/yes/no" environment, in which many actions are allowed and many objects can be manipulated (yeses), with only a few actions and objects being prohibited (nos) (Bergen, Smith, & O'Neil, 1988).

Because toddlers are developing autonomy, exercising motor skills, and exploring all aspects of their environment, they must have opportunities to perform autonomous actions with objects that are safe to handle in "creative" ways. Accidents are most likely to occur in environments without enough "yeses." Young children do need to learn self-regulation, of course, which is why there should be a few nos planned into the environment. Paired with the nos, there should be alternative yeses, however. For example, you might prohibit climbing on chairs or cabinets, but encourage climbing on the sturdy loft, stairs, and slide steps.

Health-promoting environments are free of noxious air, chemicals, and other contaminants. They have separate areas for diapering and toileting, preferably where educarers can still observe other activities in the room, and separate areas for food preparation and storage, as well as sufficient accessible but safe storage space for cleaning items. There should be a well-established set of health and emergency policies, and educarers should be trained to act in accordance with such policies. There should also be a place for secluding children who become ill. Convenient water sources for both adults and children are needed, and the indoor temperature should be kept within a comfortable range. Because fresh air and outdoor experiences also promote health, it is useful to have a covered area outdoors so that infants, as well as toddlers, can have outdoor experiences on most days and in every season. Well-designed rooms have direct access to the outdoor play area, which should have natural materials such as grass with gentle hills, umbrella-type trees for shade, and places to store toys and loose materials, in addition to fixed toddler-sized large equipment. Toys should be free of lead paint, small hazardous parts, and other noxious qualities.

In most environments designed for infants and toddlers, safety and health concerns are considered carefully. However, if you are using buildings that were originally designed for other purposes (e.g., homes, churches), you must carefully examine potential hazards and take steps to remove any dangerous and unhealthy aspects. Outdoor settings must also be evaluated for safety and health features. Appendix B provides criteria for setting up educare programs to be sure that they are safe and health-promoting.

A Green Design Environment

The building materials and furnishings that are used in the construction and equipment of educare facilities can have an impact on the health of the children and adults who occupy the environment. Since infants' immune systems are not fully developed, they are much more susceptible to the effects of poor-quality air, resulting in an increase in allergies, asthma, and other health-related problems. In addition to creating a healthier environment, "green" and "sustainable" building practices are longer-lasting and therefore less expensive to maintain. There are a number of web sites that provide good advice on developing a green and sustainable environment (e.g., www.spacesforchildren.com, www.edfacilities.org, www.designshare.com, www.sustainableschools.dgs.ca.gov) and there are also published resources (e.g., Wolverton, 1997). Some general strategies that can improve air quality and building health include:

- *Reducing the quantity of construction materials containing volatile organic chemicals (VOC) that can be released into the air.* These include paints, adhesives, synthetic carpeting, and particleboard, which can be replaced by "green" (nonharmful) woods, paints, stains, carpets, and furnishings that have few (or no) VOCs, toxins, and other irritants.
- *Installing heating and ventilation systems that provide appropriate ventilation and air filtration.* Classrooms should be designed with

windows that open and ceiling fans, thus allowing fresh air to circulate. Since infants and toddlers spend so much time on the floor, a simple and inexpensive health practice is to implement a no shoe or indoor-shoe-only policy This prevents dirt and oils that often adhere to outdoor shoes from entering the classroom.

- *Giving careful attention to lighting within classrooms.* The design should include generous amounts of natural light; should have interior windows between rooms to provide a more transparent, open feel; and should use energy-efficient interior artificial lighting. The interior lighting plan should be "sculpted" to the overall layout of the classroom, and should include a variety of recessed, pendant, and track lighting. All of these fixtures accept energy-efficient compact fluorescent bulbs (avoid long-tube fluorescent bulbs, however). Newly developed, super-efficient LED lightbulbs mimic the feel of natural daylight and use 1/30 of the electricity that an incandescent bulb uses.
- *Monitoring the acoustics to prevent high noise levels.* A noisy classroom is distracting and can have a negative impact on the emotional tone in the classroom. Using high-quality acoustical tiles and having "soft" features (e.g., drapes, pillows, carpet) in the environment will help to mitigate the noise.

A Comfortable, Convenient, and Flexible Environment

The physical environment should be a comfortable and convenient one for both children and their educarers because they will spend much time in this setting. Comfortable characteristics include soft parts of the environment (e.g., sofas, carpet, covered risers) and hard, easily cleaned areas (e.g., tile surfaces, wood cabinets). Places to support action with others and places to be quiet and semi-secluded are needed. Convenient environments have some equipment (e.g., chairs, tables, sinks, counters) at accessible heights for children, and some equipment at accessible heights for adults. Surfaces that need frequent cleaning should be easy to clean and close to a water source, with conveniently placed cabinets for cleaning materials accessible only to adults. Arrangement of the play equipment should promote children's choices, enhance their feelings of self-control, and support their development of longer interest spans, with "wet" and "dry" and "quiet" and "noisy" centers in separate locations.

Flexibility of environmental design is essential because children's needs change as they develop, and each day's activities will vary with children's interests. Equipment that folds for storage or is easily moved by educarers for space rearrangement is useful. Storage should be adequate so that all equipment and materials are not on display every day. This is especially important in home care settings because space is limited. If the environment is comfortable, convenient, and flexible for both children and educarers, both will be able to spend long periods of time there without either boredom or anxiety. The flexibility of the environment should extend to the outdoor setting. In addition to fixed toddler-size large equipment, you should have sand toys, balls, wagons, cars, tricycles, large wooden blocks, and pretend materials available outdoors. A lockable outdoor storage space for "loose parts" is preferable. Three examples of quality environments are found in Appendix C. They may be adapted to meet the individual goals and constraints of particular infant and toddler programs.

A Spacious Environment That Supports Movement and Physical Challenges

Space considerations are always included in state licensing recommendations, with typical requirements being 35 square feet per child. Although this requirement may work adequately for older groups with 18 to 25 children, they are not functional for educare settings. If that criterion is used for a group of eight toddlers, it provides only 280 square feet of space, which is the size of a large bedroom! Neither toddlers nor toddler educarers should be kept in that small a space for an entire day. Designers of infant and toddler environments should use standards suggested by professionals who are experienced in infant and toddler care (e.g., Lally et al., 1995) and provide 500 to 600 square feet of space for mixed-age groups of 8 to 12 infants and toddlers (see Appendix B).

Although young infants do not need especially spacious rooms, once children are mobile, they develop best in environments where they can move freely and explore widely, using all of their sensorimotor skills. Environmental designers may assume that because crawling infants and newly walking toddlers are small, they need less space than older children, but the opposite is true. Mobile infants and toddlers are on the go, and because their physical skills are not well coordinated, they may encounter interaction problems if they are in too small a space. Environments need to support movement and physical challenge not only to assist motor development, but also to promote cognitive, social, and emotional competence. Young children should be housed in space that gives them plenty of "action room" and access to appropriate challenge levels both indoors and outdoors.

Although the room for young infants may be smaller, nonmobile infants and infant educarers need a feeling of spaciousness, which can be promoted by large windows, open vistas into other spaces in the building, and easy access to the outdoors. Arrangement of equipment can also make a room more or less spacious and affect the amount of movement space children have. Of course, too many children in a room can make even a spacious room crowded; therefore, the number of children in a group is also important in determining space needs. Often, space can be more flexibly utilized if the room includes children of different ages and developmental levels. A room with all children who are crawling or climbing can appear too "busy" if it is not especially large.

Another option to give a spacious feeling is to give children who are in separate rooms most of the day the opportunity to flow between rooms at some times. Adjoining rooms with doors between them that can be opened for "flow time" can relieve the feeling of entrapment in small environments. Some state child-care guidelines do not permit multiage intermingling, so this option may not always be available. Young children need sufficient space to explore and play, and consequently to grow and learn. If your space is adequate and well designed, you will find that most child management problems disappear.

An Environment with a Variety of Accessible Objects and Materials

Because infants and toddlers show their longest attention spans to objects that are slightly novel (i.e., those that have familiar aspects with a few new features), you should choose play materials that can be used in a variety of ways. Often, an object can be made novel by adding another object. For example, plastic keys can be made more interesting by adding a cup into which the keys can be put. Play materials should not all be visible at one time, because familiar ones become less interesting. If you take some toys "out of service" and rotate their accessibility, you can revive infants' attention.

Some toys should be on open shelves, baskets, or tables so that children can choose for themselves; others should be kept in easily accessible storage cabinets from which educarers can replace and add materials to provide variety and challenge. Young children lose interest if an unvarying set of toys is crammed into baskets, especially if parts are separated or missing. The spatial arrangement of the materials in the room is especially important for toddler play. There should be semiprivate places for toddlers so that their tendency toward "herding" behavior is minimized (i.e., all toddlers going to the same activity when they observe one child at that activity). Because play with objects and materials is a major part of the infant and toddler curriculum, learning standards will be reached best if objects are displayed in ways in which children can access them and use them fully.

In the last 5 to 10 years, toys for young children have undergone a "technology-enhanced" transformation. Even many traditional toys, such as dolls, stuffed animals, blocks, and trains, now have computer chips that can be activated to make noise or imitate voices—features designed to direct child action. Toys for infants and toddlers often have elaborate affordances, including "learning" features such as alphabet and counting songs, "talk" that labels the child's actions, and a plethora of stimulating parts. One concern about such toys is that they may make the child reactive (to the toy's stimulation) rather than active (in charge of actions) (Bergen, 2001). Although some of these toys can be useful to help children learn particular words or actions, educarers should not overload the environment with such toys, because their long-term effects on children's play development and learning have not yet been studied extensively.

QUALITY GUIDELINES FOR SOCIAL-EMOTIONAL ENVIRONMENTS

Even when the physical environment is well designed, its effects are mediated by the quality of the social-emotional environment provided by educarers. The relationships that develop between educarers and children form the core of the curriculum. Social-emotional relationships with peers are also important because peers influence the social-emotional messages that are conveyed. Of course, children's families provide the basic building blocks on which social and emotional development rests. There are five essential social-emotional components that educarers must consider, each of which builds upon the others. They include:

1. Meeting each child's basic care, nurturance, and safety needs
2. Providing individualized, responsive, and playful social interactions
3. Giving assistance in the development of child autonomy and self-efficacy
4. Facilitating development of peer interaction skills
5. Making family members feel like welcome partners in support of educare goals

Educarers need to fulfill a number of different roles each day, including acting as nurturer, observer, teacher, coach, initiator of activity, responder, participator, environment preparer, and even custodian (Bergen, Smith, & O'Neil, 1988). Figure 2.1 describes these roles in detail. A group of educarers who gave opinions about the most important needs of infants and toddlers rated having consistent nurturing and a healthy/safe environment as most important for infants, and having a stimulating environment focused on cognitive development and autonomy as most important for toddlers (Bergen, Gaynard, & Torelli, 1985).

Peers give a "child's-eye" view of themselves and the social-emotional world, thus providing a perspective that cannot be provided by adults. Peer interactions foster development of empathy and social skills such as sharing. Families are also crucial in supporting the social and emotional growth that the educare environment fosters, providing information about individual, family, and cultural values that educarers need to consider in order to interact effectively.

A Caring, Nurturing, and Safe Environment

Although there is general agreement about the essential qualities of the social-emotional environment, state licensing standards and federal program requirements range widely in regard to adult: child ratios, overall group size, group limits in family educare, and the amount of space needed per child; thus, there can be vast differences in the quality of care that educarers provide (Gallagher, Rooney, & Campbell, 1999). For example, some states allow a 1:6 adult:child ratio for infants and a 1:12 or higher ratio for toddler groups, while federal Early Head Start guidelines mandate a ratio of 1:4 for infants and toddlers, with a maximum group size of 8. State licensing standards do not address consistency of care, although experts recommend that children should have the same educarers for 3 years (APHA/AAP, 1999; Lally et al., 1995; Lally, Mangione, & Greenwald, 2006). In planning a quality program, therefore, educarers cannot rely on licensing standards. Two levels of ratio and group size standards are acceptable: (1) "appropriate" conditions, outlined in accreditation standards (NAEYC, 2007), and (2) "high-quality" conditions, suggested by leading professionals in the field (e.g., Lally et al., 1995, 2003, 2006). Figure 2.2 shows these comparisons.

Both appropriate and high-quality guidelines recommend primary educarers (i.e., consistent adults) and continuity of care for at least 1 year. Primary educarers/consistent adults are especially "tuned in" to the social-emotional needs and temperaments of the children in their care group. Other educarers in the program should also be knowledgeable about all children's needs and responsive to their interests.

FIGURE 2.1 Educarer Roles in the Infant and Toddler Program

1. *Nurturer:* Attends to children's physical and emotional needs, conveying a sense of warmth and trustworthiness.
2. *Responder:* Shows sensitivity to children's cues, maintains interest in children's activities, gives attention to children's communication attempts, and engages in turn-taking social play.
3. *Observer:* Acts as a "laid back but vigilant" observer to monitor child initiated activity, assesses children's zones of proximal development, and is prepared to step in when assistance is needed or play enhancement is warranted.
4. *Preparer:* Plans the environment, arranging equipment and materials for accessibility, safety, and learning value, using objects with affordances that invite children's playful use.
5. *Initiator:* Plans learning activities, demonstrates elaborated play schemes, and encourages children's play elaboration.
6. *Coach:* Provides encouragement and scaffolding help when children are learning specific skills, and gives narrative accompaniment as children accomplish tasks and enjoy play.
7. *Participator:* Engages in role-play, games, and motor activities with children, and serves as a model of play skill.
8. *Teacher:* Engages in a teaching activity using the model of proleptic instruction (in which the learner sets the learning conditions).
9. *Director:* Gives specific guidance about safety rules, expected behaviors, or routines.
10. *Custodian:* Cleans up, picks up, and puts away so that the environment stays healthy and pleasant.

Note: The balance of roles will vary with the age of the children, with educarers of infants and toddlers each having a different mix of roles. For example, nurturing and responding are primary roles in early infancy, while the initiating and coaching roles are used more often with older toddlers.

Source: Originally published in Bergen, D., Smith, K., & O'Neil, S. (1988). Designing play environments for infants and toddlers. In D. Bergen (Ed.), *Play as a medium for learning and development* (p. 205). Portsmouth, NH: Heinemann. Copyright © 1988. Reprinted by permission of D. Bergen.

Unfortunately, educarers in most states are not yet required to have early childhood certification, except in early intervention/special-needs programs, although Early Head Start does require educarers to be credentialed. Educarers must be knowledgeable about young children's development and educare practices, and should receive training through degree programs or in-service education. Preferably, the staff should include both male and female educarers so children can experience nurturing, playfulness, and role modeling from both genders. If there are few males qualified for lead roles, they can be hired as assistants and encouraged to seek professional development. Other options include having a male high school volunteer, cook, bus driver, or senior citizen involved. Staff racial and cultural diversity should also be pursued vigorously.

Although ratios, group sizes, and educarer training are important, educarers' quality and types of social-emotional interactions are even more important. For young infants, educarers convey emotional safety primarily during feeding, diapering, and other care through social interactions and verbal/nonverbal communications. At later child ages, they convey this message through both care activities and play interactions. Thus, one of the most important qualities of educarers is playfulness.

A Responsive and Playful Environment

Adult responsivity to infants' expressions of need and interest are key to children's development of trust and attachment. Through social interactions, infants learn to expect that their communication attempts will get results and to rely on those who care for them. Young children's responsivity is based to a large extent on the quality of the relationship with their educarers. Your playful interactions provide infants with knowledge of the rules and signals that frame social play, that is, the boundaries of the "playframe." Your play with toddlers provides the social

FIGURE 2.2 Appropriate Conditions/High-Quality Conditions in Group Settings

Appropriate Conditions	*High-Quality Conditions*
*Ratios**	*Ratios***
1:3–1:4 for infants under 6 months	1:3 for all infants
1:4 for older infants	1:4 for all toddlers
1:3–1:4 for toddlers of 24 months, ranging to 1:6 for 36-month-olds	
Group Sizes	*Group Sizes*
For infants under 1 year: 6–8	For infants: 0–9 mos. No more than 6
For toddlers: 5–12 for younger toddlers, 8–12 for older toddlers (with 2 educarers if 10 or more)	For infants: 9–18 mos. No more than 9
	For toddlers: 18–36 mos. No more than 12 (with 3 educarers for 12)
	In mixed-age groups, 0–36 mos. No more than 8 children, with no more than 2 children under 24 mos.

*Guidelines from NAEYC, 2005   **Guidelines from Lally et al., 2006

interaction practice that assists them in playing with peers. When educarers are responsible for a group of infants, they may feel they have time only to provide basic care, not to play. Because playful interactions foster infants' attachment, however, you need to embed playfulness in much of your routine caregiving. You can sing silly songs, have "conversations," or play social games during caregiving activities. There also should be times when play is the total focus of interaction, and such play can be done with all familiar educarers. When infants play with more than one educarer, they learn about different styles of interaction and form attachments to more adults. All infants, especially those with developmental delays or those who come from abusive home environments, need the opportunity to have one-on-one play opportunities with educarers, even though their initial responses to such activities may be limited. You may have to try harder to get such children to interact, but it is absolutely essential that the children make such connections if their social-emotional development is to proceed well.

Your engagement in pretend play with toddlers is vital because adult modeling of social pretending assists toddlers in making the transition to representational thought. Parents of toddlers often facilitate their children's pretense through modeling roles, suggesting themes, and providing replica toys, but long workdays may reduce the amount of time parents have for this play. If their toddlers are in educare, the educarer must fulfill the role of pretend facilitator. You can initiate pretend themes and scripts, model roles and actions, and coach toddlers in taking roles or performing script actions. You also can act as a play participant, taking a role yourself and helping to plan the play sequence. You can draw other children into pretend play by suggesting roles.

If you work consistently with the same group of children, you will know how to adjust your playful interactions to meet the needs of each child. For example, one child may initiate social games and may need you to respond or help her engage peers in her game. Another child may be an observer, who needs to watch you pretend before performing an action himself. Some toddlers may perform many play scripts and successfully bring other toddlers into play without needing your assistance. As toddlers become more able, your role shifts to being a facilitator of autonomy and self-efficacy. As this occurs, you do more observing and monitoring, preparing or obtaining materials, and providing settings where toddlers can play autonomously with peers.

An Environment That Facilitates Autonomy and Self-Efficacy

Besides providing nurturance and reciprocal social play, educarers prepare environments that encourage infant and toddler engagement in object exploration, practice play, and social observation. You can foster infants' autonomy by assisting them in achieving instrumental ends, such as reaching toys, opening or fastening doors, crawling through tunnels, or pulling themselves up on furniture. Using the method of scaffolding, you can provide only the help needed to enable children to achieve their goals. For example, toddlers may need "coaching" through their first climb up the slide, but that should be sufficient for most then to act autonomously. One reason the physical environment should be safe is so you will not need to hover over children constantly, but instead be able to let them explore and engage in trial-and-error manipulation and sensory play with a minimum of adult involvement. The role of "laidback but vigilant observer" is one that educarers often play with toddlers. You should be ready to step in when needed but you should not be overly controlling and directive. Obtaining the right balance between interaction and observation is sometimes difficult for toddler educarers. Remember that toddlers have their own play and learning agendas; thus, adult facilitation rather than direction is needed.

Children with disabilities also need opportunities to gain autonomy. Therefore, play environments should be adapted to foster their independent play. Even children with a limited range of physical skills need to make an impact on their environment. Many types of adapted equipment, such as toys that move with pressure of a finger, arm, or head, can enable these children to interact with objects effectively. Objects that provide experience with multiple sensory stimuli (e.g., touch, sound, and vision) can hold interest for children who have a sensory impairment (e.g., touch and sound can help a child with poor vision; touch and vision can help a child with hearing impairment).

Children of both genders should engage in all types of autonomous play, with messy as well as neat materials. You should not direct girls away from rough-and-tumble play or discourage boys from dressing in a "mommy's" hat. At this age, all children should have the opportunity to use dolls and trains, take part in quiet and noisy activities, and be helped to gain self-efficacy—the feeling that they can act, do, and achieve results using their own abilities. Self-efficacy also extends to feelings of being able to interact successfully with peers as well as adults.

An Environment That Fosters Peer Interaction Skills

Infants show early awareness of peers, react with longer attention to pictures or videos of babies, and use emerging social skills to initiate interactions with infant peers. They may initially approach other infants in an exploratory manner, trying out their existing action schemes by patting another child's head or pulling a child's hair. Soon they realize that other infants are not objects because peers react differently to interactions. Infants are affected by the crying or laughing of other infants, their arousal level increases when peers are present, and they enjoy playing in the presence of peers (i.e., in parallel fashion) by the end of their first year.

Toddlers use objects as "introductory" means of initiating peer interactions. The "toy give-and-take" routine is a common one in the early part of the toddler period, and by late toddlerhood, the beginnings of social associative play may occur (usually needing adult facilitation to keep it going). When planning the social-emotional environment, you should take into account the effects (positive or negative) of the peer group and prepare the environment to facilitate positive social-emotional interactions. Although the quality of relationships between young children and their educarers is primary, the quality of relationships among peers also is instrumental in promoting healthy development, as are the relationships that you build with family members.

An Environment That Welcomes Families as Partners

The educare social-emotional environment is framed by the contributions families make to this environment. Although families are important for children at every age, their support and involvement are especially important when children are very young. For many parents, the decision to place their children in nonfamily care and education is reached only with soul searching and regret, and finding satisfaction with educarers and educare is often difficult. Depending on the family's cultural background, the transition to nonfamily care and education may result in family exposure to new ideas and practices, and members of the extended family may not approve of the parents' choice of a nonfamily educare option. Stresses of work and other roles may affect families' capability to support the goals of educarers and to be involved in ways educarers prefer.

An important way to help families feel welcome is to consider their needs in the environmental design. Even if family members spend only brief times in the environment, the space should signal comfort and convenience to them. Having a "community room" with family-friendly items, such as comfortable group seating, coffee or tea, a lending library of books for adults and children, and a toy library, distinguishes the environment as one that welcomes families. This area also can serve as flexible space for meetings, storytellers and musicians, and a display area for documentation. To make families feel welcome, especially if they come from varied cultural backgrounds, you can allow them to share their cultural artifacts or pictures, play songs related to their culture, and share traditional play activities with other families and children. You can provide a semiprivate space for mothers to nurse infants or get reacquainted with their children at day's end. A private place is also needed, where family members can talk to educarers about concerns or family problems affecting their children's behavior. A family-friendly environment lets families know that you are ready to listen to their ideas and concerns.

Because family issues provide the context in which the social-emotional environment is embedded, you must be conscious of family suggestions and concerns, and use strategies for involving families appropriately. Many programs for young children have home visit components, while others encourage families to spend time in the educare setting or to attend meetings and other events. By discussing their individual and common goals for children and working together to achieve such goals, educarers and families can promote continuity across both educare and home settings, thus providing the best social-emotional environment for young children. (See Chapter 12 for further discussion of educarer-family relationships.)

SUMMARY

While environmental design can be guided by a general principle (i.e., moderate load), and even though specific guidelines for both physical and social-emotional environments are available, one "perfect" design that is appropriate for every infant and toddler program cannot be provided. Rather, educarers must design the environments that are most appropriate for the children they care for and educate, and plan that environment within the contexts of individual child and family differences.

QUESTIONS FOR DISCUSSION

1. If you must start a program in an existing space that wasn't designed for educare, what are five important elements in the physical environment that you would consider in choosing that space?
2. What qualities would you look for in choosing educarers? What would you tell them about what is most important in a quality social-emotional environment?
3. How would the cultural composition of the children in your program affect the environment you would design?

PART II

INDIVIDUAL DEVELOPMENTAL FACTORS INFLUENCING INFANT AND TODDLER CURRICULUM: CASES AND LEARNING ACTIVITIES

The general guidelines presented in Part I help educarers maintain high overall program quality. To be responsive to individual children's needs, however, educarers must be attuned to individual and age-appropriate differences. You must build curriculum flexibility and variation, and adapt environments as children's needs change. Your curriculum must also be responsive to the values and goals of families.

In this part of the book, we present case descriptions of real children aged 1 to 36 months, and give curriculum guidelines for nine age levels. As you read these cases, imagine that these children are in your educare program. Consider how you would use information about them to make curriculum decisions and adapt the suggestions we have made. By considering each child both as an individual embedded in a particular cultural context and as a member of an age cohort, you can make responsive curriculum a reality. The questions at the end of each chapter require you to draw on information in Parts I and III, as well as Part II; therefore, you may want to discuss them again after reading Part III.

Rather than using "school-type" content fields (e.g., reading, mathematics), we divide curriculum activities into three content areas drawn from the discussion in Chapter 1 about how knowledge is constructed and how social-emotional relationships are formed. They are:

1. Knowledge construction
2. Social-emotional relationship building
3. Play development

Following Piaget's views (see Kamii and DeVries, 1978/1993), knowledge construction is further divided into four subcontent areas:

1. Sensorimotor exploration
2. Physical knowledge construction

3.   Relational knowledge construction
4.   Social knowledge construction

The first three are learned primarily through children's direct interaction with the physical environment, while the fourth requires the mediation of adults, since it is arbitrary (i.e., culturally specific) knowledge. Social knowledge includes learning cultural labels for concepts constructed during knowledge generation. As Vygotsky (1962) stressed, knowledge construction is a sociocultural experience that builds upon child-object and child-adult interactions.

The second content area, social-emotional relationship building, draws upon theories of Erikson (1963), Bowlby (1969), and Greenspan (1999), and stresses the importance of trust, attachment, and emotional-cognitive connections, which are important for infant mental health. The third content area, play development, stresses the role of play as the major medium for learning in these years (Bergen, 1998; Garner & Bergen, 2006).

At each age level, these content areas form the organizing framework for curriculum priorities and environment design, which precede the list of activities. Because educarers also need to understand how curriculum ideas connect to the early learning standards, each chapter gives examples of curriculum connections to relevant standards. (For entire set of standards see the NAEYC website, http://www.naeyc.org/academy/standards.)

Chapter 3

4–6 Weeks

Curriculum for ABBY and BRITTANY

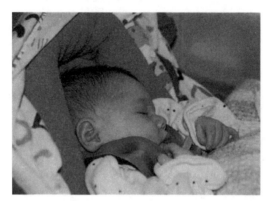

ABBY'S MOTHER HAD an easy labor, and because she had an epidural, she was able to watch the birth in a mirror without feeling pain. Abby's father and godmother were at the birth, and her godmother taped the birth sequence. Abby's mother had been happy being pregnant, and when Abby emerged, her mother already felt like she knew her. Abby had a full head of hair, golden skin, big eyes, and her dad's lips. She weighed 7 pounds, 2 ounces; was very alert; and already had two front bottom teeth.

Her mom considers Abby's birth "a miracle," because her parents had to consult with an infertility clinic before she was conceived. Now, at 1 month old, Abby has "steely" blue eyes, brownish-black hair, and olive skin. She has sucked her thumb since she was born.

She has a bottle about every 2 hours, although her schedule changes daily. She is awake more now than she was initially. Before birth, Abby was active in the evenings and woke her mom with activity around 2:30 A.M. She still has that pattern of active, awake times. After breastfeeding for 2 weeks, Abby seemed fussy and "gassy." Her mother attributed that to breastfeeding and began giving Abby a bottle. Because Abby's mother works part-time and her dad travels extensively, they needed to find good caregiving early. Although Mom had concerns about giving up breastfeeding, because of their schedule and Abby's upsets, she felt it was necessary. Abby currently eats on demand, although her mother is trying to establish a feeding routine. Her father's schedule permits him to care for Abby some days, and the family has an educarer in their home on the days when Abby's mother is at her part-time job and her dad is out of town.

Abby is more responsive now, her mother notes, and she smiles and waves her arms at objects when they come into her line of vision. Her temperament is contented, good-natured, and social, but "she already has an opinion about things." For example, she doesn't like her car seat, but she does like to be around people and to have them touch her. She is responsive to sounds and, "since day one," when she hears music play on her mobile, she stops fussing, looks in the direction of the sound, and calms down. She also attends to voices, stares at black-and-white objects, and watches color patterns on television. On her changing table, she stares at the flowers on the wallpaper. Her mom reports seeing a social smile in the past few days, and Abby grabs her mother's fingers while she is feeding. She will sit in her infant seat for about 10 minutes before becoming fussy. She prefers to lie on her stomach and is already able to push herself up with her arms. She can hold up her head when she is being held, and she shows the ability to scoot in her bed. Her eyes follow to midline, and her movements on each side of her body are equally efficient. She squeals, squeaks, grunts, and makes other noises, and she startles when she hears loud sounds.

Abby's mother wants to make sure the educarer burps Abby well because she often has gas. Mom wants the educarer to keep Abby awake to finish her 2 ounces of milk because she often falls asleep after the first ounce. Mom suggests changing Abby's diaper halfway through the bottle to keep her awake to take the second ounce. She wants the bottle warmed in water, not in the microwave. Because of Abby's sensitive skin, she prefers that water, not chemically saturated diaper wipes, be used when Abby is changed. Other advice Abby's mom gives the educarer includes, "Make sure you talk to her, have toys in front of her, hold her often, and don't let her cry herself to sleep." She wants the educarer to respond quickly when Abby wakes up, rather than letting her cry in her crib, because children "learn early you'll be there for them" and Abby's mother doesn't want anyone to "ruin her [Abby's] sense of trust."

BRITTANY'S MOTHER HAD a quick labor and delivery, with a few hours of intense back pain. Once Brittany crowned, the birth was over quickly. Brittany weighed 9 pounds, 10 ounces, and was 22 inches long. Her father and grandmother were at the birth, and a student midwife took photos that Brittany's mom proudly shows friends and coworkers. Within 5 minutes of birth, Brittany nursed for a brief time.

At 6 weeks, Brittany has dark brown hair, blue eyes, and long fingers and toes. She is wiry and vigorous in her movements and is in constant motion, even when she is sleeping. In sleep, she often grunts and snorts while moving. Although she is physically active, she was quiet, content, easily soothed, and happy during the first few weeks. Now she is often fussy for long periods of time. When she cries, it is usually because she is hungry, hot, or "just needs to be held." Brittany slept through the night in the weeks after birth. During the day, she would stay awake for 2 to 6 hours, taking short "power naps" for 15 to 20 minutes. She took to nursing well, eating vigorously until she fell asleep (within 10 to 15 minutes). She now eats 8 to

10 times a day and stays awake during and after nursing. She is a leisurely eater, often taking 20 minutes to finish. Brittany now has one nursing period at night, but when she wakes around 5:30 A.M., she is very hungry. She indicates that she is hungry by sucking her thumb. Brittany's mother is an educarer at the program where Brittany is enrolled, which allows her to see Brittany frequently during the day and nurse her.

Some things Brittany enjoys include looking at faces, mobiles, and the checkered ears on a pull toy; staring at the Mickey Mouse crib decals; watching the ceiling fan's colored streamers turn; swinging in her swing; and listening to people talking, rattles being shaken, and music. Although she smiles at anything placed in front of her, she finds her mom to be the most entertaining person. She watches Mom's every move, stares intently at her face when sitting next to her in the car, and has an instant smile whenever Mom looks at Brittany. She is beginning to laugh out loud. Being wiry and strong, Brittany can lift her head with ease while on her stomach and push against hard surfaces when her feet are against a firm object.

Brittany's mother feels fortunate to have on-site care for her daughter. Being a first-time mother, she wants to ensure that Brittany's educarers will make every effort to meet her needs. She hopes they will be sensitive to whether Brittany may be too warm, and will always burp her after feeding (Brittany's mom provides breast milk in a bottle). It is also important to Brittany's mother that Brittany have her diaper changed frequently. Mom's main concern is that the educarers spend "quality physical time" with Brittany and try to keep her happy by rocking her and talking to her frequently.

CURRICULUM PRIORITIES

Although it may be difficult to envision a curriculum for children younger than 2 months old, Abby's mother and Brittany's mother have already identified important features of that curriculum for educarers to consider. Most of their concerns relate to basic needs (eating, sleeping, diapering);

however, both mothers are aware of the need for relationship building, noting the importance of talking and interacting with their infants, even at this early age. During the first 1 to 3 months, enormous changes take place in infants' ability to perceive objects in their world, interact with people, communicate needs and wishes, and voluntarily control their body activity. In caring for children in this age range, you need to be responsive to the almost daily changes you observe in their development and learning. Abby and Brittany are already unique individuals, and it is important to keep that in mind, although many of their needs are similar. Curriculum priorities include:

1. Meeting basic health and survival needs with well-planned, regular, individualized, and nurturing feeding, diapering, and sleeping experiences
2. Developing basic trust and fostering attachment through warm and responsive caregiving interactions and predictable routines within pleasant, safe surroundings
3. Providing appropriate levels of stimulation for all of the infants' senses within an environment that has many affordances that encourage sensory exploration

RECOMMENDED CHARACTERISTICS OF THE ENVIRONMENT

- In a young infant's life, it is especially important that the environment signal respect for the parents' role. Often, parents find it difficult to leave their small infants in others' care, so the educare environment should assure parents that they are welcome. Providing sofas or rockers that parents can use and semiprivate spaces for them to nurse or care for their infants is essential.
- Group size should be small enough so that educarers have time not only to meet infants' basic needs but also to provide one-to-one social contact through holding, carrying, and talking to every infant each day. (See Chapter 2 to review guidelines for educarer-child ratios and group sizes.)
- Colors on walls, floor, and other surfaces (e.g., changing tables) should be warm but relatively bland. A variety of brighter colors and textures should be provided flexibly in wall quilts, area rugs, and mobiles.
- Low light rather than bright light is preferable when infants are visually exploring the environment; thus, glaring overhead lights should be avoided.
- Safe, cozy, and visually interesting spaces outside the line of traffic are important design elements.
- Because infants are interested in exploring human faces, there should be comfortable sofas (slipcovered for ease of cleaning) or rockers for

educarers to use when they hold and feed infants so that the infants have easy access to visual exploration of the educarer's face. Infants can also be placed on this furniture or on padded tables for closer adult-infant face-to-face interaction.

- For ease of care for basic needs, there should be protected and easily washable surfaces at adult arm level and good access to water and care items, such as diapers and clothing.
- Sleeping arrangements should include individual cribs (small size) for each infant in a quiet area that is at least partially closed off from the play area.

SAMPLE CURRICULUM ACTIVITIES

Sensorimotor Knowledge Construction

Visual Experiences

- Environments should encourage infants to focus visually on physical features (e.g., doors, walls, window shades), objects (e.g., mobiles, rattles, furniture) with colorful qualities, and contrasting patterns of light and shadows.
- Because contrasting colors and combinations of black and white are preferred by infants, you can make simple pattern "books" on white tag board using permanent black markers, or by gluing colored paper on tag board to make collagelike pages to use when you are interacting with infants during their quiet, alert states. Commercial books of these types are also available.
- Mobiles should be placed slightly offside over cribs and positioned about 10 to 15 inches from infants' faces. Since infants' heads tend to turn to one side, they will see the mobiles better if they are offside, and there will be no chance that the mobiles will fall on them. Patterns should include checkered designs, geometric shapes, and concentric circles. You can make homemade mobiles from colored construction paper or shiny gift wrap glued to cardboard. Face the flat side down and attach strings to a clothes hanger or embroidery hoop. Make simple mobiles by cutting a spiral design into a large, round sheet of heavy, colorful paper and hanging it so that it spirals down from a string and twists and turns when a light breeze is made. (Note: These homemade mobiles are safe for young infants if they are securely attached. They should not be used with infants who are in a reaching and mouthing stage.)
- Visual chains (commercial or homemade) can be securely attached to the sides of cribs so that the objects dangle over the infants. Small toys, yarn pom-poms, keys, or small household objects can be strung

on a cord or heavy elastic and securely attached. (Note: When infants begin to reach and grab, only well-tested chains without loosely attached parts should be used.)

- Positioning infants in various ways can enhance their ability to explore visually. You can hold infants in an upright position on your shoulder or in front of you with the head facing out to enable them to see moving objects like streamers attached to an air conditioner or overhead fan, or running water in a sink. As you move around the room with infants in such positions, the children can attend to decorations and pictures on walls, images in mirrors, or movements of people or animals. Holding infants in your lap enables them to see toys and books, which should be changed frequently as the children habituate to them.

- Positioning children on their stomachs on a colorful rug or quilt can be done as soon as they have some neck control. You can place toys within view, encouraging infants to arch their backs and lift their heads to look at the toys. Moving toys such as a rattle across infants' line of vision encourages them to move their bodies, strengthening neck and back muscles, as well as improving their tracking skills. (Note: Infants should not be placed on their stomachs for sleeping, because of breathing difficulties.)

- Use of gliders or hammocks can enhance visual experiences briefly as long as you either hold the infant or stay close to provide motion. Infants should not be placed alone in such devices for long periods. Because novelty and movement engage young children's attention and because they cannot reposition their bodies by themselves, young infants need close monitoring and frequent changing of position.

Auditory Experiences

- Infants enjoy listening to interesting and varied sounds. A variety of musical selections can be played using radios, CDs, tapes, or records. There should be an obvious beginning and end to each selection in order to highlight differences in tempo, rhythm, and melody. Both instrumental and vocal pieces should be used. Radios (or televisions) should not be played all day, presenting a steady stream of similar sounds, because the goal is to enhance infants' ability to discriminate and respond to a range of auditory stimuli. A steady stream of similar sound results in a "tuning out" through habituation.

- Infants enjoy being sung to as well as spoken to frequently during the day. When singing or speaking to infants, you should use a tone of voice that matches your facial expressions and body language (e.g., smile and happy voice). Speech and songs should be both repetitive and varied. If you present infants with patterns, they will learn to anticipate events and engage in "turn-taking" vocal patterns.

When infants make any type of vocal response, you should be reciprocally responsive.

- In addition to being calmed by human voices, restless infants can relax while listening to rhythmic sounds like a washing machine or clothes dryer, which are found in most homes and centers. Tapes of water sounds and other soothing sounds may also calm infants who have difficulty self-calming; however, you need to observe reactions closely because some infants may be aroused rather than calmed by rhythmic sounds.
- When infants are awake and alert, they can often be stimulated by sounds such as a music box, rattles, bells, or recordings of bird calls. Such sounds, as well as human singing voices, are especially interesting to young infants.
- To help strengthen intermodal coordination (vision and hearing working together), you can hold rattles, bells, maracas, or even empty film canisters filled with seeds or beans (with lids securely attached) in the infants' line of vision. You can shake the object and slowly move it from side to side or in a slow circular pattern as infants follow it with their eyes and ears.
- Auditory directionality can be strengthened by placing infants on their backs and standing behind them while whispering or making other sounds in one ear at a time. This encourages infants to turn their heads and seek the direction of the sounds.

Tactile Experiences

- Physical stimulation is a necessary part of building basic trust in young infants; the younger they are, the more they need to be held. You should plan to hold and carry all children during much of their waking time. This will also promote intermodal coordination (visual, hearing, and tactile).
- You should also engage in gentle touching activities such as stroking infants' faces, hands, and feet or moving infants' arms and legs in rhythmic patterns.
- Touching includes giving infants experiences with a variety of textures (e.g., rough, smooth, fuzzy, wet, dry). You can use swatches of fake fur, velveteen, corduroy, and satin on infants' cheeks, arms, hands, and other body parts. Gently rubbing with a warm, damp cloth is useful, especially if an infant needs soothing.
- Rocking infants promotes the sense of balance and infants' awareness of lateral movement. Most infants enjoy being rocked every day, although some may respond adversely when rocked even though they like being held and walked about. You should be cognizant of the signals given by infants and respond with the type of movement each infant most prefers.
- With infants, touching and moving through space should never

involve shaking or violent, abrupt movement. These types of movements can result in brain injury.

Olfactory Experiences

- Infants are already sensitive to various odors, and their early recognition of parents and educarers is probably based partially on the difference in the way each of these persons smells.
- You should be aware that many objects have odors as well as other sensory qualities; usually infants show little aversion to many odors that are unpleasant to adults.
- Many creams and cleansing products have odors associated with them, and infants learn to recognize odors related to caregiving activities.
- Intermodal perception (sight, touch, smell) is enhanced by activities such as feeding, in which these sensory experiences are integrated.

Gustatory Experiences

- A major activity of infants this age is feeding; differences in taste of various forms of liquid (milk, water, juice) provide one of the earliest learning experiences.
- From birth, infants can distinguish tastes and grimace at sour or bitter tastes; they already have a preference for sweet tastes. In trying to soothe infants who are upset, you should pay attention to the tastes they prefer.

Social Knowledge Construction

- To help infants understand that they are separate beings, you should provide activities that help them focus on their own body and on how their actions affect objects and people. Rudimentary cause/effect understanding can be enhanced by placing a colorful cloth hair scrunchy or an elastic band with a large jingle bell securely attached on infants' wrists. You should monitor and note how infants attempt to focus on the scrunchy as it passes their field of vision and/or how they stop moving momentarily to listen each time the bell rings.
- Touching activities that involve infant body parts also stimulate their sense of separateness.
- Young infants actively push against objects with their feet. You can place a board covered with soft fabric against a wall or at the foot of cribs. If infants lie on their stomachs or backs with bare feet touching the board or wall, they will scoot away from the board by pushing with their feet. As noted earlier, activities involving infants on their stomachs should be used only with close supervision, and infants should not be placed in that position for sleeping.

- If you place noisemakers on cribs or other places that cause a sound when infants move, the infants will begin to show intentionality of movement. They realize quite early that their movements control the sound-making.

NAEYC Accreditation Criteria 2.L.01 (Social Studies) Standard 2: Curriculum: "Children are provided varied learning opportunities that foster positive identity and an emerging sense of self and others."

Social-Emotional Relationship Building

- You should provide many opportunities for infants to hear the human voice, especially as an accompaniment to caregiving activities; these activities should not be done in silence. Describe what you are doing as you engage in routine tasks such as diapering or feeding, or comment upon the infants' activities (e.g., "You're making your legs go fast.").
- As infants begin to vocalize, you should respond as though carrying on a conversation in order to encourage further vocalization. When infants coo and grunt, your approving and enthusiastic responses will encourage them to produce more vocalizations.
- Encouraging infants to imitate the actions of others helps them to develop their nonverbal communication skills. You need to show a variety of facial expressions to help them understand faces and the emotions they express, and to learn to recognize familiar faces with varied emotions.

NAEYC Accreditation Criteria 2.B.01 (Social-Emotional Development) Standard 2: Curricula: "Children have varied opportunities to engage throughout the day with teaching staff who are attentive and responsive to them, facilitate their social competence, and facilitate their ability to learn through interacting with others."

Play Development

- You can use simple rhymes and songs. While touching infants' fingers and toes, you can play "This Little Piggy Went to Market" and "Whoops, Golly, Golly." (This rhyme pattern consists of gently pinching each finger beginning with the little finger and saying "Golly, golly . . .," then saying, "Whoops," while making a slide down from the top of the index finger up to the top of the thumb and saying "Golly.") Soon an anticipatory expression will begin to show on the infant's face when the words of such rhymes begin.

NAEYC Accreditation Criteria 2.D.02: (Language Development) Standard 2: Curricula: "Children are provided opportunities to experience oral and written communication in a language their family uses or understands."

For children whose first language is not English, songs and rhymes should be provided in the child's home language as a way to support the child and family's cultural integrity. Carol Brunson Phillips describes this as teaching children in a "culturally consistent context" (Phillips, in Mangione, 1995, p. 4).

QUESTIONS FOR DISCUSSION

1. How are the curriculum needs of Abby and Brittany similar, and how are they different, given their mothers' priorities?
2. What other activities would enhance their development? Would these activities work equally well with boys? Why or why not?
3. How might some activities be adapted for a particular infant who had low muscle tone or a sensory disability (e.g., a hearing impairment)?
4. How might care of infants who had a difficult birth or who were premature differ during this age period? Would their parents have similar or different concerns?
5. How could you work with a family whose first language differs from your own to ensure that you are hearing the family's concerns and addressing them effectively?
6. How could you explain to a parent ways that these experiences lay the foundation for later science learning?

Chapter 4

3-4 Months

Curriculum for CHARLAYNE and BARNIE

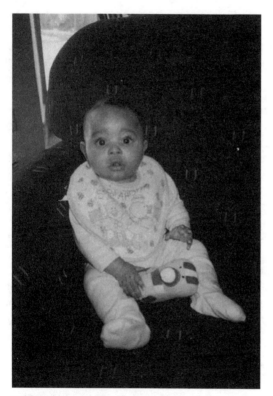

CHARLAYNE'S MOM REPORTS that when she held her adopted daughter for the first time 3 days after she was born, she seemed to be a calm, even-tempered baby. She had a normal, healthy birth with no complications. At 4 months, Charlayne is still a "predictable" child, who has slept through the night since she was 2 months old. Charlayne has black curly hair, large dark-brown eyes, and light brown skin, attesting to her biracial heritage. She now weighs 10½ pounds, up 3 pounds from her birth weight, and is 3 inches longer than her birth length of 21 inches. Mom says Charlayne got on a feeding and sleeping schedule quickly and only fusses when she is tired or hungry. She now has rice cereal in her evening bottle; she is not taking cereal from a spoon.

Charlayne's muscle tone has been good from birth. She held her head up well and now enjoys being pulled up to sit. Favorite positions are in her jumper chair or propped on her parents' laps, where she watches everything that is going on, especially the actions of her 2½-year-old sister and 7½-year-old brother. She shows excitement when her brother comes home from school and greets her. In new environments, she "takes everything in." Her mom thinks her motor development will be early because she is motivated by her siblings' activity. Her "social smile" started at 2 months, and now she laughs when her parents play tickling games at diaper-changing or bath time. Her brother also makes her laugh by making faces and funny noises. Although she will lie quietly in her crib looking at her stuffed animals and mobiles, when she sees family members, she smiles broadly.

Charlayne's fine motor skills are developing well, and now she holds onto her bottle while she is in her mother's arms. When she is hungry and sees her bottle, she reacts by shaking in anticipation. She reaches for and grabs objects, and tries to hold her pacifier and teething bear and bring them to her mouth. She likes reaching for and holding onto hanging toys. She tries to flip or spin toys and watches her actions in the mirror. She has begun to look at books with her parents, and she vocalizes often, especially when other family members are talking as they engage in tasks such as cooking dinner. Although she is fond of social interaction and her disposition is upbeat, when she is tired she wants her mother and cries until Mom takes her.

When Mom goes back to work in 3 more weeks, Charlayne will stay with the same educarer who looks after her sister. Mom has been satisfied with this educarer because she keeps the children on their home schedule, interacts with and talks to them, and provides many stimulating toys. She hopes the educarer will note Charlayne's capabilities and her likes and dislikes. For example, Charlayne likes to have the side of her face stroked to help her go to sleep and to "nudge" up into the neck area of the adult when she is being held. She doesn't like being cold, doesn't sleep well if she is not warm, and she gets upset when other children cry. Since Charlayne likes to be in an upright position, her mom wants the educarer to put her in sitting-up positions to observe what is going on. When Charlayne is fussy, hungry, or tired, the educarer should take a few minutes to give her attention, not ignore her fussiness. This educare setting has a multiage group of children, so Charlayne will not be isolated, which is important to the parents, who believe that children learn much from siblings and peers, and that concept understanding is greater when children of different ages are together. The family lives in a culturally diverse area, and they believe it is important for Charlayne and her sister (who is also adopted and biracial) to be exposed to many racial and cultural groups.

BARNIE WAS BORN in an eastern state, the home state of his mother, and has only recently moved to a midwestern state. When Barnie was born, he weighed 7 pounds, 5½ ounces, and was 21 inches long. His mother says she had an easy delivery and Barnie "came out screaming." He had a full head of black hair and big brown eyes (he still has both). His mom had her own mother, father, and sister at the hospital, and she and Barnie stayed until recently at the family home of her extended African American family. Although they were living with her family, Mom provided most of Barnie's care because she wanted to be sure he bonded well with her.

At first, Barnie just ate and slept, with a relatively regular 4-hour schedule. Barnie's mother nursed him for a week, primarily because her doctor told her that the early breast milk would help him get the nutrients he

needed. She "never intended to nurse," however, so Barnie has been fed by bottle since then. He never had a fussy period; he just gradually began to stay up for longer time periods. He still wakes once during the night to be fed and takes about four short naps during the day.

At about 2 months old, Barnie began looking around more, and was especially attracted to voices. Mom started reading to him from a children's Bible and some other books every day because reading calmed him, and she still shares this reading time with him. She remarks that "he didn't get playful" until about 3 months; it was about then that he started to hold onto objects, such as rattles, toy keys, and pacifiers, and to engage in social interactions. At 4 months, Barnie weighs 15 pounds, 11 ounces. He bites on "whatever he gets his hands on" and drools, so his mother thinks he will be getting some teeth soon. He eats cereal, likes to ride in his stroller or rock in the stroller-glider, and is alert and friendly when people talk to him, getting excited when he hears people's voices.

When they lived in the house with many people, the noise and activity sometimes made Barnie too active, so Mom prefers her present location, which is an apartment that she and Barnie share near the campus of the university she attended. She says he sleeps better now than he did when he was living in the noisy family home. Barnie had no difficulty with the plane trip and has made a good adjustment to the move, although he cried when he first saw his father, who lives in the present area. He sees his dad regularly now, but his parents have no plans to marry.

Barnie exhibits motor skills that include pushing himself up with his hands when he is lying on his stomach (he doesn't like to lie on his back), sitting while propped up to look around and reach for toys, and having his mom hold him up to stand. He enjoys tickling and other touching games and laughs delightedly with Mom as the game patterns continue.

Barnie started in educare when he was 9 weeks old because his mother was working. She chose the program because her sister worked in the building. He seemed to get along well, never crying when his mother left, but smiling when she came to get him. The main thing Mom was concerned about in the group program was that it be clean, with changing tables cleaned routinely and educarers washing their hands often. She wasn't too concerned that the educarers didn't play much because Barnie really didn't play then, but she was upset because they didn't seem very personal and warm. When she was there observing, she noticed that the educarers "yelled at the children."

In her new location, she is looking for work, and she will have subsidized educare to enable that. She visited four home educare sites from the list Community Coordinated Child Care (4C) provided because she wants a home program where Barnie can "feel like he's at home." She has selected the one that is cleanest and well organized, with an educarer who "talks to the children with respect." She thought some of the other programs seemed to be "in chaos." She says she "saved up to come here so I could have time to be picky about a program for Barnie." Her main advice to educarers is that "the biggest thing is not to be afraid to be affectionate. Babies can feel it if you don't like them. They get scared and distant." When mothers can't care for their children because they have to work, they still want their children to feel like they are being loved.

CURRICULUM PRIORITIES

A change from the 2- to 3-month period is that infants of about 4 months enjoy being held or propped in an upright position. Their head stability is well established, and their torso is gaining strength. With increased gross motor control, they reach for, bat at, and grasp objects within reach. These voluntary reaching behaviors are an important developmental milestone (Bushnell & Boudreau, 1993). Now that their range of vision has become more similar to that of adults, they exhibit more curiosity about their world. With refined visual discrimination, they practice visually guided grasping as their eyes and hands begin to coordinate. They have discovered their hands and watch intensely as they repeatedly clasp and unclasp their hands. As the mothers recognize, their children have established distinct preferences for how they are held, played with, fed, diapered, and soothed, and thus it is important to have consistent educarers who know their preferences. The infants remember routine events and can indicate anticipation of the sequence of events (e.g., arching their bodies in anticipation of being picked up, calming down when they see their bottles being prepared). Their communication efforts are more distinct and varied, and they enjoy turn-taking dialogues and games. They play with making sounds like cooing, laughing, and screaming/ shouting to garner attention. They are better able to self-calm, especially in peaceful environments. These children demonstrate that they recognize family members and consistent educarers and respond differentially to them. They distinguish between familiar and unfamiliar faces, although they do not show stranger anxiety yet. Although they love social play, they engage in solitary activities (primary circular reactions, Piaget, 1952), playing with their hands, voices, and sounds. Curriculum priorities include:

1. Nurturing consistently, accounting for child preferences and individual differences, with primary, consistent educarers who establish routines that the children can anticipate
2. Meeting children's communication attempts with responsiveness; learning each child's way of communicating; interpreting children's feelings of anger, fear, or unhappiness; and helping them to self-calm

3. Providing opportunities to practice developing motor and sensory skills (e.g., reaching, grasping) in a safe but varied environment

RECOMMENDED CHARACTERISTICS OF THE ENVIRONMENT

This environment is similar to that recommended for younger infants. These children still need a homelike and calm environment with sensory richness but moderate load. A welcoming environment for parents continues to be especially needed because parents often start their children in educare at this age. In addition to the suggestions given for younger infants, the environment should include the following:

*   Safe sling-type chairs that permit infants to be in more upright positions are a good addition, as long as they are not overused. A good way to help infants observe their environment is to hold them on your lap facing outward, so it is essential that you also have comfortable seating.
*   The environment must be more interactive than it was previously, with many objects that infants can use to exercise their sensorimotor schemata. Most objects will be mouthed first, then grasped and shaken; therefore, they must be cleaned often and should have no loose parts.
*   A low mirror is a good addition. Although infants will not yet recognize themselves, they will respond to the image with smiles and playful behavior. Faces hold more interest to children of this age than do inanimate objects.
*   Objects that can dangle safely in infants' line of vision are of interest. With their increased ability to touch and handle objects, they will reach or hit such objects to make an effect.

SAMPLE CURRICULUM ACTIVITIES

Knowledge Construction

Sensorimotor/Physical/Relational Knowledge.

Most sensory activities for younger infants can be continued with elaborations that challenge 3- to 4-month-olds. These activities build infants' knowledge of the physical world and their understanding of the physical relationships between aspects of that world.

*   For visual experiences, mobiles and chains hung over the crib within children's reach are of interest. Small crib gyms can be placed over supine infants. Mobiles, gyms, and chains should be commercial products that are well tested for safety because infants of this age

may pull apart homemade chains. When infants combine visual and motor activity to reach for and engage objects, they practice intermodal coordination, furthering their relational knowledge. Cause and effect is explored as the child discovers that his or her movements can affect objects that are dangling overhead. Infants' increased memory skills enable them to habituate to stimuli more quickly. Thus, you should change mobiles and crib/wall decorations frequently when infants lose interest. You should also change their positions frequently to keep the visual environment challenging.

- For auditory experiences, toy sound variety can be increased; some toys should emit sounds when they are accidentally batted. This early cause/effect relationship shows one of the first ways infants intentionally learn to cause an effect. You can give them rattles and small balls with bells inside, or attach wrist or ankle bands with bells on them to help them locate and activate the sound. You can attach a cushion with squeakers inside to boards at the end of cribs so that if infants' feet press against the squeakers, they will learn that kicking the board causes the sound. Objects that make sounds when jiggled or batted also encourage practice play (secondary circular reactions, Piaget, 1962).
- For tactile, olfactory, and gustatory experiences, expand the range of types of touch, smells, and tastes.
- Daily excursions outdoors give infants a new set of sensory experiences of wind, sun, birdsong, changes in air temperature, and a variety of visual environments.

NAEYC Accreditation Criteria 2.G.01 (Science), Standard 2: Curriculum: "Infants, toddlers/twos are provided varied opportunities and materials to use their senses to learn about objects in the environment, discover that they can make things happen, and solve simple problems."

Social Knowledge Construction

Although even 2-month-olds demonstrate some understanding of social turn-taking rules, 3- to 4-months-olds show greater understanding of the arbitrary social knowledge embedded in language, sound play, and song, and they show active participation in turn-taking patterns. Because of their unique environments, they may each learn somewhat different patterns of interaction, but all children of this age are ready to learn social knowledge.

- Through observation and reading infant cues, consistent educarers become familiar with infants' preferences and individual needs.

You can then establish individualized communications patterns and practice varied strategies that particular children will like and respond to positively. Charlayne's and Barnie's mothers shared preferences that their children exhibit that would help an educarer (e.g., their favorite positions). You can ask parents from various cultures to assist you in understanding how their individual child's preferences and the family culture affect their social interaction patterns.

- Because infants this age understand basic social routines and anticipate routine events, you should provide continuity of care and play routines to help them gain social knowledge. You can also talk to them about what is going to happen next and describe events as they happen so that they learn signals for routines.

- You can communicate the social knowledge embedded in colorful books, photographs, or drawings to infants of this age. Hold the infant on your lap and look at such materials while talking about what you are seeing. Children's interest span will be short, but over time it will lengthen and infants will begin to anticipate this "book-reading" script.

Social-Emotional Relationship Building

Activities that build social knowledge also build good social-emotional relationships because children's knowledge of the meanings and practices of the social world and their feelings of competence, trust, and attachment are complementary.

- Because infants' knowledge base now enables them to distinguish between familiar and unfamiliar faces and anticipate routine events, consistency of educare staff is even more important. Consistent educarers help children gain a sense that the world is a predictable place. Once the children in your care recognize that familiar events are about to take place or anticipate that their urgent needs will be met, you should follow through and not abruptly stop or delay the activity that has started. If follow-through is inconsistent and/or your emotional tone or activity style varies with your moods, infants may be confused and unsettled.

- Infants' enjoyment of both "conversations" and play activities with educarers greatly facilitates the establishment of an attachment bond for both participants. Remember, attachments between infants and educarers do not interfere with family attachment bonds. Families are usually helpful in suggesting how you and their infant can strengthen your relationship. By having a good relationship with the infant, you will also strengthen your relationship with the family. This will also help you to show respect for the family's cultural practices.

- Often, infants this age begin to eat cereal or other solids. If solids are fed with a spoon, the infant can experience the distinct flavors and textures of each. You need patience to acclimate infants to solid food, but because it is an important way to build social-emotional relationships, helping children learn to take food from a spoon is worth doing with full attention and engagement. You should also talk about what you are doing (e.g., "Taste this good cereal!"). Keep a positive emotional tone when introducing infants to new textures and tastes so that they will see eating as a positive social time. (Note: Don't put cereal in the bottle; this may lead to choking or middle-ear infections, because the structure of the infant ear does not allow good drainage.)
- Now that infants are more physically active, you must be vigilant when changing diapers or clothing on a table surface. Often, playing social games can keep infants' attention and make them calmer during routine care activities. They can learn to anticipate that diaper- or clothing-changing time is interaction time.

Play Development

As an educarer, your repertoire of social games can be used in a variety of settings and circumstances. Here are a few examples:

- During caregiving activities, you might play "Round and Round," in which you trace a finger in a circular motion on the infant's stomach while chanting "Round and round and round and in the hole" when touching the infant's navel.
- Variations of peekaboo can be done from behind your hand, with a blanket, or popping up from around a corner or below furniture.
- "So Big" is a lap game and muscle stretcher: Say "How big is baby? SOOOO big!" while holding the infant's hands together in front, then stretching them out wide to the infant's sides at the end of the chant.
- To strengthen muscle control, play a game of pulling the infant from a supine to a sitting position and then to a standing position. You can then reverse the action to sitting, then to lying down. Accompany the actions with a chant, for example, "Barnie is sitting up, Barnie is standing up, Barnie is sitting down, Barnie is lying down." It is likely that the infant's anticipation will be evident and many repetitions may be called for.
- Every activity can include a singing game. For example, when feeding cereal to an infant you can make up words to include the infant's name: "Charlayne is eating lunch, eating lunch, eating lunch; Charlayne is eating lunch, in her chair" (sung to tune of "Mary Had a Little Lamb").

NAEYC Accreditation Criteria 2.E.01 (Early Literacy) Standard 2: Curriculum: "Infants have varied opportunities to experience songs, rhymes, routine games and books through (bullet one) individualized play that includes simple rhymes, songs, and interactive games (e.g., peekaboo)."

CULTURAL CONSIDERATIONS

It is important to learn about families and their cultural backgrounds, goals, and aspirations for their children before beginning educare of a child. One way to do this is to provide a questionnaire at intake that gathers information and identifies expectations that parents have for the educare of their child. Questions might include ones about the family size and ages, primary language, child's ethnicity, discipline methods, special occasions celebrated, foods that religion or culture forbid, nicknames, and sleeping patterns (Mangione, 1995; see Appendix D). Extended families like the one in Barnie's life often have multiple caregivers to whom the child learns to relate. Children may sleep with other children or with their parents, making it more difficult for a child to fall asleep alone in a crib or on a cot in an educare setting.

QUESTIONS FOR DISCUSSION

1. Charlayne's mother says she gives the infant cereal in her bottle. Since doctors discourage parents from doing that, how might you discuss this issue with Charlayne's mother in a way that would be respectful of her views and practices?
2. If this is when children begin educare, how can you learn about their established preferences and help them adjust and feel comfortable with the educare routines?
3. How would you meet the needs of children whose parents want them to have experiences that are congruent with the child's racial and cultural heritage?
4. What would you do to help a child with a "difficult" temperament learn to self-calm if that skill did not seem to be developing well?

Chapter 5

6-7 Months

Curriculum for RYAN and JORDAN

RYAN'S MOTHER COMMENTS that her son is a "big baby," falling in the 99th percentile for both length and weight. At 6 months, he weighs 22½ pounds and is 29 inches long. He has big blue eyes, brown hair, long curly eyelashes, and "a wonderful smile." During his first few months, he was colicky. His mother spent much time holding and rocking him, and nursed him 12 to 14 times a day. He seemed ravenous when he was not in pain from gas. Because Ryan's mother had chosen to be a single parent, she went through this period taking full responsibility for his care, without the support of his father or other relatives.

Despite her concern that Ryan was never going to be a happy child, at about 8 weeks of age, he began to coo, gurgle, and smile frequently, and he was soon laughing out loud. Now Ryan is a cheerful, friendly child who has a smile for everyone. He is happy 90% of the time, and fusses only when he is hungry, tired, bored, or gassy.

During his first month, Ryan was a light sleeper, napping frequently during the day. He nursed on demand and awakened two or three times a night to nurse. Now he wakes once a night and takes 2- to 3-hour naps at home, sleeping more soundly than he did previously. His mother and Ryan "co-sleep" (i.e., he sleeps in her bed), which she believes is a natural and essential part of her parenting role.

Ryan finds many things in his home environment entertaining. He loves looking at books with colorful pictures, listening to music, watching the disco light on his bedroom wall, playing with his toes and fingers, and watching birds. He enjoys splashing in the bathtub and dipping his feet in the creek to which his mother frequently hikes, carrying Ryan on her back. He especially likes watching and listening to running water. He also enjoys banging and chewing a rattle on his walker. He grabs his toes and chews on them when entertaining himself in his crib. He holds his arms out and watches his fingers. Although Ryan prefers to be with people, he entertains himself for about a half hour in the early morning and in the evening. Ryan's greatest strength is his sociability. He quickly seeks eye contact when he is spoken to and he will become vocal in response. His mother calls him "nosy" because he is so interested in people.

Ryan demonstrates strength in his ability to maneuver objects from hand to hand and then into his mouth; thus, he now enjoys eating solid foods. He has learned to roll from front to back and vice versa when attempting to get objects that are just out of his reach, and he has recently begun to play while on his stomach. He used to fuss right away if someone put him down stomach-first. Whenever he rolls over or pushes himself up on his arms, he shows pride in his growing abilities by smiling and looking at his mother. He also shows pleasure when he is propped in a sitting position.

Ryan has been in an educare program since an early age because his mother works outside the home. She states that she wants his educarers to have lots of contact with him in order to get to know him well. They should be aware of his emerging skills and encourage him to practice them. She wants all of his needs to be met; food, clean diapers and clothes, and safety issues must be attended to, but most important, he needs to receive love and attention.

JORDAN IS A PETITE, dark-haired child with blue eyes and a dimple on her left cheek. At 7 months, she is wiry, active, and in constant motion when she is awake and alert. She's also a verbal child, frequently crowing to get others' attention. Jordan's mother describes her as having a "light switch" personality: One minute she's on, happy and content, and the next she's off, fussy and contentious. As a newborn, she was sensitive, demanding, and colicky.

Jordan does nothing by halves. Whatever her mood, it is intensely expressed. During her first month, she cried often and could be calmed only by forceful patting, rocking, and bouncing accompanied by verbal soothing. She nursed every 2 hours around the clock, taking only short naps in between. She did not develop a routine schedule for months, and she still likes to nurse every few hours during the day. Her mother has seen significant changes in Jordan since her first month. She is more self-controlled and relaxed, and although she cries when she is hungry, tired, or hurt, she can be more easily distracted and is less demanding than she used to be. When Jordan wakes from a nap or finishes nursing, she is full of energy and ready to play. She is not one to stay quietly in her crib after waking.

Jordan loves people, and when playing alone, she frequently "checks in" with family members. She has a playful relationship with her 4-year-old brother and an exciting rough-and-tumble relationship with her father. At the present time, Jordan's parents are separated and in the process of getting a divorce, but her father is living next door now, so she still sees him often.

After people, her next love is movement, and lots of it. She likes being pushed in her stroller and swinging in her wind-up swing. She sits well without support, but because she is wiry and strong, she is in constant motion even while sitting. She successfully reaches for and grasps objects without toppling. Jordan now pulls herself up on furniture or when holding someone's fingers. She can get up on her hands and knees and rock if someone steadies her knees. While sitting, she attempts to turn her body to reach toys. Jordan is beginning to drink from a cup and experiment with putting a spoon in her mouth.

Jordan's play style is as intense as her personality. She demands constant stimulation and requires frequent changes in her environment. Her mother says that when Jordan is presented with a new plaything, she is cautious at first, then jumps right in with a "rough, tough" manner, grabbing, banging, and throwing the object. Water play consumes her for a long time, as she splashes and swishes her hands in a tub on the floor. She enjoys manipulating and exploring playthings. She plays with her voice, making raspberry sounds and repeating "da da da da."

Jordan's mother is a home educarer who cares for Jordan and other children. If Jordan had to have a different educarer, Mom would like them to be flexible and relaxed. They need to be willing to experiment to find what techniques work best with her, and the environment needs to be calm and relaxed because Jordan is easily overstimulated. Her mother says that Jordan can sense when adults are uptight and that can set her off. She jokes that Jordan's educarers need to have "strong arms and earplugs" to work with her highly sociable and very vocal child.

CURRICULUM PRIORITIES

By the age of 6–7 months, individual differences in infants' development become more apparent, and personality characteristics that differentiated them from birth are major mediators of the way they learn about their world. These two mothers recognize the unique characteristics of their children and have been successful in adapting their caregiving and play interactions to accommodate their children's preferences. They know the strengths of their children, and although they don't have major concerns, they do provide suggestions to educarers about the ways they want their children's development fostered. Both Ryan and Jordan are already fully social beings with strong attachments to family members.

The thrill of emerging mobility, combined with growing curiosity about how things work, are hallmarks of the 6- to 7-month-old. Gaining the ability to sit up changes children's experiences and their "worldview." This developmental milestone also alerts educarers to the need to monitor the "inexpert" phases of sitting (e.g., when there is a likelihood of falling over) and to meet individual needs while still supervising the group of children. Sensory and physical development of children this age is of major importance, and curriculum should incorporate opportunities for children to exercise and master sensorimotor coordination of fine motor and gross motor skills. Children this age are beginning to show intentional goal-directed behavior in experimentation with objects, and they are fascinated with cause-and-effect phenomena. Although babbling sounds still gives them sensory satisfaction, they show evidence of intentional attempts at communication, and thus, the curriculum should provide opportunities for social, play-related communication attempts. As infants reach out to their world, they need to have adults describe their actions and give names to objects. Frequent dialogues with children are critical for reinforcing and encouraging repetition of vowel and consonant combinations as well as varying intonation. Curriculum priorities include:

1. Meeting emerging individual preferences in regard to basic care and fostering children's ability to communicate those preferences.
2. Building on children's strong parental attachment by having consistent and responsive caregiving and play interactions, especially if children enter educare at this age (This is even more important if children do not have secure attachments within their families.)
3. Providing opportunities for children to exercise their sensory, physical-motor, communication, and social skills, in particular assisting them to develop fine and gross motor skills, gain a sense of control over objects, and enjoy their practice play, and thus, their "thinking in action."

RECOMMENDED CHARACTERISTICS OF THE ENVIRONMENT

Although many of the environmental characteristics for younger children still apply, there are a number of additions needed for children of this age.

- Safe and well-defined activity spaces are needed so that the infants can explore and manipulate many different objects.
- The presence of low mirrors that are securely attached will enhance the development of identity.
- There should be many objects that encourage examining, shaking, banging, dropping, and throwing, all of which are "thinking in action" schemes.
- For infants who are just learning to sit without support, as well as for newly sitting infants, placement within soft "walls" to cushion slumps and falls is important. These "observational" locations will enable children to be onlookers at the activities of mobile peers.
- For active infants who may be rolling, creeping, or pulling up, a safe space in which to move is needed so they can "travel" without danger to themselves or others.

- When infants can sit alone, small chairs (5½ inches) and tables (12 inches) are preferred over high chairs. High chairs take up more space and are not as safe; thus, they require close supervision. If children cannot sit up independently to eat, they should be held while being fed rather than propped.

SAMPLE CURRICULUM ACTIVITIES

Knowledge Construction

Sensorimotor/Physical/Relational Knowledge

- Because they now have motor skills to make toys work, rattles, squeakers, and other types of sound toys are of interest, and there are many well-made commercial ones available. If there is close supervision, you can make rattles inexpensively with dried beans, beads, popcorn kernels, and other small materials placed in small juice cans, plastic pill bottles, or other hand-sized containers. You must cover them with plastic tape to close them securely and you must be present when they are used. Such objects can be handed to infants in order to encourage them to reach with alternate hands each time the object is offered. Infants of this age may also pass objects from one hand to the other, thus gaining practice in crossing their midline.
- For infants who are not yet sitting alone or comfortable being on their stomach, visual exploration while lying on their backs is very important. These infants can also benefit greatly from being placed on your lap to observe and manipulate objects.
- For infants who are sitting or lying on their stomachs, toys can be placed just out of their reach to encourage them to stretch to retrieve the toys and to use a pincer grasp.
- If infants are seated in small chairs (or high chairs), they will shake, bang, drop, and begin to throw toys. You can tie objects to the chair for easier retrieval; however, to encourage object permanence and cause/effect thinking, when objects are dropped, the objects should be unobservable to the infants until they look down to view them.
- You can present other homemade items to seated infants to encourage them to explore cause and effect. Large objects that roll when pushed are appealing, such as oatmeal, corn, or salt boxes (with sealed lids) and paper towel rolls. You can place colorful objects such as shiny paper, buttons, or strings of beads inside sturdy, clear plastic boxes and tape them shut. These encourage shaking, twisting, and turning motions. There are many commercial toys that serve similar purposes.
- Infants of this age enjoy placing smaller objects inside larger ones. In addition to commercial nesting toys, many types of scrap

materials can be used to make nesting toys and containers. You can use various-sized cardboard boxes or plastic food containers with items such as large beads or bells, clothespins, or measuring spoons. Anything given to infants must be large enough not to be swallowed and sturdy enough to withstand their use, because their motor control is not yet refined and mouthing actions are still in evidence.

- These infants also enjoy exploring different textures. There are many interesting surfaces for infants to explore, both indoors and outdoors. You can carry infants around and let them touch textures on walls or press bubble wrap, pieces of fabric, corrugated cardboard, and other textures, or you can tape a variety of texture squares on walls or make them into a quilt or book. Offering small, commercial rubber balls with textures or bumps (about 4 inches in size) also encourages tactile exploration.

- Six- to 7-month-olds love water. Ryan enjoys listening to and watching flowing water. Jordan plays for long periods in small tubs of water on the floor. For this activity, you should place towels under and around tubs for easy cleanup, and provide infants with support as they lean into the container to splash and swirl their hands in the warm water. They should probably also be wearing only a diaper for this kind of play.

- By 6 months, infants become intrigued by their image in the mirror. If a hand mirror is held to their faces, they will react with interest. A peekaboo mirror can be made by covering the mirror with fabric and letting an infant look under the fabric to see the "other" infant. Photos of familiar people can also be hidden behind cloths. These activities give infants practice in understanding object permanence (i.e., knowledge that objects still exist even if they are out of sight).

NAEYC Accreditation Criteria 2.C.02 (Physical Development) Standard 2 Curricula: "Infants and toddlers/twos have multiple opportunities to develop fine motor skills by acting on their environments using their hands and fingers in a variety of age-appropriate ways."

Social Knowledge Construction

- There is an infinite number of language activities that educarers can provide infants of this age. You can sing songs, play lap games, recite poems, and engage in finger and toe play. There are many commercial tapes and CDs available with international lullabies and other songs sung in a variety of languages (see Appendix A).

- You should use every opportunity to carry on "conversations" with infants. When they babble, you can imitate the sounds made to encourage the infants to make more sounds. You can talk to infants about every action as you change, feed, or dress them; use their names frequently; and give labels to objects as you point to them (e.g., "This is your shoe"). At this age, children's understanding of the meanings embedded in language is beginning, so they will gain much social knowledge through your communications with them.

NAEYC Accreditation Criteria 2.D.01 (Language Development) Standard Curriculum: "Children are provided with opportunities for language acquisition that align with the program philosophy, consider family perspectives, and consider community perspectives."

Social-Emotional Relationship Building

- Many "exciting" social routines can be used with infants of this age, such as "gonna get you" or tickling games, but only after you have established a good attachment relationship. If infants have played such games with their parents, they will be familiar with the routines and will react with pleasure if a well-known educarer initiates such routines. These activities can be scary to infants, however, if an unknown person initiates them, if the infant's attachment to the familiar person is anxious or avoidant, if the interaction style is too intense, or if it is very different from that which the child experiences with parents or other familiar individuals.
- Many of the relationship-building actions that educarers use with younger infants continue to be important. Infants who have been in the educare program from the time they were 2 to 4 months old will now have a good attachment established with their consistent adults. However, some infants begin educare at about 6 months, and if that is the case, you need to be sure that you are focusing especially on the many relationship-building actions that were suggested for earlier-age children. You always need to pay special attention to providing a warm and nurturing environment to help children's initial entry into educare, no matter what their age of entry.

NAEYC Accreditation Criteria 2.B.03 (Social-Emotional Development) Standard: Curriculum: "Children have varied opportunities to learn the skills needed to regulate their emotions, behavior and attention."

Play Development

Social play is extremely prominent at this age, and educarers can give infants practice in a number of social and emotional skill areas through responsive interactions in social routines such as peekaboo. Any handy covering device can be used, including hands, blankets, or furniture to peek around. You should be aware that because children are good at anticipating the activity, they may be ready to initiate it when they are in a location or at a time period in which it usually occurs. Therefore, your responsiveness when they initiate social gameplay is very important.

Infants of this age are very involved in practice play, much of which focuses on motor coordination skills. You should provide opportunities for this type of play and, because these infants are good imitators of actions, if you initiate a new way to interact physically with objects, they will be very likely to absorb that new action and use it in future practice play. For example, if a child is putting blocks into a plastic box, you might show the child how to dump the blocks out of the container, saying "Whee" as the blocks spill out. It is very likely that the child will then imitate that action and sound, thus establishing a new practice play routine that might be elaborated with other objects and other containers.

NAEYC Accreditation Criteria 2.C.01 (Physical Development) Standard: Curriculum: "Infants and toddlers/twos are provided an environment that allows them to move freely and achieve mastery of their bodies through self-initiated movement. They have multiple opportunities to practice emerging skills in coordination, movement, and balance, as well as perceptual-motor integration."

QUESTIONS FOR DISCUSSION

1. How can the same environment be arranged to accommodate both children like Ryan and those who are more like Jordan? Does Jordan need different types of toys from Ryan? Why or why not?

2. What are some other gamelike social routines that could enhance these children's development? What are some other object play activities?

3. Jordan and Ryan had somewhat similar temperaments as very young infants, but their temperaments seem to be different now. How would you have met their care and social-emotional needs if they had both started in the educare program at 2 months of age?

4. One of these children's parents is a single mother and the other is presently divorcing, although the father may stay active in the child's life. Are there some things that educarers can do to support single and divorced parents' needs and to assist their children's social-emotional relationship building?

5. What are other activities that could support these children's growing ability to "feel accepted and gain a sense of belonging," as stated in NAEYC standard 2.L.02?

Chapter 6

9–10 Months

Curriculum for GARRETT, DARA, and STAN

WITH HIS BIG BROWN EYES, long eyelashes, and sweet smile, Garrett looks like the "ideal" infant pictured on the jars of a popular baby food. Garrett's mother reports that from birth he was good-natured, not fussy, calm, adaptable, and predictable. Although he has a good disposition, she also attributes his ability to fit into a predictable routine to the child-rearing practices his parents use. (They took a class before he was born that advised them on establishing routines.) Garrett quickly adjusted to a 3-hour feeding routine and began to sleep through the night at 2 months old. As he grew older, he demonstrated good ability to play by himself. When he woke from his nap, he would "talk" and manipulate toys for a while rather than scream to get up. He vocalized often and was aware of colors, shapes, and sounds, especially musical ones. He watched a musical shapes videotape from 3 months, giving it sustained attention and vocalizing while watching. He also loved manipulable toys that made noises.

At 9½ months, Garrett exhibits many of the same traits in behavior and temperament that his mother noted earlier. Although he is more strong-willed and less adaptable, he can be easily distracted. He is good-natured, likes routines, and is not temperamental. His sleep patterns remain regular (from 7:00 P.M. to 7:00 A.M.), and he takes two naps of 1½ hours each. He was breastfed for 4 months; now he holds his own bottle (while lying in his mother's arms), but he does not yet drink from a cup. He feeds himself cereal, crackers, cheese cubes, and other finger food, and is on "Stage 2" baby food. His mother also feeds him soft regular foods (e.g., squash, mashed potato). He has six teeth and "bites" the spoon when he is fed. Although his birth weight and height were typical (7 pounds, 3 ounces; 20

inches), he presently has a long (30 inches), lean (20 pounds) body.

His overall coordination is good, but he is not advanced in motor skills. He sat up well at 6½ months and now propels himself around the room with a rolling "commando" crawl. He has strong legs, having used a "jump" seat, and enjoys holding onto adult fingers while he is in a standing position. He does not yet stand alone or walk around furniture, and he does not get himself into a standing position.

His ability to entertain himself has continued; he sits and plays with toys for 10 to 30 minutes at a time, especially if they are toys with high affordance. He examines them, spins or otherwise moves their parts, responds to changes that result from his manipulations, and "talks" to them. His finger-thumb grasp is present, but he still uses a whole-hand grasp of objects. He looks for toys when he drops them, deliberately dropping or throwing them and then searching for them. He uses action schemes appropriate for the objects (e.g., he shakes keys, spins dials, looks at pictures in books). His intense interest in his toys is a quality noted in children characterized as "patterners."

His responsiveness to people can be seen in his peekaboo play, in which he manipulates the blanket himself, and in patty-cake, although he does not always respond on command. He looks at objects when his mother says "where's (a familiar object)" and he understands routine statements. He babbles nonspecific consonant-vowel combinations such as "ba ba." Recently, he said "ma ma" and now says this "word" when his mother walks out of the room. He is attached to both his mother and father, but he is not strange with new people, although he stares at them and then looks at his mother for reassurance.

Garrett's mother would like him to learn to stand alone, understand more words and questions, eat chunkier food, point to objects, and manipulate more complex toys. She wants him to learn sign language because she is taking another class in which the instructor suggested that children of this age can be taught signs to make their basic wants known (e.g., "more," "all done") so they will not be frustrated in communicating. She was concerned that Garrett was slow to crawl; however, his recent unconventional but effective crawling technique has allayed that concern.

Garrett is presently in an educare program two mornings a week while his mother works. Because he is such an adaptable baby and so good at entertaining himself, she is concerned that he might not be getting enough attention from the educarers, who spend a lot of their time with "fussier" children. Her main advice to educarers is not to ignore the adaptable children. Mom also has Garrett in a play group with three other children. He is the only child who is not yet walking, and he spends most of his time watching rather than interacting with the other children.

AT BIRTH, DARA was in the typical weight and height range (6 pounds, 9 ounces; 19 inches), but at 9½ months she is on the wiry side, weighing 16½ pounds and being 27 inches long. She has red-blond hair and

hazel eyes and is just getting her first tooth. Dara's mother describes her baby's temperament as "patient." Dara has never been a demanding baby, but from an early age she spent long periods gazing at patterns (e.g., her quilt) and people (e.g., faces). Other words her mother used to describe her were "charming, sweet, sociable, and happy." From her first months, she has wanted to make eye contact with people, and she began to smile at family members at about 2 months. Except when she was sick, she was not a hard crier, and although she required feeding about every 2 hours, she moved to a regular schedule of every 4 hours by the age of 3 months. It took her a long time to sleep through the night, however; 4 hours was about the longest amount of time she could go without eating. She started cereal at 4½ months but is still being breastfed twice a day, although she feeds herself crackers and cheese pieces and eats some baby food. She presently goes to sleep at 9:30 or 10:00 P.M. at night (the family's preferred schedule), and then sleeps until morning. She takes a long morning nap and sleeps for a short while in the afternoon at her educarer's home, when Dara's mother is at her part-time teaching job.

At 9½ months, Dara is very active. She sat without support at 5 months and began crawling at 7 months. Now she pulls herself up to a standing position without support, although she has not yet begun to take steps. When she falls, she cries for a minute or two, then goes on with her activity. She can stoop and recover her balance and presently spends much of her time changing her position from sitting to standing and vice versa; it looks like her crawling days will soon be over.

Dara's fine motor skills include having a finger-thumb grasp and being able to bang cubes and manipulate a range of toys. She enjoys playing ball and interacting with the family dog. She likes toys that make noise, such as bells or musical toys. She can uncover hidden objects and remembers some previous actions. For example, she unrolled the toilet paper once and now does that whenever the opportunity presents itself.

She babbles a range of nonspecific consonant-vowel combinations, such as "la la" and "da da," and is beginning to understand her name and the word *no*. Because she is now routinely getting to places in the home that have out-of-bounds objects, this word is one she hears frequently. Some of her imitative actions, such as clapping and waving, were learned at her educarer's home. Although Dara is sociable, she primarily focuses on interactions with adults. When she is with other children, she watches their activity. She is showing separation anxiety, clinging to her mother when it is time to separate at the educarer's home and the church nursery. She also cries more if her mother is there when she falls than she does when other adults are present.

Dara is in a home educare setting because her parents don't want her to be with a large number of children. Her mother has definite ideas about what she wants in terms of educarer behavior. She doesn't want Dara put in a playpen for a long time, preferring her to have attention when she is awake. Mom does not want Dara to watch videos; she wants firm, consistent discipline (such as the use of the word *no*); and she expects that the educarer will help Dara learn skills. It is important that Dara's educarer have Christian values and exemplify them by having a religious emphasis at holidays. Her parents especially don't want Dara to hear about Halloween witches or other such non-Christian entities.

STAN'S PARENTS KNEW from the prenatal amniocentesis examination that he had Down syndrome (trisomy 21, which is an extra chromosome); however, his mother experienced a normal pregnancy and he was born at full term. He weighed 8 pounds, 6 ounces; was 21¾ inches long; and received an Apgar score of 7. Unfortunately, 20 hours after birth he developed a septic infection, resulting in his heart stopping and a reversion to fetal stage in breathing. He was placed in intensive care and remained there for 1 month. According to his dad, Stan had "20 wires and tubes," and heavy respirator use resulted in his getting a perforated lung, requiring that lung to be collapsed until it had healed. Because he was a "Down child," the medical staff thought that there would likely be abnormalities in his immune system, thyroid, and/or heart. Thus, he was subjected to numerous tests to determine which physical abnormalities might have contributed to his illness. His dad says that Stan had "every medical test" during his first 6 months of life. His heart was monitored and he was on steroids until the determination was made that his physical systems were sound.

At his present age of 10 months, Stan is off medication. His parents think that his early problems were a result of an infection. A few hours after his birth, his mother had a fever due to a mild bacterial infection, and this may have been communicated to Stan at birth. Because the medical team knew about his disability, however, they saw him through that lens, and conducted extensive medical procedures to make sure no physical disability was a contributing factor to his early trauma.

His mother reports that he was 8 days old before she was allowed to hold him and she could not begin breastfeeding until he was 2½ weeks old. The traumatic start to his life may have had some effects on Stan's early social-emotional experience; during the first month at home, he was shy with nonfamily members. His overall pleasant and outgoing temperament prevailed, however, and at 10 months, he is a responsive, warm, and friendly child. He is blond and blue-eyed, just like his dad. He is an excellent sleeper, sleeping 10 hours at night and taking two short naps during the day. Stan now weighs 22 pounds and is 29 inches long. His head circumference is slightly smaller than typical. He is a good eater, "rarely missing a meal," and is beginning to feed himself cereal pieces. Both parents and medical personnel have remained "overconservative" about his health.

He was "involved with early intervention before he was born," and since he was 3 months old, he has had an Individual Family Services Plan (IFSP; explained further in Chapter 12). Stan initially received visits from a physical therapist, occupational therapist, speech therapist, and early intervention specialist every other month, and next fall, these visits will continue on a monthly schedule.

Presently, Stan is not showing any major developmental delays. His verbal skills include responsive cooing and babbling, laughing during parent play, understanding both motor and verbal cues, and vocalizing while playing with objects and people. He is responsive to faces but also enjoys toys, and he is curious about his environment. He watched his hands, tracked objects visually, and had a social smile at the typical ages. However, his gross motor development is delayed. He began to roll at about 5 months but did not roll purposefully until 9 months. He can now sit securely when placed in position, but he doesn't get in and out of a sitting position easily by himself. He is not yet interested in crawling or standing.

His fine motor skills are developing, and he can now transfer objects from one hand to the other, pick up small cereal and pasta pieces, bang two objects together, and take rings off (but not yet put them on) a stacking toy. He is beginning to clap his hands and drop objects in containers. He enjoys playing turn-taking and roughhouse games with Dad, such as "gonna get you" and being lifted in the air. He will also look at books when Mom holds and talks about them, and he likes music and the color orange. He notices peers and has brief "object-giving and object-taking" interactions with them.

Stan's parents own an educare center and have clear expectations of how Stan, as well as all infants, should be treated. They believe that children grow at their own rate and that if responsive care follows the children's leads, development will progress. Although Stan had an educarer at home until 8 months old, he is doing well at the educare program now. His parents want him to have time to explore and learn on his own with educarer facilitation rather than direct instruction. They want the educarers to be involved in the IFSP process, but they want Stan to be treated first as an individual, not as a "Down child." Although they have valued the therapeutic assistance that Stan has received, they are concerned that doctors and therapists have "preconceived notions," sometimes using words that describe Down syndrome rather than the actual child's behavior (e.g., calling Stan's 3-month responses "floppy"). They don't want assumptions made without close observation of what Stan can do, and they want him to have the opportunity to master things on his own, rather than having people assume that he won't learn without their intensive intervention.

CURRICULUM PRIORITIES

The period around 9 to 10 months is when many parents and educarers realize that they truly have a "person" to educate and care for. Although much is going on in the infant's mind and body before this age, the evidence that children are beginning to understand routines, the object world, and social situations becomes stronger around this time period. Concerning 9- to 10-month-olds, adults make comments such as, "He recognizes different people and shows expectations about their behavior," "She understands what I say even if I don't gesture," and "He seems to be trying to tell me something." This is an age when children begin to explore the "wider world" and test relationships between their body space and the spaces in the environment. Many infants at this age are accomplished "space explorers." Children's newfound mobility combines with a growing curiosity about their surroundings. Most children this age are crawling or actively rolling with intent, many are traveling upright by holding on to furniture, and some are walking independently. Children who are ready to stand and walk often have short attention spans for object play because they are focused mainly on moving their body in space.

Not all children of this age will master the same curriculum goals; within each child's zone of proximal development, the goals can be adapted to their development and learning styles. Children like Dara need careful monitoring by educarers as they move quickly from place to place exploring every part of the educare setting, even those that are off-limits. They may experience many situations requiring them to learn the meaning of the word *no*. Children like Garrett and Stan need encouragement to extend their mobility. Making interesting things visible but slightly beyond their mobility range will encourage them to practice their motor skills and explore their environment. If educarers can build on their interests, the children will enjoy the challenges of greater mobility. They will express strong preferences for certain objects and people, making them less compliant, and their improved memories may cause them to become bored with the familiar. Fortunately, "old" objects and activities can become "new" with just a little change or elaboration. Curriculum priorities include:

1. Offering opportunities for children to experience the effects of their actions on objects, to learn about the movement of objects in space (both inanimate and animate objects), and to find out more about the appropriate social uses of objects
2. Providing assistance for children to gain self-regulation of eating behavior, social routines, and body control, and to become more aware of the effects of their actions on objects and other people
3. Encouraging children to use gestural communication methods to express their needs, to respond to the gestural and speech requests of adults, and to attach word labels to common objects and actions, including introduction to iconic symbols such as pictures that represent objects or people and that begin to make them aware of themselves as persons

RECOMMENDED CHARACTERISTICS OF THE ENVIRONMENT

Because there is so much variation in mobility preferences and communication motivation at this age, and because there are noticeable individual differences in abilities in these two domains, the curriculum must be varied to meet these individual differences. The physical and social environment needs to be much more complex than that for the less mobile and minimally communicative 6-month-old. All children this age need a safe physical environment that encourages exploration by whatever mobility means they are using.

- The environment should have as many supports for motor skill development as are present in environments for slightly younger and slightly older children. As Garrett, Dara, and Stan demonstrate, some children are ready to "take off" in walking, while others will not be ready for that for 3 to 5 more months. The environment should have features that allow children to pull up, stand, walk around furniture, and walk alone, along with more secluded areas where less mobile children can play for long periods without constant interruption.
- The environment should include a wide variety of responsive and slightly novel objects that are accessible but not overwhelming in number. It is best to have sufficient objects so that they can be rotated throughout the week to maintain novelty. Children this age show strong preferences for some objects and may search them out every day, so those preferred objects should be available as long as continuing interest is demonstrated. Of course, almost every object is of interest to the 9-month-old, and in the home educare setting, pots, pans, lids, and other sturdy kitchen utensils may be of even more interest than conventional toys. In that environment, there should be some cabinets or drawers that are safe and permissible for mobile children to access.
- Low (4–5 inches), deep (12 inches) steps for climbing up and down are of interest to mobile children. The steps should be carpeted or

padded. Low ramps (18 inches) are of great affordance, especially
for new crawlers. Well-stabilized tunnels made of wood or foam,
with a foam or padded ramp attached for children to crawl down
after emerging from the tunnel, are good examples of challenging yet
safe environmental features. Large foam-filled pads of a variety of
levels that can be fastened together can also be useful for crawling.
Safe, enclosed spaces for climbing into and out of are needed,
and children need to know where such activity is permitted. For
example, educarers need to decide if children can lie on low shelves,
or crawl into floor-level cabinets without doors. If not, then similar
affordances should be provided, such as boards on low trestles and
large cardboard boxes.

- A good solution for climbing, crawling into and out of, and pulling
up on is a low platform or loft that is sized to allow more than
one child to engage in an activity simultaneously, and that is also
big enough for an educarer to be part of the action while also
supervising.
- The physical environment needs to have partially isolated areas for
the more sedentary play of nonwalkers. Low shelves or padded
area dividers can provide just enough of a barrier to protect these
children from walkers during active play periods.
- Manipulable objects and stuffed animals should be placed on low
shelves that children can reach by crawling or pulling themselves up.
The shelves should be sturdy, however, and should not be able to be
tipped over by a child's weight (e.g., wall-attached).
- A "print-rich" environment that includes pictures and symbols at
children's eye level and that are related to children's experience will
be of interest.
- A box of simple musical instruments such as shakers, rattles, and
tambourines is useful for seated infants to explore. Soft cloth or
plastic blocks about 2 inches across will encourage the use of a pincer
grasp, and balls or stuffed animals with squeakers or bells hidden
inside will encourage cause/effect exploration.
- "Activity centers" that include doors or windows to open, flaps
to lift, and large buttons to push to elicit interesting sounds are
recommended. Gadget boards can be made using a smoothly sanded
wooden board and attaching items such as different types of latches,
a small wheel that spins freely, small knobs that turn, and a light
switch.
- "Activity quilts" with a variety of interesting objects attached
to them are good to add, if they were not already provided for
6-month-olds. These quilts have flaps to lift up to see plastic mirrors,
pictures of children, or drawings of familiar objects.
- Small containers such as cardboard boxes with lids that are easy to
remove and a set of strings of large beads, small balls, and plastic
figures or cars are also good additions. Children this age love to
remove lids to find out what is inside, and then dump out the

objects. These objects must, of course, be large enough not to be swallowed, since some children still mouth objects before they use newer action schemes.

SAMPLE CURRICULUM ACTIVITIES

Knowledge Construction

Physical/Relational Knowledge

- The plastic rings that were of interest for mouthing by 6-month-olds can now be used for other types of manipulation. Children will continue to chew on them, but may also bang them together, spin them, and take them off the cone, and some may attempt to place them on the cone, but will not yet be concerned about ordering. You can demonstrate this concept casually, and some children will begin to imitate and practice ordering (e.g., Garrett). You can tape down a variety of textures such as fine sandpaper, corrugated cardboard, cut-up egg cartons or bubble wrap on a low table top that standing infants can reach so they can poke, pinch, or rub the various textures. Children this age enjoy exploring small balls wrapped in double-sided tape in contrast to balls that "let go" when dropped.
- After children have explored musical instruments, you can demonstrate shaking and banging them together or tapping one on your hand. The children will imitate the actions and elaborate on them.
- Blocks provide many opportunities for physical/relational knowledge development. To encourage children's ability to reach across the midline of their bodies, you can offer them one, two, then three blocks, holding them on different sides. Because plastic blocks make an interesting clacking sound, this will entice children to bang them together.
- Children can now understand that a string tied to a toy can be used as a tool to draw the toy closer. When children are seated in chairs (or high chairs), you can offer toys that are attached to a cord so that when they drop a toy, they can retrieve it by pulling the cord. Other objects attached to a cord can be given to a child to encourage exploration of cause and effect when the child pulls on the cord. Obviously, you must closely supervise such activities; do not leave children alone when cords are involved.
- Although object permanence isn't fully established, children this age love social games that offer the anticipation of surprise. You can play simple peekaboo games by hiding behind a towel or cloth held up to the face and looking around it at the child at unpredictable intervals. A puppet can play peekaboo with a child from around the back of the high chair or from the side of the changing table.

- A child like Stan, who has shown only minimal interest in crawling or standing, might be encouraged to look for and retrieve a favorite toy if he sees it placed just out of reach, especially if you are there to encourage his efforts.
- Cause-and-effect exploration is assisted by toys that have affordances suggesting that they be pushed, pulled, pressed, turned, or squeezed in order to produce a sound, light, opened door, pop-up of an object, or other effects. Activity centers, gadget boards, and rugs with action objects to be explored are of great interest to children this age because of their developing understanding of cause/effect relationships. If children like Dara have these opportunities, there will be less occasions to have to say "no."
- The places children can crawl into and out of help them explore how their bodies fit in different-sized spaces. This not only helps spatial awareness but also promotes self-identity knowledge.

NAEYC Accreditation Criteria 2.6.01 (Science) Standard: Curriculum: "Infants and toddlers/ twos are provided varied opportunities and materials to use their senses to learn about objects in the environment, discover that they can make things happen, and solve simple problems."

Social Knowledge Construction

- By 9 months, some children can point to body parts when asked. You can give children a rag doll, and point to and label its body parts. You can also label its clothing ("She's wearing white shoes"), and talk about its hair ("What soft brown hair he has!"). You can also describe its actions as you make it walk, sit, stand, or dance.
- You can provide plastic, cloth, or cardboard books that children can handle on their own as well as books that you read to them. Picture books are most appropriate, since children this age cannot yet follow a storyline. You can hold a child on your lap and talk about familiar objects and events in each picture. Books should be only five to six pages long and should be very sturdy.
- Spontaneous recitation of familiar poems, fingerplays, and nursery rhymes are appropriate while changing children's diapers, during transition times, or when children are involved in activities. For example, while children play in a large cardboard box or sit in an open cabinet, you can recite the poem: "Here is a box/And here is the top/Lift the lid/And out (child's name) will pop!"
- Lap games are a big favorite because children can now sit up for longer periods of time. "Patty-cake" and "This Little Piggy Went to Market" help with recognition of body parts.

- You should use children's names frequently to capture or retain their attention during routine activities such as feeding or diapering, and to make them aware of the effects of their own actions ("John, you made the bell ring!").
- You can tape your own voice as well as the children's and then play the recording. The children will show signs of recognizing familiar adult voices and their own, and you can label them with names.
- While talking to children, you should modulate your voice so that children hear a variety of tones, volumes, and pitches.
- Children enjoy looking at themselves, toy animals, or dolls in a mirror, although not all children know that they are seeing themselves and the objects they are holding. You can label what they are seeing and point from the object or person to the image in the mirror.
- You can make a foot puppet by taking a baby sock and drawing a face on the toe with a permanent ink marker. Place the puppet on the child's foot to encourage the child to grasp and remove it. Because Stan is attracted to faces, this activity might encourage an understanding of his own cause/effect actions. It also could extend his social engagement.

NAEYC Accreditation Criteria 2.E.01 (Early Literacy) Standard: Curriculum: "Infants have varied opportunities to experience songs, rhymes, routine games and books through: (bullet two) daily opportunities for each child to hear and respond to various types of books including picture books, wordless books, and books with rhymes."

Social-Emotional Relationship Building

- The children can now read adults' facial expressions and respond accordingly. You can make a happy/sad puppet by using the bowl of a wooden spoon and painting a smiling face on one side and a frowning or sad face on the other. This can also be done using a paper plate. Show children one face (smiling face), and then switch it (sad face) while you imitate the facial expression as the spoon is turned. You can accompany this action with verbal labels of happy and sad. Soon the children will anticipate the emotion and their faces will mirror it.
- Your supervision is essential when children are together because they still treat one another more like objects than like other thinking, feeling beings. They may crawl over and step on one another, oblivious of their actions. Your modeling of empathy and verbalizing children's feelings can help them gain awareness of others' needs. Imitative behaviors emerge as a result of children's observation of the people in their lives. You can provide a number of activities to

strengthen the quality of children's relationships with you and help them begin the process of relating to peers.

- Simple hand or finger puppets and soft dolls are attractive at this age, and children often attempt to "talk" to them. They babble to dolls or stuffed animals as they hug them or gently pat their heads. You can model conversations using dolls and puppets, and encourage children to show affection by modeling hugging, patting, and kissing the toys.

- When a child cries or is otherwise upset, you can explain to other children why the child is upset and label the child's emotions. This demonstrates that feelings are a natural part of being, and that you recognize and have names for them. You need to help children find ways to self-calm by speaking in a quiet, soothing manner even while recognizing the child's distress.

- This is the age when children begin to understand limits. When a child's behavior is unacceptable, you can follow limit setting with an explanation stated in positive terms. For example, "Your cup stays on the table."

- To foster self-identity and peer recognition, you can seat two children in front of a large mirror and draw their attention to their images. You can talk about things as what they are doing and what clothing they have on.

NAEYC Accreditation Criteria 2.B.03 (Social-Emotional Development) Standard 2: Curriculum: "Children have varied opportunities to learn the skills needed to regulate their emotions, behavior and attention."

Play Development

- At this age, practice play is beginning to take the place of simple exploration of objects. Children like Garrett are already involved in extended practice play routines. Children like Dara are more likely to have a short attention span for fine motor play because they are more focused on practicing their gross motor skills, and children like Stan are not yet engaged in extended practice play. You can engage most children in fine motor practice play by playing with them. You might bring out interesting sound-making or puzzlelike toys and start the play; then, as they become engaged, you can leave briefly while staying in their sight, returning frequently to acknowledge their activities. Although children like Garrett are good at entertaining themselves for long periods, they also need your involvement in their object play. You should resist allowing object-oriented children to spend a long time in practice play at the expense of social interactions with them. As Garrett's mother noted, such children should not be overlooked even though more active children or children with special needs require much attention.

- This is the age when children begin onlooking play. They watch interactions between other people with rapt attention, and are fascinated by the comings and goings of others. Children like the three in this age group, whose social interactions have been primarily with adults, need encouragement to respond to other children. You can start social games between children by placing them facing one another and helping them roll a ball back and forth or alternate giving one another a toy. This face-to-face physical arrangement can facilitate social interaction. You need to stay close in order to scaffold these interactions, however.

- Play development at this age can be strengthened by building on children's emerging interest in other people, their need for novel experiences, and their growing ability to imitate social behaviors. Simple props, such as toy telephones, dishes, and soft dolls, encourage pretend play as you model their uses. For example, you might pretend to drink from a cup and offer it to the child, then demonstrate giving the doll or stuffed animal a drink.

- Play with language should be encouraged, since children are now babbling more in response to others' vocalizations and saying what may sound like real words (i.e., "ma ma," "da da," and "ba ba" for "bottle").

QUESTIONS FOR DISCUSSION

1. How would you handle Dara's mother's request that Halloween activities not include witches? What if you had specific requests like this from parents who come from other religious groups? What about other parent preferences, such as using videos or sign language (Garrett's mom) or not using videos or playpens (Dara's mom)?

2. What adaptations in curriculum will help Stan? Will you need to communicate more with Stan's parents than with Garrett's and Dara's, given the differences between his rate of development and theirs? How can you respect his parents' wishes about the kind of program they prefer?

3. With the increasing diversity of fine and gross motor abilities of children this age, what are some activities that might engage children whose gross motor skills are progressing well but whose fine motor skills need practice? What about those who need gross motor rather than fine motor facilitation? How can you accommodate many levels of mobility when you may have eight infants in one room?

4. What are some ways you can help children at this age become more aware of one another, and how can you support positive peer interactions?

Chapter 7

12–14 Months

Curriculum for ASHLEY and EDEN

AT 13 MONTHS, Ashley is a compact, wiry child with fair skin, white-blond wispy hair, plump cheeks, and alert blue eyes. She weighs 21 pounds and is 30 inches tall. Ashley's mother says she was a happy, alert, and interested child—the classic "easy baby." She fell into a comfortable routine once she came home from the hospital, slept through the night early on, and took catnaps right after nursing. Although Ashley's mood is still predominantly happy, she becomes clingy when she is tired. She takes two naps, except when she is teething. She has trouble going to sleep at night if it is still light outside, but giving her a pacifier calms her down. When she wakes up in the morning, she throws all her toys out of the crib, and then calls demandingly to get out of the crib. When awake, she is on the go now that she is walking.

Ashley's mother describes her play style as focused. Ashley plays with one toy at a time before moving on to another, and plays by herself for long periods. Ashley is interested in everything. She loves to run, climb, chase balls, play in water, and dance to music. She enjoys sound toys such as her toy piano, pressing the piano buttons and listening intently to the programmed melodies. She also sits for a long time looking through a book on her own, and likes to push her dolls in her new baby stroller.

Ashley shows social interests, watching her 4-year-old brother, mimicking his behavior, and bringing toys or books to adults to get them to interact with her. When she is with other children, she watches them intently. Ashley's mother describes her as "busy."

For her age, Ashley shows strengths in gross motor skills. She walks with control and self-confidence, is adept at using push toys as she weaves in and around furnishings, and climbs on the staircase at home. She is cautious while climbing up and is able to turn around and scoot down on her bottom. She easily climbs on the couch but is still uncertain in her descent. Her fine motor control is also good. She can spend a long time putting coasters in and out of their holder, one at a time. She enjoys feeding herself with a spoon. One of Ashley's pleasures is eating for long, leisurely periods. Ashley's language skills are increasing rapidly. She says "thank you," "baby," "apple," "cracker" and calls out "down" in the game "Ring Around the Rosy." She mimics songs and conversations. Mom calls her a "chatterbox," talking constantly as she plays and explores her environment.

Ashley dislikes having her movements constrained and balks at limits to her climbing. She is impatient if she doesn't get something immediately, causing her to throw a tantrum. She screams if her brother gets up on Mom's lap. When her mother doesn't want Ashley to have something, she can usually replace it with a comparable alternative

Ashley's mother considers keeping her daughter safe and happy as the main priorities when Ashley is at her educare program. Mom wants the educarers to be warm, loving, and caring people who give her daughter lots of attention. She hopes Ashley will have opportunities to engage in a variety of stimulating activities with other children, and states emphatically that she doesn't want Ashley sitting in front of a television. She sees her daughter as a loving, happy, empathetic child who is fun to be around, and she wants educarers to know that Ashley is "just a wonderful little girl!"

AT 14 MONTHS, Eden is a slim child about 30 inches tall and weighing 20 pounds. She is a "Celtic baby" with creamy skin, reddish hair, a pixylike appearance, and her dad's large gray-blue eyes. Her slight build and small appetite have been an ongoing concern for her parents. Eden's mother says that in her early months, Eden was assertive, letting her parents know when she needed something. She was fussy at times and never slept well, being on a reversed schedule, where she slept more in the day and was awake at night. Eden nursed at least every 2 hours, but when introduced to the bottle at 6 months, she had no trouble making the transition. Now Eden sleeps through the night except when she is hungry and wants a bottle. Her parents describe her as a happy, playful child who thoroughly enjoys being with Mom and Dad.

Eden likes to load and unload objects in and out of any kind of container, including the household laundry basket and her toy box. Her parents say she is fascinated by animals and mimics their sounds, especially dogs barking. She loves to listen to her father play his guitar and she strums it with his help. When music is played, she attempts to dance by twisting and turning her body even while sitting on the floor. She has discovered that the foyer in their home has interesting acoustics when she plays with her voice, talking or screaming.

Eden has been crawling since she was 6 months old, and now she pulls herself up on furniture and climbs on it. She is not yet walking well alone, however. She walks using push toys or a chair for balance, and spends time exploring different objects in her path. She has a rocking zebra at home that she repeatedly climbs on and off. In the morning, she likes to jump on her parents in bed, squealing with laughter and vocalizing. Her favorite time of day is when her father arrives home from work. Once she knows he is home, she crawls to the door and waits for his entrance.

At educare, crawling through a foam tube occupies much of Eden's time. She also loves balls and carries them with her as she moves from one activity to another. Often, she can be found sitting on the floor flipping through the book pages, talking to the books as though she is reading them.

Both parents express concern about Eden's eating habits and describe mealtime as an ordeal. They distract Eden with props in order to get an adequate amount of food into her, which makes mealtime a long, drawn-out affair. Eden's pediatrician is concerned about her slow weight gain and poor appetite.

When Eden engages in unacceptable behavior, her parents speak in a gentle, matter-of-fact, but firm tone of voice that is usually effective. Her dad says Eden is very sensitive to adults' tone of voice and that they need to say "no" only once for her to respond. They may need to comfort her if she is upset. It is still easy to distract her with a more acceptable object when another object must be removed, however.

Eden's parents want her educarers to be kind and loving and to provide her with a sense of security. Her mother stresses that educarers should talk and play with her frequently. Her dad says they want the environment to offer lots of things to do that will interest their daughter. Although her parents see Eden as basically happy, content, and adaptable, they know it is important for Eden to have a sense of security when she is at educare.

CURRICULUM PRIORITIES

Two of the hallmarks of this age are children's need to practice and elaborate upon their newly emergent mobility, and their urge to touch, taste, and manipulate every object in their path. Ashley and Eden typify this stage of development, with a few apparent differences in their skills and interests. They need a setting that is specifically planned to encourage mobility and stimulate their curiosity.

Children who are not yet adept at walking need a physical setup that offers supports to assist their upright mobility as they explore their surroundings. Once they begin walking, they seek portable objects to carry around with them. Repeatedly filling containers with objects and then dumping them out is an interest of all children of this age.

These children spend much time observing their environment and imitating many of the actions they see. Because they usually have strong attachment bonds, stranger anxiety may be evident. Social encounters are important but not well defined. One-year-olds typically sit and watch others. To find out more about peers and their activities, their explorations begin to take the form of showing, giving, or taking objects.

Children's first words usually emerge at this time. Some children engage in babbling that sounds like true sentences because of the intonation, but the language is undecipherable. Others point a finger or grunt to indicate a desire for something. More verbal children may become fascinated with labeling objects in the environment and imitate the names that adults give to objects. They also attempt to engage in social communication with educarers, and their understanding of requests is growing. Because of limited verbal skill, however, they may become frustrated by communication problems. Practice play skills are increasing rapidly, and pretend play is beginning. Curriculum priorities include:

1. Providing opportunities for children to construct physical and relational knowledge (i.e., comparing sizes, shapes, quantities) through independent actions, using well-differentiated action schemes (e.g., hugging stuffed bears, stacking blocks)
2. Encouraging engagement in in-depth and expanded communication interactions with adults, using both gestural and verbal means, as well as with peers
3. Affording children opportunities to learn self-regulation through improving their self-help skills (e.g., feeding themselves) and social behaviors (e.g., following simple requests), and honoring their requests to "do it myself," even when adults may still not be ready to let them

RECOMMENDED CHARACTERISTICS OF THE ENVIRONMENT

While the complexity of the environment needs to increase, many recommendations for 9- to 10-month-olds are still important. Some environment features need to be flexible, because children of this age vary greatly in mobility, communication, and social-emotional development.

- For children who are not yet walking well, low tables, bannisters, push toys, child-size shopping carts, or baby strollers will assist them in walking. Some children will be beginning to attempt walking at 12 or 13 months, so they will need stable objects on which to pull themselves up and walk around.
- You should provide safe stairs to climb, tunnels for crawling, and boxes to get into and out of to enhance motor skill development for

children who are ready for practice play with their own bodies.

- Structures that offer practice in crawling in and out, climbing up and down, and going over and under are of great interest. You can also use them for opportunities to play social games such as peekaboo and follow the leader, which are extensive at this age.
- Many portable objects that can be carried safely should be in easily accessible bins, buckets, and baskets, or on low shelves. Individual containers facilitate practice play and make cleanup easier.
- A sturdy floor-level cabinet without a door can provide a space for a child to have privacy while playing with a toy, sitting with a friend, or just "watching the world go by."
- Objects of various sizes, shapes, quantities, colors, and affordance should be available to aid relational knowledge construction. Objects that foster social knowledge, such as dolls of various types and racial appearances, doll bottles, sturdy child-size (not miniature) dishes and cups, and baby blankets, are also recommended.
- A variety of distinct play areas around the room facilitates children's desire to be on the move and to explore every nook and cranny.
- In home settings, you can make a kitchen cabinet or a low drawer available for exploration. The cabinet or drawer may hold a variety of objects (e.g., spoons, pans, cups, toys) that children can safely use in practice play (e.g., taking out and putting in, carrying about, using as noisemakers).
- A book area with an inviting display of books is needed. The books should be made of vinyl or laminated cardboard and should be sturdy and washable. You should provide books with pictures of people who reflect the cultural diversity of the children's community and educare setting.
- Posters, photos, and drawings that reflect the children's social world should be placed at children's eye level around the room, on walls, in cabinets, under the climbing structure, and next to the changing table. To prevent them from being torn, you can laminate them or use contact paper. An alternative is a Plexiglas case for pictures and objects for viewing.
- The environment should be routinely inspected for potential hazards that actively exploring children might encounter (e.g., outlets, shaky cabinets). You should look at the environment with a child's eye in order to predict what the hazardous environmental attractions may be. Make sure that all corners, cabinet edges, and low windowsills have rounded edges so that unsteady walkers do not injure themselves.
- Easily cleaned surfaces that permit children to engage in self-feeding, even though the activity may be messy, are preferable. Use other environmental adaptations such as child-size sinks (or wooden stepstools to the home sink) to encourage children's ability to "do it themselves."

SAMPLE CURRICULUM ACTIVITIES

Knowledge Construction

Physical/Relational Knowledge

- Large pegs and peg-boards, shapes that fit into specific holes in the lid of a container, and simple one-piece puzzles or form boards give practice in problem-solving strategies.
- Objects of various sizes and shapes that can be placed in and dumped out of a container give experience in spatial relationships.
- Nesting cups, cans, or boxes assist in the understanding of size relationships.
- When children are playing in, out, and around a box; going through a tunnel; or climbing up or down a structure, you should label the actions with spatial positioning words (e.g., "Up and down, up and down, Ashley is going up and down").
- Toys with levers, buttons, knobs, dials, and handles that cause doors to open, things to pop out, or sounds to be produced give children experience in anticipating an effect from their actions. Small squirt bottles filled with water can be added to a low water table.
- Children use simple musical toys for cause/effect experimentation. Toy pianos, large bells, maracas, and musical balls should be available. Also, toys with pull strings that activate animal or vehicle sounds are of interest.
- A clear plastic tube (18 to 42 inches long) strapped to a wall or climbing structure through which balls, toy cars, or other small objects can be dropped and their trajectory observed showing a cause/effect sequence is of great interest. Pictures or photos hidden in the drawers of small boxes encourage children to open these to see the pictures.
- Small (but too big to swallow) plastic animals or plastic colored eggs can be partially hidden around the room and a hunt can be initiated. A favorite toy hidden in the room with an invitation to come help the adult find it encourages the development of the sense of object permanence.
- Peekaboo played from inside a large cardboard box or playhouse or from around a doorway is a more complex form that extends both children's knowledge of objects and their sense of their own bodies in space.
- You can tape down clear shelf paper with the sticky side up on a low table surface. Offer children small wheeled toys to roll across the sticky paper to explore the sound and feel of each toy.
- Place thick soap bubbles made from baby shampoo on a table surface for children to explore and watch them disappear.
- Partially fill small zip-lock plastic bags with different colors of finger paint. Tape the closed bags to a table surface and encourage children

to explore them, using their fingers. Name the colors as the child
plays.

NAEYC Accreditation Standard 2.F.01 (Early Mathematics): Standard Curriculum: "Infants, tod-
dlers/twos are provided varied opportunities and materials to . . . see and touch different
shapes, sizes, colors and patterns."

Social Knowledge Construction

- You can provide good language models by routinely labeling your
  own and children's actions and objects in the environment. Using
  new words in meaningful contexts is important.
- Snacks and meal times offer opportunities to introduce the terms
  for different flavors such as sweet and sour as well as new taste
  experiences.
- Name the child's body parts while diapering, putting shoes and
  socks on, or changing the child's clothing. You can rub baby lotion
  on a child's hands, feet and arms to combine a sensory experience
  while naming body parts.
- When children make communication attempts (e.g., by pointing
  or grunting), you can state in a short but complete sentence what
  the child is trying to say, while also being responsive to the child's
  request or comment.
- Telephones are fascinating to children of this age. If you have toy
  phones in the room, you can invite children to hold spontaneous
  "conversations" alone or with you.
- Scaffolding can be used effectively at this age to facilitate language
  development. You can label animals and objects in picture books
  and ask the child to point to those named pictures. After a few
  times of pointing to named pictures, the child will likely be able to
  repeat some of the names you have provided. This is a place where
  books showing cultural diversity in the pictures can be effective in
  broadening sociocultural knowledge.
- Emerging literacy experiences are fostered by adult-child book
  interactions. You show children that a book contains meaning
  when you demonstrate appropriate ways to hold it, turn pages,
  and talk about the objects and people in the pictures. Themes that
  are of interest to the 1-year-old child include familiar objects (ball,
  cup, spoon, doll), interesting faces, or people engaged in familiar
  activities such as eating, sleeping, or walking. Animals are of interest
  to children who actively seek books with familiar animals in them.
  The pictures may elicit a child's imitation of the animal's sounds.
- Puppets are of interest to children of this age. Animal puppets
  give children the opportunity to imitate the animal's sound. New

vocabulary can also be practiced while conversing with various animal and people puppets.

- Many children are attracted to music and will sway, twist, and turn in response to it. You should play a variety of types of music at specific times. Children will sit mesmerized if you or a guest play a guitar, banjo, or wind instrument for them.
- Nothing draws a crowd of young toddlers like a novel event presented at their level. You can place appealing objects on the floor or on a low table and invite children to see what is offered. Activities such as water play, scribbling on a paper-covered table, or even a favorite snack will attract 1-year-olds.
- You can provide inviting, large play spaces like boxes, lofts to crawl or climb upon, and tunnels or other crawl spaces large enough for two children to encourage rudimentary social play.

NAEYC Accreditation Criteria: 2.E.02 (Early Literacy) Standard Curriculum: "Toddlers have varied opportunities to experience books, songs, rhymes, and routine games through . . . experiences that help them understand the pictures represent real things in their environment."

Social-Emotional Relationship Building

- Songs, chants, poems, and fingerplays are even more enjoyable for this age group because they enjoy the companionship of familiar adults. You should insert children's names in the songs in place of the original proper names or personal pronouns to give them a self-identity experience.
- At this age, the presence of consistent educarers who know the children well is especially important. The children will not explore as confidently without the security of a good social-emotional relationship with educarers, even if they are familiar with the physical environment.
- Because stranger anxiety is often evident now, introducing new individuals (either new educarers or visitors) into the environment is likely to cause unease for some children, especially those with a "slow to warm up" temperament. You should introduce new adults carefully and not encourage their immediate interaction with children who do not initiate interactions themselves. Some children will initiate, and as the new adult and the initiating child talk or play, the other children will get the message that this person is welcome in the environment and will gradually become friendly.
- You should continue to talk about what is happening or sing to the child during routine care activities. Your patient encouragement when children are learning self-help skills is a good way to

strengthen relationships. You can make positive comments on the child's self-feeding attempts (e.g., "You ate the applesauce all by yourself!"). This interaction is a relationship-building experience as well as a way to motivate children to improve their self-help skills.

- Children of this age are sensitive to others' tones of voice and facial expressions, providing an excellent opportunity for you to expose children informally to verbal labels for basic emotions such as happiness, fear, and anger. You can look them in the face to make sure they hear what you say and the tone you use. This facilitates their comprehension through observing your body language and tone of voice. Seeing you demonstrate facial expressions of surprise, joy, sadness, and even pretend crying will fascinate children and help them label emotions.

Play Development

- This is the beginning of the most extensive practice play period. Children play with objects, people, and their own bodies (e.g., repeatedly walking or climbing in different ways). Variety, moderate novelty, and accessibility are important factors in supporting quality practice play, as is the modeling and encouragement of adults.
- Imitation that extends into elaborative play is typical of the 1-year-old. When you sit with one or two children and make a variety of faces and sounds, you encourage mimicry from the children. You can also ask children to play games that require them to clap their hands, nod their heads, or kick their legs to strengthen their ability to listen and to follow directions. Soon they will be doing their own variations of these actions in independent play. You need to be sure that the actions and sounds you demonstrate are ones you want them to imitate and elaborate on in their play.
- Pretend play begins at about this age, usually with the scaffolding assistance of adults, who first imitate simple pretend actions and then encourage the child to repeat those actions. The earliest pretend sequences involve activities with which the child is familiar, such as eating and sleeping. You need to provide play materials that encourage such pretend, to be models and initiators of pretend, and to comment on their pretend actions (e.g., "The baby went to sleep when you covered her with the blanket").

NAEYC Accreditation Criteria: 2.J. 03 (Creative Expression and Appreciation for the Arts)
Standard Curriculum: "Infants, toddlers/twos have varied opportunities to express themselves creatively through freely moving to music. Toddlers/twos have varied opportunities to engage in pretend and imaginative play."

QUESTIONS FOR DISCUSSION

1. Are Eden's walking attempts at 14 months within the range of typical development? How might you provide scaffolding experiences for her that would help her to perfect this skill?
2. What social behaviors will you encourage for children like Ashley and Eden? How can the environment support such behaviors?
3. At this age, would boys be doing very different things from girls? Would the environment need any adaptations for boys?
4. What would you say to parents who have concerns such as those expressed by Eden's parents about her poor eating behaviors? What about Ashley's parents' concerns about her screaming when her mobility is constricted?
5. What other musical experiences could you suggest to parents that they could provide for their children to complement what is offered in your program?

Chapter 8

18–21 Months

Curriculum for LEAH and WILLIAM

LEAH IS A TALL 18-month-old with soft, curly, dark hair; large brown eyes; and curly lashes, which prompt her parents to call her "Betty Boop." She has been a healthy child, never having had an ear infection or a cold. Leah's mother describes her as an easy child with a pleasant personality. She is always in motion, "like a locomotive" from morning until night. Even as an infant, she preferred physical play with Dad and Mom and the rhythmic action of her swing to lying passively in her infant seat. She spent little time crawling; she walked at 11 months. She has never been a snuggler, which disappoints her parents. As an infant, she didn't sleep much during the day, but she did well at night, waking only once or twice to be nursed. Her dad says she is a picky eater who has a big breakfast, but prefers to snack lightly all day. She has difficulty staying interested in food at mealtime. She can feed herself using a spoon and fork, drink from a cup, and use a straw successfully.

Leah pursues many focused interests and seems oblivious to others once she is involved in her activities. She loves music, appearing to "go into a trance" while listening to the radio or television. She is fascinated with gadgets, including telephones (especially her ringing play phone) and the TV remote control. She wants to know how things work, so anything that makes a noise receives her attention. She explores kitchen cabinets, taking out pots, pans, and plastic containers. According to her dad, she is fond of water and thoroughly enjoys bathtime. She will hold her hands out to catch water flowing from a faucet whenever the opportunity arises. She is also fond of playing with the family's large dog, but she calls the dog "cat." She spends long periods of time taking her toys in and out of a basket. Her mother says she is so self-directed, she never seems to run out of things to do.

Leah's father cares for her much of the time, but when he is not caring for her, she goes to an educare center. At educare, she is constantly on the go, pulling out a bin of plastic blocks, talking on a toy phone, or climbing up and down the loft. She also watches other children play, and on occasion she will hug another child or try to lift her. She follows directions well when asked to do a task and has a good memory for routines. She is able to communicate her needs clearly through her actions, words, and tone of voice. She asks the educarer for her bottle by lifting her arms and saying "ba ba." She can scribble with a crayon and sing with her favorite TV show, *Barney*. She also likes to practice saying "One-two-three."

When she wants attention, she grabs her mom or dad around the legs and whines. Leah's mother reports that she is the family disciplinarian, even though Dad is the primary caregiver. Mom says that if Leah is into something she shouldn't be, Mom just changes her tone of voice as a warning. Leah responds well to redirection and easily turns her attention to the new stimulus. She has small tantrums, but they are short-lived, although they have been increasing lately. Leah has contact with many other family members, staying with her paternal grandparents once a week and seeing her other grandparents frequently. She interacts with aunts, uncles, and cousins when visiting her grandparents.

Leah's mother wants educarers to "be there for Leah." She says they need to be calm, cool, and collected because Leah will pick up on their tone of voice if they are tense or angry. Mom wants them to pay attention to Leah, know what she enjoys, and make those things available to her. Her dad wants them to be with her "down at her level" and "just have fun with her."

AT 21 MONTHS, William weighs about 25 pounds, which shows his good progress from his premature birth weight of 2 pounds, 14 ounces. Now he is an active and sociable child with light-brown curly hair, brown eyes, and a ready smile. His parents, who are African American, were not prepared for his birth 2 months early, but when the doctor saw signs that the infant might have had a prenatal stroke, she decided to induce the birth. Mom says the doctor "never told me exactly why." Mom and Dad were both upset because they didn't get to hold William after his birth, because medical personnel "just took him away." William was in the intensive care unit until he gained an additional pound, and no complications occurred. Mom and Dad went to the hospital every day, but it was a traumatic period for them. Although his mother "really wanted to nurse," because they gave him bottles

in the ICU, she was not success-ful. For 2 months, she used a breast pump and gave him breast milk in the bottle, to get him off to a good start.

William's mother dropped out of college to stay home with him for 3 months. Because he was so small, she didn't feel she could have anyone else stay with him. She says he just slept and ate during that period. Because of his prematurity, doctors had concerns about his vision; thus, his development has been moni-tored by a pediatric specialist. When William's weight reached 5 pounds, his mother went back to college for one term, paying for home care 3 days a week. She found the home care through a friend, and it seemed to work well for about 5 months, but then she got a part-time job working at a mall. She was able to receive subsidized child care so she could work and finished her college degree part-time.

The first educare program she took him to was near her worksite, and William adjusted well, with no separation problems. She thought the pro-gram provided adequate care for William's needs at that age level (9–15 months). Now that she has graduated and taken a position in her profes-sional field, she has William in an educare program near her home. She drops him off before she goes to work, which is an hour's drive away, and his dad picks him up when he gets off work, feeds him, and cares for him until she gets home (about 7:00 P.M.). The family is planning to move out of the city to a suburban area closer to their workplaces.

As far as William's development is concerned, his mother says that for a long time, she was worried because it seemed "he was never going to do anything." He did smile at 5 months, but it took him "a while even to roll over," and she thought he crawled for a long time (from 11 to 13 months) before walking (at 13 months). "All of a sudden," soon after he started walking, he showed progress in many areas. His parents' concerns about his vision are over, since there are no signs of problems. Recently, he has shown the ability to climb stairs on his hands and knees, run, "dance," and jump up and down. He plays ball with his dad and enjoys tickling and other roughhouse games. Although he prefers gross motor activities, his fine mo-tor skills are progressing. He can fill and dump objects, stack blocks, and press the numbers on his small play phone to make a sound.

At educare, he likes to make scribble pictures, and he recognizes the A-B-C song, although he does not sing it. His mom says he has started to do the "imagination thing," such as pretend eating. He imitates words he hears, and routinely says "bye-bye," "hi," and "bah bah" for his bottle and his sippy cup. He also "talks" in strings of sound that aren't understandable. He gets upset when he doesn't get his way, and his educarer reports that he sometimes hits other kids over toy conflicts.

William has always been good-natured, even when sick, and he enjoys being with the older children of the family friend who sometimes cares for him. He thinks he "can do anything," which Mom calls "having an attitude." She says he has always been independent, preferring to sleep in his crib rather than in bed with her (which she preferred), not liking to be rocked, and wanting to walk without holding her hand.

William's mother would like to see some changes in educare. First, she wants educarers to "go by what my child's needs are," and she cites problems in the present program with forced potty training, using sippy cups instead of allowing bottles, and not allowing pacifiers. She didn't feel her child was ready for some of the things the educarers expected all children to do. Second, she would like more planned learning activities, especially those that will help speech and literacy develop. Third, she wants consistency in educarers. In William's present program, "the staff changes all the time," with only the director being consistent. Fourth, she thinks educarers "could talk more to me about ideas of things I can do with William. I am a first-time mother and don't always understand." She would like educarers to write down what William did each day and tell her how she can support his learning at home. She feels that William's dad could also benefit from these suggestions because he "doesn't know much about being a dad, since he didn't have a dad around when he was growing up." She hopes to find an educare program after they move that will meet some of these needs, although she is generally pleased at how well William is now developing.

CURRICULUM PRIORITIES

Children of this age show great achievements in gross and fine motor development. They are now stable walkers and enjoy going for walks of short duration. Running is a new thrill, and they seem to go everywhere at a run. Most can climb purposefully to get to a desired object, walk up and down stairs, use riding wheeled toys by pushing with their feet, and "dance" to music. They can throw a ball using their whole arm, but can't yet catch it. They no longer routinely put things in their mouths, but use appropriate action schemes with objects. For example, they "drive" a toy car but "hug" the toy doll.

They have better control over the small muscles in their hands and fingers, and handedness is emerging. They are adept at scribbling, turning knobs and book pages, and doing sorting tasks. They still like putting objects into and out of containers and making collections of objects. They want to know how everything works and what substances are like, so they smear, spread, pound, squeeze, dab, and poke the substances. They are not at the point yet where they create products, however.

This age marks the transition from sensorimotor to representational (preoperational) thought. Children can remember where things are, even things that adults have put away, hoping toddlers would forget about them! They use not only trial-and-error strategies, but also problem-solving strategies. They have perfected imitation skills and are great imitators of adult and peer behavior, and spend much of their time observing others.

Their language is developing rapidly, although children's styles vary. Some like to label objects or ask, "What's that?" to collect label names. Others chatter to imitate adult conversation patterns, especially on the phone. Most have about a 10- to 12-word vocabulary and use two-word (telegraphic) speech, although others are beginning to use complete sentences. They can respond to routine adult directions, such as pointing to their body parts when questioned, and they can obey other simple requests (when they choose to do so). They like to hum and attempt to sing familiar songs.

Their social-emotional skills are emerging, but are problematic. Children this age still may treat other children like objects (e.g., poking or pinching them), and are possessive with toys, not yet capable of sharing. This is a peak period for oppositional behavior, with *no* being a favorite word. However, they respond to praise and show affection to dolls and animals. They recognize themselves in the mirror or in pictures and can say their own name.

Most toddlers take only one nap a day. They can perform self-care acts such as undressing themselves, feeding themselves with a spoon or fork, drinking from a cup, pouring with fewer spills, and washing their hands (or at least going through the correct motions). However, they have a low frustration level, especially when they are tired. They know how to use adults as resources, being able to ask for help when they need it. Curriculum priorities include:

1. Providing opportunities for children to extend their autonomy of action to a wider range of settings and experiences within an environment with many "yeses" and a few calmly and consistently enforced "nos"
2. Encouraging them to learn prosocial behaviors that facilitate adult-child and child-child interactions, especially ones that further positive peer interactions
3. Helping children extend their self-regulation to additional self-help skills (e.g., beginning to dress themselves) and social behaviors (e.g., delaying gratification, using words to express needs)

RECOMMENDED CHARACTERISTICS OF THE ENVIRONMENT

In most educare programs, 18 months is when children make the transition from infant to toddler. The environment in a toddler room (ages 18 to 36 months) more closely approximates a preschool room than an infant room in physical setup and daily schedule. Learning/activity centers are identifiable and similar to the types used for older children, although they have features that are more appropriate for toddlers. In multiage settings that include both infants and toddlers, some parts of the environment need to be more like infant rooms and some parts more like toddler rooms. The environment needs the following features:

- You should provide many opportunities for practicing gross motor skills to foster motor consistency (i.e., the ability to use those skills on a range of surfaces and structures). Toddler-size climbers, slides, rocking boats, and other such equipment should be in both indoor and outdoor environments. Wagons or carts to pull and push, cars to sit in and move with the feet, push-type tricycles, slightly raised boards to walk on, and soft bolsters or mats to jump on all allow children to practice motor mastery. Because toddlers are still learning these skills and may not have reliable balance, all equipment should be sturdy and untippable. Moderate-size balls and baskets to throw them in are also recommended.

- Because of toddlers' great interest in exploring objects, they need sturdy, untippable shelves at their level with a variety of manipulative toys to turn, shake, take apart, and fit together. You should provide pop beads, stacking rings, toddler-size plastic bricks and table blocks, nesting cups, puzzles, form boards, and busy boxes. Ideally, shelves should be open so that toddlers can access some materials by themselves. Not everything should be accessible, however. There should also be wall-mounted shelves directly above the child-accessible ones for storing some toys. Rotate the items on the closed shelves with items on the open shelves to maintain the novelty level and to maintain children's interest level. Young toddlers have a tendency to take everything out, carry objects around the room, and leave them abruptly as something else strikes their interest; thus, only a moderate amount of objects should be accessible at one time. Wall shelves provide easy access so you can change materials but don't take up floor space.

- In the "house" area, you could include a toddler-size sink, refrigerator, stove, pans, dishes, soft plastic food, telephone, dolls, doll bed, stroller, high chair, a variety of hats, purses, and lunch boxes. Toddlers do not need dress-up clothes; hats, vests, purses, lunch boxes, and briefcases are sufficient. Items should represent both male and female clothing and accessories. There should also be a double-width, full-length mirror (42 inches by 42 inches) that allows two or three children to see their body images simultaneously. Because toddlers engage primarily in parallel play, they do not need a wide variety of dishes, but they do need a large number of the same kinds so that more than one child can set the table or feed a doll. The doll beds and high chairs should be large enough to hold a child safely, since toddlers enjoy finding out how their bodies fit into various spaces.

- A comfortable, inviting book area is essential. Children's expressive language is built on exposure to images that help them learn new vocabulary. Books should be sturdy cardboard or cloth because toddlers enjoy tearing paper. Pictures should be of familiar objects, people, and animals, and should include people of diverse age, gender, race, and culture. Books with textures to explore are of interest. Children this age are not ready for books with a storyline; they generally have trouble following a long sequence of events. The book area should have visual privacy from other areas and should be out of the footpath of other children.

- There should be an area for play with sensory materials, such as water, sand, nonmentholated shaving cream, and finger paint. Messy activities should be near a water source, preferably with a drain in the floor in order to clean the area efficiently. For exploratory water and sand play, children can use plastic dishwashing basins filled with materials placed directly on the floor. If the room is large enough to accommodate a low water table, you can also provide that. Such containers should be large enough to accommodate more than one child. Because children spend extended time digging, scooping, and pouring the sand, an outdoor sandbox should have an awning over it. It should be large enough to accommodate several children to encourage social interactions.

- A child-size sink should be available for hand washing and teeth brushing. Children will play with whatever water is available, often spending extended time at the child-size sink if no water is provided elsewhere.

- The outdoor area should have equipment that is appropriate in size for toddler climbing, a sandbox, and a hard surface area for vehicle pushing or scooting. The climbing area (either indoor or outdoor) should have a well-padded ground/floor within the "fall zone" area.

SAMPLE CURRICULUM ACTIVITIES

Knowledge Construction

Physical/Relational Knowledge

- Toddlers often collect small items from around the room, examine their physical features, place them in containers such as purses or trucks, and carry or drive them to other room areas. Thus, you should provide a varied selection of such objects. Children may select the same objects each day or vary the collection as they gain knowledge about the objects' features. You can use descriptive terms such as *more than, less than, bigger*, and *smaller* to describe and compare the found objects.

- Small table blocks for stacking and lining up (toddlers are not yet ready to construct buildings); peg-boards with large, cylindrical pegs; and mechanical boards with sliding bolts or latches on hinged doors all contribute to toddler problem-solving ability.

- Simple puzzles or form boards can be of interest. Puzzles with knobs to grasp, large wooden puzzles with only three or four shapes, and form boards with two or three pieces are best. Pictures should be of familiar objects, animals, and people, including diverse images. Place puzzles, peg-boards, and beads on a tray on the table. Plastic trays with 1-inch sides will hold the puzzle or other item and keep the materials on the table. Because toddlers are not always well coordinated, they may bump or swipe table materials to the floor if the materials are not contained.

- Water play is a major attraction, and will keep toddlers happy for a long time. Buckets, cups, and other containers of various sizes for filling and dumping enable children to explore physical quantities of liquid. You can provide water wheels and other devices that demonstrate properties of water to aid concept learning.

- Sand is another universally popular medium for toddlers. Having a selection of spoons, buckets, and other containers is necessary. Sand has physical qualities that are very different from those of water, and combining the two (water and sand) creates another set of physical properties for children to explore.

- Bubble activities provide opportunities for attention- and motivation-building, intermodal coordination, and elaboration. Toddlers will chase and grab bubbles and frequently ask you to make bubbles available. Bubbles are an unusual material that sustain toddlers' interest, and they can be used both indoors and out.

- Because nonmentholated shaving cream feels and smells like soap, toddlers find smearing and squishing it an appealing pastime. You can spray the shaving cream directly on a table, or use an empty water table. For children who enjoy playing with small cars, having some cars to push through the shaving cream will extend their attention. A mixture of cornstarch and water ("ooblick") poured on a cookie sheet or activity tray will also encourage toddlers to pat, rub, and handle this viscous substance. Often, toddlers are squeamish about getting their hands dirty, so they may shun finger painting and ooblick activities. Toilet learning is usually introduced around this time, and children may be sensitized to the idea that "messy" is not good.

- You can place a variety of textures around the room for children to touch, rub, and walk on with bare feet. A sheet of bubble wrap taped on the floor will give toddlers experience with both texture and sound effects when the bubbles are stepped on with bare feet. Use of such materials should be supervised closely, and the materials should be stored when not in use.

- Art experiences must be simple for toddlers. They can paint with a brush at an easel or on a table using washable tempera paint.

Outdoors, toddlers love to paint walls and sidewalks with clear water from a bucket. They should not be given food to play with, (e.g., pudding) to use as fingerpaint. They are just beginning to figure out what is edible and what is not, so using edible substances as play materials can be confusing. Also, some parents object to using food as a plaything.

- Paper tearing is appealing to children this age. You can provide different kinds of scrap paper and old magazines to be ripped and torn. This is an example of a "yes" activity to balance a "no" activity (i.e., tearing up books or adult newspapers or magazines). One or two rules that differentiate this activity from tearing other materials are needed. You might say, "These are old magazines that you can tear sitting here at this table."

- Another popular activity for young toddlers is to give them objects wrapped in colorful tissue paper. They enjoy ripping the paper off to find a familiar toy inside. They continue to enjoy opening drawers to find different pictures or objects inside them.

- Scribbling with crayons is a good activity for children this age. Tape a large piece of paper to a table and give each child a few different-colored crayons. Art materials now come in a variety of colors, including various skin tones. Offer black, brown, and tan crayons and paper as routinely as red, green, blue, and white, being careful not to imply that earth-tone colors are somehow less desirable than primary and secondary colors. Toddlers will enjoy the physical activity of scribbling and observing the results of the scribbles, but they will not be concerned with making a product.

- Although almost all manipulatives encourage cause/effect knowledge, busy boxes with switches and dials that make sounds or have other actions are especially fascinating to toddlers. Children enjoy other cause/effect toys, including wind-up or battery-operated toys. They may not know how to use a wind-up key or remote control, but they will see you as the "cause" and repeatedly request that you make the action occur. Closely supervise the use of such toys, because they may have small parts. Battery-activated toys are particularly enjoyable for children with motor delays or disabilities because they can use one action, such as pressing a panel, to activate the object. Another experience can be provided by slitting the lid of an empty shoe box and filling it with several scarves tied together. Children enjoy pulling the seemingly endless number of scarves out of the box. These activities promote autonomy experiences, which may be few and far between for children with disabilities.

Social Knowledge Construction

- Your involvement in emerging literacy activities continues to be important. Toddlers learn the concept of "book reading" and "sense of story," gain language labels, and learn cognitive information from book-related experiences. Let them carry around their favorite books as part of their collections. Even young toddlers learn that books are treated differently from other objects. They are adept at asking you to "read" books with them, and you should respond to those requests, even if it is not a planned "book reading time." Touch books can also be made by sewing various fabric scraps to cardboard pages and linking them together with yarn. The commercial *Pat the Bunny* book is a universal favorite.

- From 18 to 36 months, most toddlers experience a language explosion, from expressing a few words to having a vocabulary of at least 50 words. Since language is learned as social knowledge (i.e., transmitted by other people), the more language interactions you have with toddlers, the better. Many children achieve bilingualism at this age. All parents, including those whose primary language is different from the dominant language, should be encouraged to speak often to their children and engage in playful social interactions. Unlike second-language learning at later ages, the brain at this age is capable of incorporating more than one language into its system of organizing language. You do not have to be concerned if a child hears two rich languages; you only need be concerned if there is a paucity of language interactions at home and at educare.

- You should listen and respond well to children's communication attempts during this period because the motivation to communicate comes from having a sense of self-efficacy when communicating. It may be hard for you to be a patient listener and strive to understand what the child wants. However, it is vital that you persist in trying to understand and respond. Young toddlers often use gestural and vocal means at the same time, which will help you understand, and then restate the request or comment in an expanded version (i.e., "Oh, you want me to give you more crackers"). For the language-delayed child, as well as for typically developing children, you can begin teaching simple words and phrases in sign language to help children express themselves more successfully. You can also use some simple words and phases from the child's home language that the parent often uses to support language learning in the home.

- Adults expect toddlers of this age to understand and follow a few rules of social behavior. Toddlers can understand that there may be different expectations at home and at educare. Your best approach is through modeling the behavior (e.g., saying "Thank you" to them

---

NAEYC Accreditation Criteria 2.D.03 (Language Development): Standard Curriculum: "Children have varied opportunities to develop competence in verbal and nonverbal communication by responding to questions; communicating needs, thoughts, and experiences; and describing things and events."

when they give you something), giving calmly stated but persistent reminders of social expectations, and giving simple verbal signals, such as "not that," "wait a minute," and "calm down."

Social-Emotional Relationship Building

- Although toddlers will look at books alone, they gain socially, emotionally, and cognitively from adult companionship in reading. The best reading style is warm and interactive, promoting child responses to items on the page. You can converse about the items the child finds interesting, and label the emotions the books suggest (e.g., "This bear looks happy"). The emotional support toddlers gain from book-reading times cannot be overestimated. It is an especially good way to strengthen attachment bonds with educarers.
- Your consistent caregiving is still extremely important, even though children are doing more on their own. The scaffolding approach is helpful when children are learning self-help skills. You can put children's feet through pant legs and then tell the children to pull the pants up. Food containers that are sturdy and designed to permit toddlers to use them independently are needed. Use pitchers with small openings filled only partially full to assist children's pouring. Your expressions of appreciation for child performance of self-help skills are highly motivating to toddlers (e.g., "You poured the milk all by yourself!"). Often, busy educarers think it would be easier just to dress the child or pour the milk for the child. Because this is the age when children want to "do it themselves," it is a mistake to miss the opportunity to provide scaffolding for self-care skills. Depending on family goals, toilet training may begin at this age. Both eating and toileting are autonomous skills that are under the control of toddlers, not adults. Thus, an approach that is calm and supportive works best, with patient but timely reminders and matter-of-fact attention to accidents.
- Since most toddlers are not ready to share with peers, to facilitate positive peer interaction, you should have more than one of most individual play objects (e.g., puzzles, dolls, cars, buckets, shovels). Toddlers' early social interaction often involves showing objects to one another and exchanging objects. Even in a well-designed environment, you should be prepared for some conflicts. Rather than jumping in immediately to resolve the problem, you should first observe how the children are handling it. Often, the children

---

NAEYC Accreditation Criteria 2.K.01 (Health and Safety) Standard 2: Curriculum: "Children are provided varied opportunities and materials that encourage good health practices such as serving and feeding themselves, rest, good nutrition, exercise, hand washing, and tooth brushing."

will come to a resolution that satisfies both of them without adult intervention. This "wait time" avoids children getting into the habit of instantly turning to adults to solve their social problems.

Play Development

- As noted earlier, practice play is pervasive in toddlers, and repetition and elaboration in play are extensive. Almost every object that toddlers encounter becomes a practice play incentive, including objects that adults think are designed for pretend play and objects that adults think should not be played with at all. During the period from 18 months to 36 months, children gain much of their mastery over the physical world from practice play. With toddlers, practice play is primarily solitary or parallel in social content. That is, children play alone or in the company of other children, but without social contact. However, associative play in which children have brief and sporadic social interactions through smiling at one another, making sounds together, and giving and taking objects begin to be seen during practice play.

- Pretend play is also of a solitary or parallel nature at this age. For example, three children may be in the house area, but each is feeding a doll or putting containers on the table, without reference to the other children. They may interact briefly, but there is no social theme to the play. Since they are not talking about what they are doing (as older children do), it is difficult for the adult to know whether a child is pretending or merely using the realistic objects in practice play. Your modeling of verbal narratives during pretend sequences (e.g., "Let's put the baby to bed. Does she need her blanket?" or "That car is going into the garage") is of great importance for increasing the quality of toddlers' pretend play. One way to make parents aware of their children's ability to pretend is to ask them to bring in familiar empty food containers. These may engage toddlers in more elaborate pretend play.

- The social games of young toddlers are still played primarily with adults. However, most toddlers know a variety of such games and initiate the game or request that an adult play a particular game. Some rudimentary peer turn-taking games may be seen, such as run and chase (with toddlers exchanging roles), or give-and-take routines with toys. If laughter accompanies the peer interaction, it is likely to be a spontaneous social game.

NAEYC Accreditation Criteria 2.L.04 (Social Studies) Standard 2: Curriculum: "Children are provided opportunities and materials to explore social roles in the family and workplace through play."

QUESTIONS FOR DISCUSSION

1. What are some additional ways you might help toddlers achieve representational thought or emerging literacy skills? What goals might you have for Leah? For William?
2. Some children (e.g., Leah) have extended families involved in their early experiences. How would you make grandparents and other family members welcome at educare? How would you deal with disagreements among parents and other family members about goals for the child's development?
3. Premature infants usually exhibit some delays during the first 2 years, but tend to catch up if they have no major problems. Is the environment suggested for 18-month-olds appropriate for 21-month-old William? Which aspects of the environment suggested might already be appropriate for 12- to 14-month-olds who are walking and talking well?
4. What concerns might you have if a child did not show the desire for autonomy that Leah and William express? How would you help such children gain a secure base from which to expand their world?
5. How could you explain to parents the way you are helping children lay the foundation for later understanding of mathematical concepts as related to NAEYC Accreditation Criteria 2.F.01 (*Early Mathematics: Standard 2: Curriculum:* "Infants and toddlers/twos are provided varied opportunities and materials to use (bullet one): language, gestures and materials to convey mathematical concepts such as more and less and big and small; to see and touch different shapes, sizes, colors, and patterns"?

Chapter 9

23–24 Months

Curriculum for BRANDON and NANCY

ALTHOUGH BRANDON HAS blond hair and hazel eyes, he tans deeply in the summer and his mother believes this is because he is part Native American. At 24 months, he is tall and slender and already wears boys' size 4T clothing. Brandon's mother says he was a happy, quiet baby who mainly slept and ate. He was never colicky. Although he spent most of the time sleeping, he often woke up at night. Then his mother would take him into her bed.

She recalls that the age of 17 months seemed to be a turning point for Brandon because he began to sleep through the night, although he still had occasional nightmares. Recently, he has been "off his feed," possibly due to his constant motor activity since he has become an accomplished walker. He takes a nap every afternoon; without it, he becomes cranky.

Mom observes that although Brandon is more independent, when she is around, he wants no one else. This is a change from his past behavior. Brandon's mother was in her teens when he was born, and she and Brandon live with her parents. Brandon's grandparents shared in the caregiving, and he shows a strong attachment to them. Although friendly, he is more cautious now, even to people he knows well, which has been hard for his grandparents to understand.

Brandon's mother describes him as an independent child, playing by himself for long periods at home, although he must be sure that she is near. Brandon's most recently developed interests are in tractors and the riding lawn mower, which he rides with his grandfather. Blowing air from his mouth is a new skill, which he uses to blow out candles and to blow bubbles. Another favorite pastime is playing with the garden hose. He likes to spray others, although he hates to get sprayed. He relishes the chance to water house plants, and he uses a watering can to wet the rocks in the garden.

In his educare program, building block towers to knock down is a favorite activity. He spends much time at this, and also likes to kick and throw balls, especially shooting baskets into a small basketball hoop. At educare, he pretends to eat plastic food, plays with small train cars, and looks at books. He frequently talks to himself as he plays. When he is with peers, he observes others' play and on occasion will sit or stand near another child who is looking at a book, engaging in water table play, or using pretend carpentry tools. His social play with other children is usually in a turn-taking game, such as repeatedly running to look for a child who knocked on the climbing structure. This game can go on with screams of delight for over 5 minutes.

Brandon has mastered using a fork and spoon, and he can serve himself at mealtime. He pours his milk and juice, and drinks from a cup without spilling. He is beginning to use the toilet independently, and will take off his clothes and diaper with encouragement. He also can brush his teeth, take off his shoes and coat, unzip and untie, put pennies into his piggy bank, and get toys out of his toy box. He goes up and down stairs unassisted, using a handrail, and he tries to use alternating feet while holding his mother's hand. He is mastering pedaling a trike. He helps put away toys with assistance. His mother is trying to wean him from his pacifier, which has not been an easy task.

Brandon is a child whose mood in the morning predicts his day. If he wakes up grumpy (or happy), he will be that way all day. He loves to be chased and tickled and makes a game of it with Mom. She says he lives to play!

The only concern expressed by his mother is Brandon's speech articulation. He will begin speech therapy soon. According to the speech pathologist, Brandon has difficulty using the back of his tongue to form words. His two- to three-word sentences are often not understandable. He says "please" and "thank you" and other words with prompting.

His mother reports that Brandon throws tantrums when he doesn't get his way. She usually ignores him and lets the tantrum run its course. When he hits her, she makes him sit on the couch in time-out. He still prefers to drink a bottle in the morning, but she gives him a sippy cup instead, despite his protests. She has a hard time keeping him in his chair to finish a meal. He prefers to pop up frequently and wander off to play.

Brandon's mother's advice to educarers is to have patience and to keep in mind that he is only 2, despite the fact that he is large for his age. She wants educarers to "get down on the floor with him," to help him to learn, and to read to him often. She wants him to be taught right from wrong and disciplined appropriately for his age.

A SLIGHTLY BUILT 2-year-old who weighs 25 pounds and is 33 inches tall, Nancy has shoulder-length, white-blond hair; fair skin; and blue eyes. She is active, alert, and in constant motion. Her mother described her as being a hungry, demanding, and active infant. She slept well at night but did not sleep more than 5 to 10 minutes during the day and only after she was nursing. She was fussy around 5:00 P.M. each day. Now Nancy still eats well, but she has developed a sweet tooth, according to Mom.

Nancy and her mother have just moved to a new apartment (her mother is a single parent). Since moving, Nancy sleeps through the night only if she is in her mother's bed, and she will not take naps at home. Nancy has begun toilet learning and now has bowel movements in the toilet.

Nancy has many interests, most of which involve gross motor activity, and she prefers to be outdoors, rain or shine. She likes to jump on the sofa cushions at home. Her mother reports that Nancy is learning to put plastic bricks and puzzles together, and she is putting on her own shoes. She occasionally watches children's videos, but isn't interested in television. Mom says that she "gets nothing done" when she and Nancy are at home.

Nancy is also "a dynamo" in her educare program, where she is always on the move, although she does nap briefly each day. She tries to climb and jump off furniture at educare, as she does at home. She has been developing fine motor skills, putting together pop beads and pulling them apart, and placing large puzzle pieces of geometric shapes in the correct spots. She enjoys listening to tapes of nursery rhymes and stories. She frequently uses the play phone to imitate adults talking, pausing and laughing as though she is responding to someone on the other end. She enjoys sensory activities like drawing, painting, and sand and water play.

Both Nancy's mother and her educarers agree that Nancy's activities are brief and occur in rapid succession due to her constant mobility. At educare, she flits around a room, changing activities about every minute. For example, in a short time she may engage in water play, try puzzles or manipulative toys, climb and jump on structures, dump the dishes into the water table, push a truck around on the floor, and repeatedly climb up to view a construction vehicle outside the window. She likes activities that include other children, although she watches or plays next to them rather than interacting with them. In a short time period, encounters with children may include seeing a child shake a homemade paper-plate instrument and running to get one for herself, dancing around the room with other children, taking a toy from or giving one to another child, jumping on mats with peers, and running to get her hat when it is time to go outside.

Recently, Nancy was screened for a speech and language delay. The examiner found that her expressive language is in the 15- to 18-month range. She has just begun to mimic words said to her, and she has about 15 meaningful words in her vocabulary. Because of her delayed speech, she will be receiving speech therapy.

Nancy's mother reports that Nancy has violent temper tantrums during which she kicks and throws objects. Generally, Mom ignores her or tells her, "You're really angry because . . ." She has found that time-out doesn't work with Nancy, but says that holding and rocking Nancy while talking softly to her usually does. Redirecting her to another activity, such as taking a soothing bath or watching a video, also works.

Nancy's mother wants educarers to take care of Nancy as she would, that is, to hold her, hug her, and pick her up when she needs loving. She also wants a program of age-appropriate activities provided, focusing on hands-on learning through play. She believes in the philosophy of meeting the needs of the whole child. She emphasizes that health and safety issues are also important in group care settings. Most of all, she wants Nancy's educarers to appreciate Nancy's unique personality.

CURRICULUM PRIORITIES

Toddlers at age 2 are still gross-motor-oriented, although their balance has improved enough so they can perform more sophisticated movements, such as walking on a line, balancing in rocking boats and on bounding boards, dodging obstacles, walking on tiptoe, climbing stairs unassisted (although not always on alternating feet), getting up quickly from a seated position, climbing to high levels, jumping in place, pushing wheeled toys, stacking big blocks, and pedaling low-slung tricycles. Balance has continued to improve, and many children can now walk backward on a line. Their aim is better when throwing a ball or beanbag, or when trying to kick a ball. They are interested in exploring the outdoors, but they still like to squeeze themselves into confined places such as cabinets or shelves.

Regarding fine motor skills, their handedness is usually established by this age, they can turn one page of a book at a time, and they alternate their hands when exploring objects. They are able to pack dirt or sand into a container, dig with tools, unscrew jar lids, string large beads, hold crayons and markers in a fist grasp, and make scribble circles and straight lines. They are adept at putting together simple puzzles and lining up blocks, cars, or shapes in rows.

Their self-help skills have improved, and they have the ability to brush their teeth with minimal assistance, control eating utensils and cups, turn a tap on and off, put away playthings, and zip and unzip clothing.

Now they are better able to solve problems by thinking about them rather than using trial and error, sort and classify objects, and grasp simple concepts of time (now versus later), number (one, two, more), and color (at least two or three colors). Their improved spatial awareness allows them to construct a cognitive map of familiar surroundings. Object permanence is more sophisticated; they can verbally predict the movements of hidden objects.

Their use of symbols has expanded rapidly, not only in their language but also in their ability to imitate actions when the actor is no longer present, to substitute ambiguous objects for realistic objects in pretend play (e.g., using a round puzzle piece for a cookie), and to briefly sustain a pretend theme (e.g., mother caring for a baby by feeding, putting to sleep, or taking a walk). Their understanding of spatial relationships (up and down, in and out) is greater, and they now understand that objects have different attributes and can label them (e.g., heavy-light, soft-hard). They can point to less obvious body parts (e.g., elbow) when asked where they are, and they know that objects have specific uses (e.g., balls are for throwing).

They can name most familiar objects and persons in their environment, and many children have an expressive vocabulary of 50 to 300 words. By age 2, children have discovered the "power of words," and this is reflected not only in their constant echoing of adults' words, but also in using words to get reactions and assistance from adults, understanding communication signals for future events (e.g., getting a coat when told it is time to go outside), and using the words I, me, and mine to stake out their territory. Their vocabulary is influenced by their experiences, that is, their words are for familiar people, animals, food, playthings, and events. Their brains' synaptic connections are rapidly expanding. They constantly incorporate new words into their language system, and they are highly motivated to do so, frequently asking, "What's that?" and asking "where" and "what" questions. Toddlers' interest in music continues to expand as their motor abilities and facility with language improve. They can now march and play an instrument at the same time.

With motor and communication skills expanding daily, their feelings of autonomy are at a peak. Their words and actions show that they have a stronger sense of self, and they can use words to express feelings. "Me do it" is a common refrain. They may be bossy with both peers and adults, ordering others to do their bidding. Their own feelings are hurt easily, however, and they may fear adult disapproval. They are likely to express feelings of caring toward a favorite educarer, although they can begin to share educarer attention with other children. They are developing a sense of empathy, expressing self-conscious emotions (e.g., shame, guilt, pride), and considering others' feelings on occasion. The intensity of their emotional reactions is at a peak, with tantrums evident when they are frustrated, resulting in screaming, throwing things, or physically lashing out at peers or adults. They may have wide emotional swings; their emotions seem to turn on a dime.

Because they now have a "life of the mind," fantasies and fears are more common. By being able to think about a fearful event and anticipate fearful things, children occasionally scare themselves, especially at night, so that sleep problems may occur, and in their play, they may enact a fearful theme with dolls and stuffed animals.

Not all of these characteristics are seen in every child of this age, however. As children get older, the range of their skills and their learning interests vary more. When educarers prepare the 2-year-olds' learning environment, therefore, they must know each child's strengths, interests, and needs in order to provide appropriately challenging activities and materials. Items should be changed frequently to reflect children's growth and emerging interests. Levels of difficulty must provide for the least mature as well as the most mature child in the group. Curriculum priorities include:

1. Continuing to provide opportunities for children to exercise autonomous actions to extend their physical, relational, and social knowledge, by having many choices of developmentally appropriate activities available, including ones with symbols such as pictures, numbers, and letters
2. Encouraging children to practice more complex prosocial and social communication behaviors (e.g., sharing with peers, using social conventions in speech such as "thank you") and to gain the ability to express ideas verbally rather than motorically
3. Supporting children in self-regulation of self-help skills (e.g., dressing, toileting) and emotional-control behaviors (e.g., learning ways to deal with fears and anger, using verbal means of expressing emotions, delaying gratification)

RECOMMENDED CHARACTERISTICS OF THE ENVIRONMENT

Because the curriculum for 2-year-olds builds on that provided for 18-month-olds, the general appearance of the environment is similar to that for younger toddlers. However, it has a number of additions and modifications:

-   More than one telephone should be available, to encourage two children or a child and adult to talk to one another.
-   Baby bottles, receiving blankets, toddler-size washing machine and dryer, iron and ironing board, broom, mop, sponges, and other objects (e.g., stuffed animals) that suggest play themes should be added to the house area. Dolls should reflect diversity of race, culture, skin color, and gender.
-   Simple dress-up clothes that are easily taken on and off, such as adult-size jackets, vests, and low-heeled shoes should be added for dressing up, and they should include both traditional male and female clothing. A double-width, full-length, nonbreakable mirror

(42 inches by 42 inches) is useful so children can observe the results of dressing up and trying on a variety of roles. The clothing should be hung on large, rounded pegs for easy access instead of being stored in baskets or drawers, which encourages dumping.

- Books should reflect children's growing vocabulary. Picture books about familiar objects and events encourage children to label and identify what is happening on each page. Because children of this age can begin to gain a sense of story, books with a storyline about familiar, everyday events such as getting ready for bed, using the potty, visiting a relative, or playing with a pet are recommended. In addition to having books with stories about diverse people in their own communities, the books should reflect people of all ages and men and women in nontraditional as well as traditional roles. Stories that elicit feelings of happiness, mild sadness, or mild fear provide a chance to help children use words to describe these emotions. Toddlers enjoy books with nursery rhymes and repetitive chants or phrases. They like to find a familiar object or animal hiding on each page, because they like mild surprises. For example, in *Good Night, Moon*, they can find such objects and animals on each page.

- Because 2-year-olds demonstrate better fine motor control and eye-hand coordination, their marking and drawing can be encouraged. A writing center with a variety of writing/drawing utensils and different types of paper and surfaces is recommended. Two-year-olds can hold paintbrushes and make broad strokes on paper, so they need places to paint—an easel or a table surface. One or two easels with crayons and paintbrushes hanging from strings (with one or two colors of paint) can encourage large scribbling movements as well as social interaction with peers.

- Sensory materials can be expanded (e.g., wood shavings, seeds), although sand and water continue to be favorites. Play-Doh (or cornstarch and water) is an attractive substance for many 2-year-olds. Various tools can be offered to use with dough, such as plastic knives and small hammers for pounding; however, most 2-year-olds cannot use a rolling pin or cookie cutters. They are primarily interested in how this substance feels when handled in various ways.

- Water play is best provided with a sand/water table because toddlers have moved from an exploring phase (spilling, splashing) to a practice play phase (pouring in or pouring out of one container, or pouring in many containers).

- Most of the manipulatives provided in the 18-month-old children's environment still hold interest for 2-year-olds. Other materials to add further challenge include small table blocks, a variety of beads, animal or vehicle puzzles with four to eight noncontiguous pieces, plastic animals, small cars and trucks, small trains with two or three cars, and more complex sorting or cause/effect toys.

- Because jumping is a favorite 2-year-old activity, a variety of levels should be offered in the room to provide safe jumping-off points.

A collection of large foam mats, cubes, and ramps can be combined in interesting ways for children to leap from safely. Good padding underlying the equipment is essential. Another choice for jumping is an inflatable air mattress, which is heavy-duty and flexible (with an electric air pump). These are especially good for outdoor use.

- Blocks of different sizes and materials should be available both indoors and out. Commercially made wooden blocks are preferable; however, well-made cardboard and plastic blocks can also be used. Wooden or plastic figures of people of different ages, genders, races, and cultures will enhance block play. Figures that portray occupations should not be stereotyped (e.g., only male doctor figures and female nurturing figures).
- Pull and push toys should be available both indoors and out. Inside, such toys can be more interesting to children if something happens when they are pulled: if they make a noise, if small beads pop inside them, or if the feet flop on a frog or duck. There should be trains and small wagons to push or pull, large wooden trucks to ride on, shopping carts, and doll strollers and carriages for dolls to ride in. Outdoors, small wheelbarrows, wagons, and sleds should be present for children's use in collecting leaves, grass, dirt, and other natural found materials. Riding toys of various types should be available. Some 2-year-olds are able to successfully pedal big-wheel trikes. Two-passenger buses or cars encourage cooperative effort.
- Throwing is of growing interest to 2-year-olds. Targets can be made from hula hoops taped to a wall, empty laundry baskets, small trash cans, and cardboard boxes. A frame can be made from a sheet of cardboard or plywood in which holes of different shapes have been cut. Objects to be thrown include beanbags and foam and rubber balls of all sizes.
- Low, fairly broad balance beams can be provided both indoors and out. Other materials that encourage precise movement can be used as well, such as squares of carpet children can step on.

SAMPLE CURRICULUM ACTIVITIES

Knowledge Construction

Physical/Relational Knowledge

Although a well-designed environment provides many opportunities for child autonomous actions that strengthen knowledge about the physical world, you can enhance its effect in many ways.

- Many inexpensive outdoor activities provide physical knowledge construction. You can allow children to draw on sidewalks with large pieces of washable colored chalk. On hard surfaces, you can draw lines for them to walk on to practice balance, and chalk squares or circles to jump into and out of or to aim and throw balls at. You can help children search for leaves, sticks, or rocks, and categorize them by size or color. With your help, toddlers can be surprisingly good observers of the natural environment.

- You can take toddlers on short "theme" walks to discover interesting aspects of the environment. After a rainstorm, you can take them for a "worm walk" or "puddle walk" (with all children wearing boots); in spring, they can go on a "flower walk" when blooming bulbs and pussy willows may be found, or a "bird walk" near trees or bushes that birds frequent; in winter, they can take an "ice puddle walk" when the ground is dry except for a few frozen puddles that are good for stomping.

- In city environments, walks around the block allow children to explore store signs, store types, city parks, neighborhoods, and truck and car traffic. You should use sturdy loop ropes for each child to grasp for walks in such locations, however, and there should be at least one adult for every three or four children.

- Indoors, you can give children many opportunities for classifying and sorting. They can sort plastic animals by color, wild/domestic, type (horses/cows), or other features that can be discriminators (pets/farm). Ambiguous objects (e.g., blocks, plastic shapes) can be sorted by color, shape, or size.

- You can provide simple matching activities, such as matching three-dimensional objects to pictures of the objects; finding pairs of shoes that go together; or playing lotto-type games that involve matching.

- Children this age love hiding games. You can hide objects in the room (preferably in plain view or only slightly hidden) for children to find.

- Because older toddlers are able to unscrew jar lids and remove lids from plastic storage containers, a number of activities that involve getting lids off containers to find interesting objects, pictures, or other surprises can be of interest. (Note: This is another example of a "yes" activity paired with a "no"—i.e., not being allowed to unscrew medicine or household cleaning bottles.)

- To assist fine motor development, you can provide large beads to string on round shoelaces and clothespins to drop in plastic bottles or coffee cans.

- Containers into which two or three differently shaped objects fit challenge children to focus on spatial relations, and toys that help children predict outcomes continue to be appropriate. Toddlers still enjoy rolling a ball down a large slanted tube into a bucket or placing balls into holes and watching them travel down tunnels.

- If an old record player is available, you can put a record-shaped piece of paper on the turntable and let children hold a crayon on the paper as turns on the table. Two-year-olds find this a fascinating activity.

- Some toddlers are comfortable finger painting with commercial finger paint or with finger paint made from nonmentholated shaving cream. You can add drops of food coloring to make it colorful and appealing.
- Many 2-year-olds love playing with toy cars and trucks. Usually in-between sizes, slightly larger than miniature ones but not extremely large, are best. Some children like to bring their favorite cars from home and may be more likely to play if they can use their own toys. You can provide a block "road" to drive on and small boxes to use as "garages." Other children like trains with small tracks that the trains can ride upon. While children manipulate the toy vehicles, you can use number names in a conversational tone to count the toys as they play.
- Water and sand continue to be all-time favorites. You should provide different-size shovels, scoops, buckets, and other containers, both indoors and out. These may be more elaborate than those for 18-month-olds. (Note that food substances are still not appropriate as playthings; see Chapter 8.)
- A number of other sensory activities are challenging for 2-year-olds. For auditory stimulation, you can sit on the floor with a few children and place a low screen between yourself and them. After they have seen a collection of objects that make noises (e.g., a bell, talking doll, rattle, or drum), have them shake or otherwise activate the noise; then you activate them behind the screen and ask the children to identify which object they hear. They can take turns being the noisemaker and letting others guess.
- A good tactile activity involves placing various textures in the compartments of an egg carton. Turn it upside down and let children poke their fingers into the small holes at the bottom of the carton and try to describe what they feel (scratchy, soft, smooth, rough).
- Many activities involving food provide sensory knowledge. Two-year-olds are more adventurous in trying new foods than either younger or older children. You can have a tasting party, offering children different fruits or vegetables to try (e.g., star fruit, guava, mango, fresh pineapple). Be sure to select nutritious foods for this activity, because many 2-year-olds already prefer sweet, salty, or fatty foods. Children also like to dunk fruit into cottage cheese dips made in a blender. You can remark on the taste, texture, appearance, and sometimes the sounds of eating different foods. Experimenting with taste activities should be done at snack time because families from some cultures believe food should not be a plaything.
- Two-year-olds enjoy watching popcorn come spewing out of a popper and holding the bowl to catch it. You can sprinkle it with a little melted butter and grated Parmesan cheese. Watching the entire sequence from kernels to expanded popcorn gives children an understanding of physical change, in addition to the sensory experience of tasting, touching, and smelling the popcorn.

NAEYC Accreditation Criteria 2.L.05 (Social Studies) Standard 2: Curriculum: "Children are offered varied opportunities and materials to learn about the community in which they live."

NAEYC Accreditation Criteria 2.K.02 (Health and Safety) Standard 2: Curriculum: "Children are offered varied opportunities and materials to help them learn about nutrition, including identifying sources of food and recognizing, preparing, eating, and valuing healthy foods."

Social Knowledge Construction

- Use every opportunity to sing to children, making up songs or chants for any occasion. This works especially well during transitions and times when children must wait for something. While children are washing their hands, sing, "This is the way we wash our hands" to the tune of "This Is the Way We Wash Our Clothes." A song or chant to help with cleanup time is "Clean up, clean up, everybody, everywhere. Clean up, clean up, everybody do your share."
- To enhance children's understanding of social situations in stories, you should read slowly enough to allow them time to absorb the ideas and pictures. It helps to let children control the pace by turning the pages themselves. You should encourage the use of "where" and "what" questions while reading to children. By using books with simple, repetitive plots, you can facilitate children's development of a sense of story.
- Songs that use children's names catch and hold their attention. An example is the song, "Oh, Do You Know This Friend of Mine?" sung to the tune of "Oh, Do You Know the Muffin Man?" The last verse states, "Her name is. . . ." Songs with repetitive motions and words appeal to children this age. Examples are "Where Is Thumbkin?," "Did You Ever See a Lassie?," and "Head, Shoulders, Knees, and Toes."
- Because children at this age are experiencing a "naming explosion," this is the time to use less common adverbs, adjectives, and pronouns in your everyday encounters (e.g., "You made a huge building! His building is longer but not as tall."). You can also give two-part or three-part directions (e.g., "Go to the counter and bring the washcloth. Then you can wash the doll's face."). Remember that when you increase children's vocabulary, you support their literacy development.
- Because toddlers' speech may be only about 70% intelligible, it is important to listen carefully when they try to convey a message or ask a question. When you use puppets, you can help children who are hesitant to speak find a medium for self-expression. Puppets can

be used to tell stories, sing songs, and be the leader of games that require following directions. Oral storytelling also helps children learn that stories have a sequence.

- You can help children use words when they want something instead of grunting, pulling, or gesturing to you to get it. When you use complete sentences to restate what the child is trying to gesture or to say (e.g., when the child says "My cup," you can ask, "Do you want juice in your cup?"), the child will have a good model to imitate.

- When you take photographs of children as they play and show them pictures in which they can easily identify who is in the photo and what they are doing, you aid both symbolic and social knowledge. The photos can be placed on a low bulletin board at the children's eye level. Photos of children can also be hidden in unexpected places, such as in the texture table or under pillows. Take the opportunity to talk with children about the photos when you see children looking at them. Use of a digital camera gives immediate feedback.

Social-Emotional Relationship Building

- Books can be made with photographs of children engaged in activities (cooking, feeding dolls, building with blocks), and stories with a beginning and end can be told about those activities. Because toddlers can identify themselves and peers in pictures, this activity builds peer relationships and self-identity, also aids representational thinking.

- For children who have difficulty controlling their anger, the paper-tearing activity mentioned earlier can be a good redirection and a way to reduce frustration. You might like to try it, too!

- By arranging the environment to encourage parallel and associative play, you encourage peer friendship and social interactions. Having a wide easel for two children to paint on at the same time or large paper that can encourage two children to color together on the same piece of paper will give them the opportunity to begin finding friends who share their interests. When you observe children's interests, you can facilitate these friendships during block, train, doll, water, or any other play by making room for two children to play happily alongside one another. Your occasional participation will draw them into associative play and help these friendships develop.

- Food preparation activities from the children's cultural backgrounds also build social relationships. Invite parents to help children prepare food that they eat at home. A parent might show how to make tortillas with a tortilla press or pasta using a pasta machine that children can crank. Two-year-olds love to make pizza using muffin halves, pizza sauce, and shredded mozzarella cheese. They can also cut out biscuits and cookies with minimal assistance. Cooking activities are one of the best ways to involve parents in the program because this is an area in which most parents feel competent to share their skills.

- You should be collecting children's art and sensory products in a portfolio to document each child's progress from scribbling to drawing shapes and people to making letterlike marks (prephonemic writing). You can share this portfolio with parents and children at conferences or at parent visit times. When parents can discuss their child's developing skills with you and feel that you really know their child, a stronger educarer-parent relationship linkage is built, which has positive consequences for the child.

- The emotionality of children this age may make educarers feel that their task of social-emotional relationship building is difficult. Even the most patient of educarers (and parents) will at times feel frustrated and angry when 2-year-olds exercise their noncooperative emotional powers. Educarers should make a calm restatement of necessary rules along with providing opportunities for many child choices (within a limited set of options). If a strong base of attachment has been established, both educarers and children can come through this phase well. For a child who is new to educare at this age, some attention may need to be paid to earlier types of interactions (holding, reading, attending more) in order to establish such an attachment base.

NAEYC Accreditation Criteria 2.B.04 (Social-Emotional Development) Standard 2: Curriculum: "Children have varied opportunities to develop a sense of competence and positive attitudes toward learning, such as persistence, engagement, curiosity, and mastery."

Play Development

Both the practice play and the pretend play of 23- to 24-month-old children can be greatly enhanced by educarers who systematically use facilitation strategies and brief but attentive play participation, such as the following:

- Take advantage of opportunities to play briefly with children during their practice play in the learning/activity centers. While there, help children describe what they are doing and serve as a model for play elaboration, language, and social behavior. Because 2-year-olds are more interested in one another, look for opportunities to encourage turn-taking and social play. It is important to make positive comments that reflect the act (not giving nondescript words of praise like "good boy" or "you're great") to children when they cooperate with one another or resolve their conflicts with words instead of actions. For example, you might say, "I see that you are sharing the puzzles well today." Although you must be alert to potentially harmful interactions, give toddlers the chance to settle their resistance over sharing the trucks or puzzles first before stepping in to resolve the conflict. Social play requires the ability to negotiate with the play partner, and it is not too early for toddlers to begin to learn those skills. Because playing with others is enjoyable, it is highly motivating for children to use their social skills to keep the play going.

- You can introduce simple pretend play themes to extend the range of children's pretense. You can line up chairs to make a "train" and give children engineers' caps to wear and a train whistle to blow. You can place a large cardboard box on its side and let children park wheeled toys inside this "garage," adding a cardboard gas pump and short piece of hose or tubing to create a "gas station." Or you can make a simple "doctor's office" by adding pretend stethoscopes and bandages to doll play. Besides providing these props, you should model the pretend sequence once or twice to get the pretense started, and suggest roles or themes for the play. Most children who pretend well have fathers and mothers who have interacted with their toddlers in pretend ways. For those children who seem less skilled at pretending, it is especially important that you take on this scaffolding role.

- Your scaffolding for gameplay is also essential. Games can assist children in learning to follow verbal directions and to decenter (become aware of the perspectives of others). For example, "Simon Says" can be modified so that Simon always says what to do and children always do what Simon says. (At this age, there is no need for a "don't do it" part.) Another game that stimulates thinking skills and remembering names is "Who's Missing?" With a small group, one educarer can help a child hide while another asks the rest of the children in the group who is missing. You can also hide a number of familiar toys in a box and as each one is brought out, ask the children to tell what it is. Games at this age should be simple, with only one rule (or at the most two rules) to follow. The game usually breaks down completely if an adult does not stay in the game in at least a peripheral way. Good games for young toddlers let everyone participate rather than requiring them to wait for their turn. "Ring Around the Rosy" and other such games that have everyone involved in the action are best.

QUESTIONS FOR DICUSSION

1. What can you do to help children like Nancy and Brandon who have language problems? Do these children have other strengths that could help them build their language articulation and vocabulary?
2. When children have tantrums, how should they be handled?

Should there be different techniques for children with different temperaments or whose parents have differing expectations? How should these factors influence your strategies?

3. What information would you enclose in toddlers' portfolios to document their various types of knowledge construction? Their social-emotional relationship building? Their play development?

4. What are some other things to introduce into the environment as the year progresses that would help Nancy increase her attention span? Build on Brandon's interests and skills? Give sufficient challenges to various children?

5. In what ways could you take into consideration family and community perspectives in providing these children with opportunities for language acquisition and further NAEYC Accreditation Criteria 2.D.01 (*Language Development*) *Standard 2: Curriculum:* "Children are provided with opportunities for language acquisition that align with the program philosophy, consider family perspectives and consider community perspectives"?

Chapter 10

29–32 Months

Curriculum for PAUL, JEREMY, and NATALIE

PAUL, 30 MONTHS OLD, is a well-proportioned child weighing 33 pounds, and 37 inches tall. He has fair skin, strawberry-blond hair, and gray-blue eyes. He usually has a serious, thoughtful expression. At birth, Paul was a big baby, falling into the 95th percentile for both length and weight. His parents say he was calm and content except during his second month, when he had colic. Although he ate well, his sleep pattern was "so-so." In the evening, he was difficult to comfort. Fortunately, both Dad and Mom were involved in his care, so they supported one another. He developed a predictable eating schedule (every 4 hours) by his second month, but needed his parents to hold and walk with him to help him fall asleep. He never used a pacifier or sucked his thumb, but he was soothed by stroking his mother's hair. Now he takes a 2-hour nap each day and sleeps about 11 hours each night, rarely waking. His parents say that his food preferences change frequently now, accompanied by an occasional preference for particular foods. He is beginning to use a variety of eating utensils.

Paul's dad and mom have observed a number of strengths in Paul. He began to walk at 12 months after a brief crawling phase, and now he climbs stairs without fear and gets up on the seat of his dad's riding lawn mower unassisted. His language skills are advanced. He spoke his first words—*duck, ball,* and *papa,* around 10 months of age. He now speaks in complete sentences and enunciates words clearly. He always gives full answers to questions and asks many questions of his own. His vocabulary is especially rich in words related to nature; for instance, instead of reporting that he saw a bird, he will say he saw a cardinal.

Paul has become a nature lover and enjoys going into the woods near his house, picking up sticks and pretending to hunt for "big bucks" (just like Dad), looking for worms, and admiring ferns and flowers. He looks forward to watching the PBS program *Nature*. He knows the names of an amazing number of wildlife, and can name all his small plastic wild and domesticated animals. He helps in the family garden by removing unwanted rocks. He also pretends to "fly" into the woods as he thinks Peter Pan would.

Inside activities at home include playing with plastic bricks, a small train set, a riding tractor, toy animals, and small cars. He likes to organize things, lining up his toys and animals in neat rows, and he enjoys helping his mother cook and his father work with tools. He prefers talking on a real telephone to a toy phone. He will watch a children's video for 30 minutes at a stretch. Paul can play independently for 20 minutes at a time, and is frequently heard talking to himself as he plays with animals or other objects that make real-world sounds.

Paul's social skills are also strong. He likes visiting other people's houses with his parents, and is part of a large extended family. His parents rarely go anywhere without him, and he stays with other family members as though he were at home. He has always been a warm and affectionate child. His dad jokes that he has the makings of a politician. His parents have observed that Paul is capable of showing empathy for others. He finds other people fascinating to watch. He always says "please" without prompting when he asks for something.

However, Paul's parents say that when he's tired, he "gets mean." He will pinch or push someone or tear a leaf off a house plant. When he has a temper tantrum, his parents back off and then try to distract him. Reading is an effective way to get him to relax. If he hits the dog or his mother or father, he is given a time-out for a few minutes to help him calm down. He is also capable of telling his parents when he needs cuddling. He will say, "I need you to rock me in the chair."

At his educare program, he prefers playing near others but still manages to go his own way in pursuit of interesting things. Paul is mastering puzzles and creates plastic brick structures. He climbs on anything that is permitted at educare, and he is learning the meaning of the word *no*. He has yet to show interest in toilet training and is "too busy" to be bothered with a diaper change.

With regard to the educare experience, Paul's parents' first concern is that he be safe. They want him in a nurturing environment where he is treated as an individual and not expected to be like all the other children. They assume he will treat other children nicely and not act in a violent way. When he does act inappropriately, they want his educarers to talk to him about his behavior. They don't want him to develop bad habits. They want him to eat nutritious foods, and not items such as nuts and popcorn that can cause choking. It is very important that his educarers inform them of any changes in Paul's health or behavior. Neither Dad nor Mom expresses any concern about Paul's language, cognitive, or social development.

JEREMY IS A TALL, slender child with reddish-blond hair, pale skin, and light brown eyes. He weighs 30 pounds and is 38 inches tall. Adults often expect more mature behavior from Jeremy because he looks older than his

34 months. His mother describes him as happy, busy, sociable, curious, and independent. As an infant, he was content, happy, and easy to calm down. He ate frequently, nursing until 6 months, and he started solids at that time. He slept well at night, usually for 10 to 11 hours, although occasionally he would wake up and want to be nursed or rocked. He took one morning nap every day.

Once Jeremy began walking at 13 months, he lost interest in eating and focused on getting around. Now he is eating better, but he still has trouble staying seated to finish a meal. His mother says he prefers breakfast foods such as waffles or yogurt to most lunch items, but he will eat finger foods such as cheese and fruit whenever they are offered. He is adept at serving himself from a bowl with a tablespoon and at eating with a fork or spoon. Jeremy is learning to use a knife to butter his bread.

Any messy activity such as finger painting, water play, playing with bubbles, or sand play attracts Jeremy's attention. He enjoys his bath and will stay in the water a long time. At home, he plays alone for short periods, but recently, he has wanted his mother to sit on the floor near him while he plays. Jeremy's skills include being an agile climber, having good balance while walking and running, and going up and down stairs unassisted, although he doesn't alternate his feet yet. His fine motor skills are demonstrated by his ability to put together snap-on toys and large plastic bricks. He is also learning to hit a ball with a bat. Jeremy's major interest centers around anything with wheels. One of his first words was *tractor*. He loves to listen to tapes and be read to, although his mother suspects that at bedtime, wanting to be read to or listen to tapes may be his way of staying up longer. His mother is trying to get him to be gentler with family pets and to express himself more clearly.

At his educare program, Jeremy rapidly moves around the classroom trying activities, including squeezing Play-Doh into and out of a press, carrying stuffed animals, putting puppets on his hands, playing with plastic bricks, riding wheeled toys, and listening to educarers read. He loves balls and often throws, kicks, and tosses them at the low basketball hoop. He frequently stops to watch other children or to listen to an adult, and on occasion he will play near others. He is just as busy on the playground, riding wheeled toys, playing in the sand, going down the slide, blowing bubbles, and playing with balls. He plays with toy cars, trucks, and tractors both in-doors and out. He rides cars and pedals small trikes on the playground and in the hallway at educare.

Jeremy's father died unexpectedly about 6 months ago, and this has been a difficult period for both Jeremy and his mother. She says that Jeremy is beginning to talk more about his father when she shows pictures of him, or when they are looking at his belongings. Recently, Jeremy has insisted on putting a plate on the table for his father. He occasionally refers to his father while playing. It is important to his mother that his father's memory be kept alive because Jeremy was so young when he died. She wants Jeremy to remember his father and the things they did together. For example, when his father was alive, he took Jeremy for rides on his bull-dozer and lawn mower. Neither his mother nor his educarers have identi-fied major problems in his behavior since his father's death.

Jeremy's mother and educarers are concerned about his expressive language, and he is scheduled for a screening test by a speech and lan-guage specialist. He comprehends well, but his speech is difficult to un-derstand. This doesn't stop him from talking, though. He repeats nursery rhymes spontaneously, sings songs, and attempts to count objects with adult help.

Jeremy's mother reports that he is having fewer tantrums than he did at age 2 (about the time of his dad's death). Now tantrums occur only when he is tired. If he engages in unacceptable behavior, Mom first tells him "no" and redirects him to another activity. If this doesn't work, she continues to talk to him and help him focus on what she is saying. On Mon-days, he often engages in testing behavior at educare, and Mom thinks this is his way of adjusting to the transition from home, where he has her all to himself. She does see him at lunchtime when he is at educare, however, because she works nearby.

Jeremy's mother's desires for educare include having him get a great deal of attention and physical affection, be safe at all times, and be watched closely, especially if he is around animals. She also wants him to have many things to do to keep him busy.

NATALIE IS A DARK-HAIRED, brown-eyed child who is now close to 3 years old. Her parents nearly didn't make it to the hospi-tal because her birth was so quick. She weighed 7 pounds, 15 ounces, was 20½ inches long, and had "only a fuzz" of hair. Al-though she now weighs over 28 pounds, she seems slim because she is tall for her age. Her par-ents recall that she was a calm infant who took her bottle every 3 or 4 hours and didn't cry much. Instead, she "squeaked" when she wanted something. Her mother carried her around a lot because Natalie always wanted to be close, and even now she is her mother's "cuddle bug." Thus, it was hard for Natalie when the family had a new baby 3 months ago. Her father is her primary caregiver during her mother's workday, and over the past few months, her attachment to him has become stronger. Her dad says, "She doesn't want to let me out of her sight," and she screams if he leaves the room or goes outside. She is also attached to her 4-year-old sister and imitates many of her behaviors. The family is extremely close, spending most of their time together; Natalie's dad even takes the children to see their mother during her lunch break at work.

Natalie's parents didn't notice problems with Natalie's development at first. She sat up at about 7 months, loved her swing and her walker, and was compliant. When she was 9 months old, they noticed that she tilted her head in a funny way when she reached for things, and she often was not successful in getting the object. Her dad says she had a "lazy eye," and her mom says she was "seeing double." Natalie underwent surgeries at age 1 and again in the past year to correct this problem. She will now have to wear glasses, and her mom is worried that she will resist wearing them.

Her parents think her development has been slow because of her eyes, saying that she had a setback in activity after each operation. Although she walked at 12 months, she didn't crawl at all, and didn't reach for toys at that time. She has just now stopped drinking from a bottle (with much protesting), and is not yet potty trained. She never adjusted well to eating food that was lumpy or had texture; Mom says she would "act like she was gagging." Even now, she eats mostly applesauce, soup, pudding, and other soft foods, although she has been feeding herself with a spoon since she was about 1½. She understands almost everything said to her, such as "Throw your diaper away" and "Get in the bathtub," but her expressive language is delayed. She is now using a number of words, such as *bite, hello, hi,* and *yeah,* and she can say her brother's name (although not clearly).

Natalie is presently in an Early Intervention program two mornings a week, and the interventionist also visits the family's home. The program has strived to improve Natalie's physical, language, and social development. Her father says the interventionist thinks some of Natalie's delays in development are due to environment, but her parents attribute them to her vision problem. Her parents believe that because the surgeries and glasses have improved her vision, she will not be able to stay in the Early Intervention program after age 3, so they have decided to send her to Head Start. The early interventionist, however, says that Natalie could have continued to qualify for Early Intervention.

Her parents identify the following skills that Natalie now demonstrates: getting dressed by herself, putting on her shoes, opening doors, answering the phone, and drinking from a sippy cup. After her eye surgeries, she didn't play much, and her play is still not as elaborate as that of many children her age. Natalie's play includes putting together shape puzzles, driving around Hot Wheels cars (her dad collects them), pretending to feed her doll, "talking" to her troll doll, Jill, playing ball with her dad and sister, doing somersaults with her sister, making scribble drawings, playing a patty-cake routine with Mom, and "dancing" with Dad to a Kiss record. She prefers watching videos to looking at books, and she can sing songs (although the words are not distinguishable) from videos, such as a Barney song and Kiss songs. Mom says she is "her own person" but is also "prissy," because she likes to wear dresses, unlike her older sister. Dad says she now cries when she doesn't get her own way, and he handles that by sending her to her room. Both parents believe she imitates the behaviors of her older sister and plays well with her sister and the neighborhood children.

Because Natalie's father is at home, her parents have not had her in a daily educare program, but if they had needed to do so when she was younger, their expectations would have included having her fed and changed, and getting other care needs met. Now, at Early Intervention and when she goes to Head Start, they want the educarer to be sure that Natalie wears her glasses. Her dad doesn't think the family can expect much more from an educare program, but he certainly doesn't want the educarer to "teach her something bad." Mom says she would like Natalie to be read to and allowed to color. The main goal that her parents have for Natalie in the next year is for her to "say more."

CURRICULUM PRIORITIES

By this age, children's fundamental motor skills are well developed. Most can kick a ball forward without losing balance, bend at the waist to pick up objects off the floor or ground, jump with both feet off the ground, walk between two lines 8 inches apart, walk with an even gait, run with good balance, successfully throw an object at a moderate-size target, and engage in precise filling and dumping motions. Although they may still use a fist grasp when holding a writing utensil, these children can scribble diagonal lines and circles, screw lids on jars, put objects together and pull them apart, do more complex puzzles without frustration, brush their own teeth, and use a fork (but may prefer to use their fingers). The majority has begun toilet training, and many have accomplished that skill. They can remove their own clothing and put some of it on by themselves, use a drinking fountain and drink from a cup with few spills, and help put toys away (with adult assistance and encouragement).

Cognitively, they have made major strides. Most understand some space, number, and quantity concepts and can remember and explain short sequences of events. They can search for hidden objects successfully, and they may label their scribbles as representational images (Daddy, train). When asked whether they are a boy or girl, they can tell, and they can say their age, identify a greater number of body parts, and group objects by color, size, and shape (although they may not always accurately label the attribute).

Their vocabulary may be up to 300–400 words, and it includes spatial words ("in here") and negations ("no more juice"). Their sentences may still be telegraphic, with use of subject-verb ("I go") or verb-object ("go store"), but they use the word-order patterns of their native language. Many children of this age speak in complete sentences, although not all words may be intelligible. Most will join in singing songs and repeating fingerplays, point out details of pictures in books, ask for clarification when they don't understand something, and use plurals (although they overgeneralize irregular nouns: e.g., saying "foots" for "feet").

This is the age when adult concerns about a child's language delays usually begin, either about articulation difficulties that make the child's speech hard to understand, or about a lack of language production attempts. This is also the age often designated as the "terrible twos." Toddlers' use of the word *no* is at a peak; their behavior is often oppositional, primarily because they want to take charge of decisions and think they should do something because "I want to." (This often comes as an unpleasant surprise to adults who have been used to making all the decisions for a previously compliant child.) Toddlers have clear preferences for what they like and don't like, and they express them vehemently. However, they change their minds frequently, and they may have trouble making up their minds when given choices. Thus, they need routines to provide stability and security in their day.

Their social skills are improving, and they like to play near and enjoy the presence of other children, but they may intrude in peer play inappropriately and show possessiveness of toys and belongings. They initiate affection and want to please adults, but the timing of adults' affectionate overtures may be unwelcome and rejected. They are able to engage in small-group activities if allowed to proceed at their own pace, coming and going as they please, although they will sit at an art activity or listen to songs or stories for a longer time than they did 6 months ago. However, they still do not do well if they are expected to participate in large-group activities. Curriculum priorities include:

1. Increasing children's opportunities to use their wide range of motor and cognitive skills and to build upon their interests in symbolic systems (e.g., pictures, books, songs, letters, numbers)
2. Encouraging continued development of social skills with both adults and peers, of expressive language, and of initial awareness of cultural contexts in which social interactions occur
3. Providing children with opportunities to solidify their self-identity as autonomous and self-efficacious beings, through the practice of their self-regulation and self-help skills

RECOMMENDED CHARACTERISTICS OF THE ENVIRONMENT

The environment needs further enhancement to keep up with the play needs of older toddlers. Additional materials that build on their diverse experiences can be introduced at learning centers. Depending on the children's experiential base, educarers may provide many enriching materials.

- Firefighter hats, short pieces of plastic tubing for hoses, and a low structure to safely climb on can be used for "putting out fires." Wheeled cars and trucks can also become "fire trucks."
- Outdoors, a real working hose or soap and water in large buckets and wheeled toys to wash are much enjoyed. Indoors, a large cardboard box can become a drive-through car wash for toy vehicles. It may also have a pretend gas pump.
- Flat boxes to hold plastic fruits and vegetables, empty boxes of foods that children enjoy and recognize (crackers, cereal), and child-size grocery carts and shopping bags for collecting their "purchases" will engage toddlers. Cash registers are not necessary.
- Unused food containers from a nearby fast-food place that is familiar to the children will be of interest. A large cardboard box can be made with a drive-through service window through which food can be passed. Children love to "drive" their wheeled toys up to the window to pick up orders.
- Additions to the writing/drawing center may include envelopes, blunt scissors, stickers, and stamps. A variety of markers and crayons, including colors that can represent diverse skin tones, should be available.
- Some real tools, such as screwdrivers and hammers, should be provided for woodworking. Older toddlers can pound golf tees into covered Styrofoam blocks quite successfully. There are a number of commercial workbenches and tools designed for older toddlers.
- The book center should now contain vocabulary and storylines that help children with comprehension, memory, and sequencing of events. Stories should offer adverbs, adjectives, and other modifiers to give children models for sentence construction. Picture books with alphabet letters for objects and numbers for counting objects can be of particular interest to highly verbal children. Now is a good time to introduce big books, which can be looked at while lying on the floor or held up for all to see from a sitting position. Repetitive stories that allow children to predict events are especially enjoyed, such as the *Spot* books or *The Very Busy Spider* (see Appendix A). Of course, diversity of people and occupations should continue.
- There should be a variety of riding toys, including tricycles to practice pedaling and some vehicles that work best when two children cooperate. Children in rural communities love riding toy tractors and pulling wagons attached to their riding toys. Urban children use vehicles and climbing structures to represent trains, cabs, and buses.
- A variety of sizes of balls and beanbags should be available, with targets for throwing. Indoor and outdoor low basketball hoops are well used by older toddlers.
- There should be a greater selection of blocks: enough unit blocks for each child to have about 50 at one time (i.e., if four children are likely to be in the area, there should be 200 blocks). Cardboard bricks, large

hollow blocks, and foam blocks may also be provided. The block area should be between 60 and 70 square feet and located out of the major traffic lanes, to accommodate a number of children at one time and to avoid accidental conflicts caused by other children disrupting the activity.

- The music center should have a variety of rhythm instruments, CDs or tapes with players, and bells of various sizes that children can use. Children should have access to these during autonomous play, not just at "music time" (although a special music time is enjoyed by older toddlers). Tapes or CDs of music from many cultures should be provided, and music selections should be used at planned times, not in the form of nonstop background music.

- For sand and water play and easel painting, there should be adjacent rounded hooks for smocks and large towels to use to wipe up spills quickly. Such play gets very exuberant at this age.

- Climbing structures that accommodate a number of children are most important for older toddlers because these promote peer social interaction. Similarly, presence of wagons or two-seat cars encourage turn-taking (e.g., first you pull me, then I pull you) and pretend play (e.g., driving Dad and Mom to visit Grandma).

SAMPLE CURRICULUM ACTIVITIES

Knowledge Construction

Physical/Relational Knowledge

- To give toddlers opportunities for sorting and classifying foods by attributes (e.g., color, shape), you can use plastic fruits and vegetables. You can make suggestions such as "Let's put the red ones on this plate and the green ones on the other plate."

- You can encourage children to start collections of familiar objects (e.g., leaves, animal figures) and to find more objects that fit into the category. Older toddlers love to collect rocks. They can sort them by color, shape, size, or type, with scaffolding help from you. This could become a first lesson in geology! You can bring in items for various collections, and parents can help their child find objects that fit in the categories.

- When you take photos of special events (e.g., a birthday party) or everyday activities (e.g., a block tower that a child built), these can be placed on a bulletin board at the children's eye level. The pictures help them remember events that happened "last week," and encourage talk with peers and adults about the events.

- Have children help set the table for snack or lunch, placing cups, napkins, and plates on the table. This helps them learn one-to-one correspondence, an essential mathematical concept. Talk about who will sit at each place as you help them put out the right number of place settings. At this age, their understanding of one-to-one correspondence extends to three or four object-person relationships (about the number of people in their own families).

- To extend spatial awareness and motor coordination, you can give children small paint rollers to use for painting on tabletops. For painting with large rollers, hang a sheet of butcher paper on the wall or on a fence outdoors. Cardboard boxes of various sizes are also fun for toddlers to paint with rollers. Large-scale painting activities are best done outside.

- Toddlers love to paint with water outdoors on buildings and fences. Since they are still not really interested in the product, the darker shade they see produced by the water on the cement or wood is sufficient for giving them a sense of having an effect, which is an example of the often-heard phrase about toddlers that "the process is more important than the product."

- Cause/effect can be explored with a variety of sizes of paintbrushes that cover different-size areas on types of painting surfaces. Golf ball painting (the toddler version of marble painting) can promote causal reasoning. Put a paper lining in a large box with sides at least 2 inches high. Help the children use a large spoon to put a golf ball into a pan of paint. After they have placed the ball in the box, help them move the box and ball around to make a trail of paint, and then remove the ball with the spoon. Repeat the process with balls that have been placed in different colors of paint, until a design is created.

- You can also help children see cause/effect by having them finger paint on a table surface, then place a piece of paper on the markings and lift it to see the imprint. You can point out to them that the lines on the paper are caused by the paint design, which was then "printed" on the paper. Other objects, such as toy vehicles, can be used to make interesting lines in the paint.

- Printmaking can also be done by dipping cookie cutters, biscuit cutters, small butter presses, jar lids, strawberry baskets, plastic animals' feet, old puzzle pieces, or any other potentially interesting object in paint and then pressing it on paper. Observing the varied patterns and naming the object that made the pattern assists children's discrimination and categorization ability as well as causality. (This is another "yes" activity that has some "nos" attached, with certain objects being allowed and others not being allowed in the paint.)

- Tearing a variety of types of scrap paper, aluminum foil, waxed paper, and lightweight cardboard is a process activity that enhances both knowledge of physical objects (e.g., foil versus cardboard) and emotional expression, and it extends their earlier tearing experiences. A next step is to have some glue and let them attach their torn materials to paper to make a collage. One large paper for all of the children is sufficient; toddlers will not care about taking their own collage paper home yet.

- Sand and water still rank high in interest for older toddlers. Bubble-making can be added to the water/sand table repertoire if there is a variety of cones and rings to blow through. Tools such as eggbeaters, wire whisks, water wheels, sifters, and funnels of different sizes allow children to explore how these machines work in water and in sand. If you add water in varying amounts to sand to increase its packability, children's knowledge of its physical properties is expanded.

- To increase the range of sensory experiences, you can make coffee sand by combining a gallon of used, dried coffee grounds with cornmeal and flour. This substance does not smell or look like food, so children are not tempted to taste it.

- You can suggest matching activities to enhance sensory skills. Children can do a simple experiment such as tasting a tray of foods and comparing ones that are sweet with ones that are sour. They can also find the ones that taste alike. Textures taped to the bottom of film canisters can be matched by touching, and items with different odors placed in small jars can be used for smell-and-match challenges. Canisters filled with objects that make different sounds when shaken can also be matched. Care must be taken to have secure lids on such canisters. These activities can engage children with sensory impairments if they are ones that make use of their intact senses (e.g., a visually impaired child could do all of the suggested activities). Natural science activities are of interest to children this age.

- Older toddlers enjoy using plastic bricks and other building materials to make larger objects by connecting pieces. They can connect a long row of bricks or stack them to form a "house" or a "car." With some scaffolding help from you, they can string large beads following patterns that you provide, and you can talk about the placement, colors, and shapes of beads used.

- Puzzles should have a range of difficulty levels, and should be offered on racks or low shelves so children can access them. Toddlers will select puzzles that challenge them if offered a choice of levels of difficulty. A set of puzzles representing diverse people engaged in nonstereotypical activities can serve both physical and social knowledge goals. Also, children this age enjoy putting together number and letter puzzles, especially the colorful, interlocking foam number and letter sets. They also like simple obstacle courses that encourage problem solving and spatial awareness as they crawl, hop, climb, and jump. These can be varied in pattern every few days to extend the novelty and complexity of the activity.

- Another way to extend cause/effect knowledge is to help children make simple rhythm instruments (such as shakers made from cans or paper plates sewn together with yarn). The children can put small stones, beans, or coins inside; however, you need to make sure that container lids and sewing stitches are secure so that the containers do not leak. Children can experiment with various substances in such shakers and note the differences in the sounds they make, thus improving their discrimination skills.
- You can attach pockets that have pictures of objects such as a ball, doll, frog, or other familiar object onto heavy fabric to improve discrimination and classification abilities. Give children a collection of small representations of these items and let the children put them in the corresponding pockets. You can also put a label for the object on the pocket, and point to it casually when you (or they) name the objects.

Social Knowledge

- To facilitate vocabulary and comprehension, you should read to children throughout the day. You can generate participation in the plot by asking what will happen next in a familiar book or by making a purposeful mistake in naming a character that the children know well. You can point to salient words as they are read to help children make connections between the written and spoken word (to give them a sense of print and sound). It is not uncommon for a cluster of three or more children to sit together to listen to a book being read. Language-based activities that encourage responses from children are particularly important at this age, especially for those children who are not speaking clearly. They need to be motivated to continue making communication attempts. An example of a way to do this is the song "John Has Gone Away," which requires the child to jump up and say, "Here I am" on the last line.
- To help children order their activities, you can give two-step directions during routine activities. For example, you can say, "Put the book on the shelf and then go wash your hands for snacktime."
- You can make a game having children match pictures with real objects and then asking them to tell something about the pictures and objects. You should model how to "tell" about the picture or object by saying, "This picture shows the boy eating an apple. What does this next picture show that he is doing?" (Be sure to have them answer with a narrative, not just shout one word.) By giving children patterns for talking about things, you enhance their ability to express narratives in sequence, an essential element of writing, which develops concurrently with reading (two components of emerging literacy).
- Another way to help develop narrative ability is to have children

hold hand or stick puppets while you tell a story about the puppets. Stories in which children can repeat a line frequently keep them involved (e.g., in "The Little Red Hen," saying "Not I" as each animal is asked who will help).

- Simple felt-board stories encourage verbal narrative participation and enhance social knowledge. Story characters and props can be made for familiar stories with repetitive themes and language (e.g., *Brown Bear, Brown Bear, What Do You See?*). Felt characters can be made by cutting out felt, pasting Velcro-like tabs on the back of pictures, or using medium-weight iron-on interfacing. Characters can be traced onto fabric and colored with permanent ink markers or colored pencils. The sticky side will cling to a felt board. When the story has been told a few times, children enjoy putting the pieces on the felt board by themselves. They usually talk about their version of the story as they place the pieces, thus practicing narrative skills.
- You should have a repertoire of poems and nursery rhymes memorized that you can recite at just the right moments. However, because most nursery rhymes and many poems are about male characters, you will want to replace male names with female names some of the time. Gender-equal or gender-neutral poetry books (e.g., *Father Gander*) provide ideas. Because children this age are fascinated by natural phenomena (rain, wind) and animals, knowing a few poems about these topics can come in handy.
- If the windows in the educare setting are low enough, you can let children look out the windows in the room to watch traffic and passersby or natural phenomena such as snow. You can use these opportunities to talk about what children see.
- Tightly woven carpets with drawings of villages and train tracks can be purchased, or you can make your own on heavy butcher paper. With scaffolding help from you, older toddlers can "drive" small, wheeled vehicles and trains around the carpet "town." If you narrate what the children are doing and casually offer suggestions about where they are going ("to the store" or "to the restaurant") and what they are doing ("You are making the train go very fast"), the children can broaden their knowledge of social scripts and gain richness in concept learning.

Integrated Knowledge

- A love of nature is something that many children this age possess. Older toddlers should be outdoors at least once every day to gain physical, relational, and social knowledge from the natural world. All seasons have opportunities for integrated knowledge. You can point out changes in trees, shrubs, and flowers, as well as wildlife, in each season. Make a marked trail on the playground or in a neighboring park by hanging colorful string on objects to lead children to a special destination where "treasure" may be found. In winter, the "ice puddle walk" or "sound walk" can help them hear various sounds in the environment. In spring, a "color walk" gives children examples of familiar colors that they can discover (e.g., in flowers). In autumn, they can find pine cones, dead leaves, and nuts to collect and use for sorting games or art activities.

- Music activities provide physical and social knowledge opportunities. Children's tapes or CDs with simple songs and movements children can follow, such as "Play Your Instruments" and "Make a Pretty Sound," can provide many opportunities for learning rhythms and song lyrics. (Albums and song books are listed in Appendix A.) A piano, autoharp, or guitar will be of interest to toddlers, and they enjoy nursery and folk songs when played on these instruments. Older toddlers can dance and march to music, and can learn to stop when the music stops. Music encourages children to dance, and props such as scarves, streamers, or long skirts with elasticized waistbands encourage twirling and shaking. This activity provides opportunities for emotional release and social control, thus building social-emotional relationships.

- Another integrative activity is cooking/food preparation. Older toddlers have increased fine motor control and a willingness to apply these skills to food preparation. When given plastic knives to cut fruit or spread butter or cheese on bread or crackers, they understand that there is a larger goal in mind: making fruit salad or sandwiches. Another cause/effect activity is butter-making. You can fill small plastic containers with cream and have the children shake the containers. With much hopping and bouncing, they will discover that the cream has turned into butter. Older 2-year-olds love to help cook. They can assist in making cookies, quick breads, muffins, and biscuits. If ingredients are premeasured and ready to mix (since the children do not understand fractions), you can help them see that there is more of some ingredients than others and talk about why that might be. The use of prepared mixes is not recommended because it deprives the children of the opportunity to see, taste, and understand all of the ingredients in each recipe. Cooking activities also build social-emotional relationships because they duplicate activities done at home and give children the opportunity to see you in another nuturing role.

NAEYC Accreditation Criteria 2.G.01 (Science) Standard 2: Curriculum: "Infants and toddlers/ twos are provided varied opportunities and materials to use their senses to learn about objects in the environment, discover that they can make things happen, and solve simple problems."

Social-Emotional Relationship-Building

- "Circle time" may be initiated at this age but should not be required. Rather, activities should be optional and free-form, allowing children to leave when they are no longer interested. You can sit down and begin to sing songs, tell a story with a puppet, or repeat familiar fingerplays with just a few children. Others will join in, but the audience will come and go as the spirit moves them. Familiar songs and poems can be practiced by providing large felt pieces portraying characters in the songs or poems and placing them on a small A-frame felt board that can sit on the floor or on a low table. This begins the process of understanding "groupness," that is, "self as a member of a group." However, this concept will not be formed completely until late preschool age.

- Because of the sometimes volatile and unpredictable nature of older toddlers, close (but "laidback") adult supervision is essential at all times. You serve as a role model for showing concern for others and respecting others' rights. Conflict mediation is a major responsibility with children of this age. Your goal is to make children better able to resolve conflicts themselves, so you should focus on a "giving children words" strategy (e.g., "Jeremy didn't like it when you hit him"; "When Beth is finished, then it will be your turn") that children can imitate and use effectively in future conflicts.

- You can use puppets to help children deal with conflicts, by having puppets express angry or sad feelings, and comforting them, or scolding them for hurting other puppets. The children can then make the puppets interact. Young children often tend to be overly aggressive with puppets, so you need to supervise and guide the play toward resolution of the feelings in prosocial behaviors and empathetic responses.

- Poems, songs, and fingerplays help with transitions to new activities or when children need to delay gratification. To keep children's interest, you can substitute children's names in songs and poems. The most famous of these are the "cleanup songs," but any transition can be smoother with a made-up song. For example, "Let's get our coats on, let's get our hats on, let's get our mittens on, to go outside."

- Displaying photos of all the children is useful for relationship building. Now that toddlers have a clear sense of self-identity, photos can strengthen their bonds with peers, parents, and educarers. Toddlers can point out to parents a picture of their "friend." You can have a "book of friends" that can be taken home on a rotating basis by families. Toddlers love to show their parents or grandparents who their educare friends are, and this aids them in strengthening their friendships with other children.

Play Development

- Practice play continues to be of major importance and many of the suggestions made for younger children are still appropriate. However, the variety and complexity of the objects for play need to be expanded. You should try to have play materials that build on the children's natural interests and keep moderate novelty in the environment. Social interaction difficulties and random wandering often occur if the play environment becomes boring. The practice play materials should be selected to be challenging for children to master, not just the "same old stuff" that was there all year.

- Now that children are better able to imitate adult roles, a variety of pretend play themes may be introduced. You must make sure that children have a familiarity with the role/theme before proceeding. Taking walks to see stores or activities in which workers are engaging (e.g., street repair) will enhance children's understanding of a particular theme, as will any other direct experiences that you plan (e.g., going to a farm to pick pumpkins). When toddlers play out their experiences in pretend scripts, it is equivalent to older children's writing or talking about their experiences, and serves similar purposes. Play allows them to reflect upon the experience and assimilate it meaningfully. Objects that remind them of the experience will assist in their reenactments. For example, "street repair" equipment can encourage that script to be played.

- Toddlers' pretend play becomes richer when educarers facilitate it by playing with them for brief periods of time. You can take a role (e.g., mail carrier) and model appropriate actions or language for that role, and comment positively or ask questions that help to elaborate the play. For example, in a "birthday party" script, you can ask, "Where are the presents?" and bring an object from another area wrapped in scrap paper to give to the "birthday" child. It is likely that all participants will then find "presents" to give to that child. Another popular experience is to have a "tea party," serving milk or juice. Adult facilitation of pretend play increases both the quality of the play and the language that young children use.

- Children at this age love to dance, especially when props such as scarves are made available. This is a good way to introduce children to varied musical styles, including music from different countries and cultures.

- Group games are enjoyed by most children. A good group game for children this age is a simple version of "London Bridge." You clasp one child's hands and hold them high while other children go under them as you chant the song. On the phrase "my fair lady (or gentleman)," bring the arms down and lightly clasp the child who is passing under. That child is the next one to hold the bridge up with you. Because toddlers are not good at delayed gratification or taking turns, you will find that the group is not a stable one. Some children will leave as soon as they get caught. The game does provide

---

NAEYC Accreditation Criteria: 2.B.05 (Social-Emotional Development) Standard 2: Curriculum: "Children have varied opportunities to develop skills for entering into social groups, developing friendships, learning to help, and other prosocial behavior."

controlled excitement and helps children learn anticipation of an action within a sequence.

- Both pretend play and game skills increase when children this age are in mixed-age groups with slightly older children. The "almost 3" toddlers provide highly salient play models for the mid-2-age toddlers.

NAEYC Accreditation Criteria: 2.J.01 (Creative Expression and Appreciation of the Arts) Standard 2: Curriculum: "Children are provided varied opportunities to gain appreciation of art, music, drama, and dance in ways that reflect cultural diversity."

QUESTIONS FOR DISCUSSION

1. What are some contrasts and similarities between the play behaviors and preferences of Paul and Jeremy? Would it be likely that girls would have similar interests to these? How do Natalie's behaviors and play preferences differ from what would be expected of most older toddlers? Would she benefit from being in a group of children this age?

2. What could you do to help Jeremy (and his mother) cope with the death of his father? Since he seems to have no major behavior problems (but shows some indicators of unease and a language problem), should you do anything differently for him? How could you help his mother cope with single parenthood?

3. Paul seems advanced in motor, language, and cognitive skills, and at age level in social skills, while Natalie shows delays in development in all areas. What might keep Paul's interest and enable him to progress in areas where he is especially strong? What does Natalie need to help her advance in skills?

4. Some parents encourage children this age to watch videos and television, to play computer games, and even to listen to adult music tapes/CDs at home. Other parents are opposed to having young children involved with technology. What advice would you give to parents about the effects of child technology experiences? Should you include TV or pop-culture-inspired toys (e.g., Barney, Teletubbies, Kiss) in the educare environment?

5. Since the three children described at the beginning of this chapter all come from European-origin backgrounds, how could you provide appropriate and appealing art, music, drama, and dance experiences that would introduce them to cultural diversity?

Chapter 11

35–36 Months

Curriculum for QUENTIN, MEIKO, and ROSA & ROSITA

AT 36 INCHES, Quentin is of average height for a 3-year-old, but he has a slender build, weighing 30 pounds. His blond hair is worn in a bowl cut, his eyes are blue, and his cheeks are plump. Quentin sucks his thumb, especially when he is tired, when he is going to sleep, and when he is in new situations. During his first months, he occasionally had fussy spells. Quentin never liked riding in a car and so began crying 15 minutes into a car trip. He had a good appetite, ate every 2 hours, and then went right back to sleep. Now Quentin goes to bed at night without protest as long as he is read to first. He doesn't always nap at home, but he usually naps at his educare program. His parents say he has a wicked temper when he gets overly tired, and he will have an emotional "meltdown." He prefers having a huge breakfast and lunch and not much dinner.

Quentin has many interests and a long attention span. He often spends 30 to 40 minutes playing with his train set at home, redesigning the arrangement of the tracks into different configurations. He loves puzzles and does them for long periods. His mom says that when he is concentrating, his tongue goes out, just like his dad's. His father says that Quentin has a great imagination, making up stories using his stuffed animals. He enjoys watching funny TV shows and videos and laughs at appropriate times. He watches the evening news with his parents and knows the newscasters' names. His mother says they have to limit his viewing time or he would spend too much time in front of the TV.

Quentin also loves playing outdoors. At home, he rides a small bike with training wheels and he does well with tricycles at his educare program. He has his own child-size golf set, just like Dad's. They like to "hit a few balls around" together in the yard on the weekends. Quentin spends a lot of time shooting baskets into a low hoop both at home and at educare, and he has amazingly accurate aim for a 3-year-old.

Quentin's tremendous curiosity leads him to ask many questions. He has a need to understand everything that is going on around him. His parents say he has an excellent memory for people's names, remembering them after only one meeting. An only child, he plays alone frequently, both at home and at educare. He often stops to watch other children and can be drawn briefly into a group activity. He has a cautious personality and is fastidious, avoiding most messy activities such as painting and food preparation that involve getting his hands wet or sticky. Mom says that if he spills his juice, he immediately gets a napkin to clean it up, and he prefers to eat his cupcakes with a spoon!

Quentin has excellent fine motor control, putting together small manipulatives and carefully pouring liquids. His gross motor skills include pedaling a trike, throwing balls, shooting baskets, and climbing up and down stairs. He enjoys practicing forward rolls at home and is mastering putting on his shoes and socks. He likes to pretend to tie his shoes.

His language skills have always been strong. He has spoken in complete sentences since he was 2. If he talks too fast, he may stammer, but then he slows down and repeats the phrase to say it correctly. He is now recognizing letters by picking them out from book texts.

Quentin's parents say he can be stubborn, given to an occasional tantrum. When this happens, they just wait for it to run its course. Afterward, he wants to be held, which means he's ready to talk about what happened. If his parents talk to him about why he cannot do something, he needs time to think about it, then he usually complies. They find that it helps to give him ample warning before transitions or when there has been a change of plans because he doesn't like surprises.

Quentin's parents want his out-of-home educare environment to be stimulating, with many interesting activities for him to engage in. Mom says she wants his educarers to pay attention to him, talk to him, play with him, and read to him. Dad stresses that he wants the educarers to recognize Quentin's unique sense of humor and, most of all, to enjoy him for who he is.

AT 35 MONTHS of age, Meiko has already lived in three different countries. She was born in Japan, with her mother's family and her 20-month-old sister present at the hospital (her father was in his native land, Korea, at the time). Meiko was rather small at birth, weighing 7½ pounds and measuring 19½ inches long. She was quiet, even at birth, and didn't cry much. She slept more than 12 hours a night right from the start and had to be awakened to be nursed. Although she had diaper rash and cried for about 30 minutes every evening, her mother says that she was an "easy" baby

during the first 3½ months, when she was in Japan. She seemed to have a special bond with her sister, touching the fingers of her sibling's hand and noticing her actions at an early age. Meiko's first real smile was for her sister. During the time Meiko lived at her grandparents' home in Japan, she was adaptable and calm.

When she traveled to Korea with her mother and sister, her behavior changed. She became fussy and very attached to them. She wanted no one but her mother and sister to be with her. She was cautious and quiet around her father (who does not speak much Japanese), and she would not allow her father's parents and in-laws to hold her. Meiko's mother thinks that the change to a different language environment and the loss of familiar family members made this transition difficult. In Korea, her mother and father conversed in their common language, English, but everyone else spoke Korean, and Meiko's father spoke Korean to her, although her mother continued to speak to her in Japanese. Her social-emotional upset at this transition lasted about 2 months, until she was about 6 months old.

When she was 10 months old, the family made the move to the United States so that her father could go to college. That transition was smoother, although Meiko had jet lag and a formula change. Because the weather was very cold on their arrival, the whole family had some adjustment problems. Meiko cried quite a bit at first, but she remained a good sleeper.

Now, after about 2 years in the United States, Meiko is an independent child who is friendly and self-assured around both adults and older children. Her mother thinks this is because her sister has been a constant presence in her life, and the two children have had good rapport and communication. Meiko is used to playing with older children most of the time; as her mother puts it, "She doesn't think she is her age!" The family presently lives in student housing, where Meiko sees many people of varied racial and ethnic backgrounds and plays outside with older children. Her mother comments that "She says 'Hi' to everybody." Mom notes that Meiko has been independent since she began walking, and she often doesn't seem to need her mother.

Although Meiko had more transitions than most young children, which affected her social-emotional development at those times, her motor and cognitive development were not affected adversely. She sat up well at 5 months, crawled at 7 months (first in a "turtle" style on her stomach, and then on all fours). She took her first steps before her first birthday and, at

14 months, she was walking well. Now she is a climber who can scale the tallest slide without difficulty.

When she was younger, she played with balls, rings, and other manipulative toys, but now she likes her puzzles, reading books (two or three books a day), and music. She knows many songs, likes to dance, and plays a small electric piano. She also knows how to count with meaning in Japanese and in English and to recite the alphabet in both languages. Her first love is the outdoors, with the swings and slides being her favorites, which is good because her mother says, "We don't have many toys in the house."

At her present age, Meiko is a small but sturdy child who "changes from shy and quiet to outgoing," depending on the social situation. When she was 2, her mother took her to a gymnastics play group with American children about her age, but Meiko was shy and didn't play; she just watched. When she tried to interact with peers, she was "rough," touching, pulling, and pushing them. At that time, her mother used to spank her, but she no longer uses that form of discipline. Mom still thinks Meiko needs to learn how to play with children her own age. Her mother characterizes her as a child who "always knows what is going on." She learns new things easily and smiles a lot, especially at silly things. However, she is stubborn and needs to get what she wants.

Her mother speaks Japanese to her because she wants Meiko to have facility in that language, and her father usually speaks to her in Korean for the same reason. Presently, Meiko speaks fluent, well-formed sentences in Japanese, and understands both Korean and English. She speaks both of these languages with shorter sentences that are not always well-formed, but she knows in which situations to use each language. With her sister, who is now in Head Start, Meiko usually speaks English. She also can sing songs in all three languages.

If there had been an Early Head Start program for Meiko to go to, her mother thinks she probably would have been initially shy and would have needed help with the transition. Because no Early Head Start program was available, Meiko did not go to educare. If she had done so, her mother says that she would have wanted educarers to "respect what she [Meiko] wants to do" because "she knows what she wants to do and should not be ordered to do things." Her mother would like educarers to increase her curiosity, broaden her mind, and help her to learn English (her mother wants Meiko to be trilingual). When asked whether she wants aspects of Japanese culture to be promoted, Meiko's mother says she does not, because she prefers the style of child-rearing in the United States to that of Japan. In Japan, she says, "They don't respect kids" and "Kids have to follow adults' orders exactly." She adds, "Americans don't scold as much." She feels that she and her husband already are communicating the aspects of their cultures that they want Meiko to learn, so what she would want from educare would be for Meiko to learn English well and make friends with children her own age.

ROSA AND ROSITA are 36-month-old identical twins were born in the United States. At 9 pounds, 3 ounces, and 9 pounds, 8 ounces, respectively, they were the biggest twins ever born at the community hospital. Rosa, who weighed less, was longer (21 inches), and Rosita was 19 inches. There is still a similar difference in their heights. The twins were born at their mother's due date, but there was a delay of 7 minutes between the birth of Rosa and Rosita because Rosita had to be turned in the womb before she could be born. However, the twins' mother says it wasn't an especially difficult birth. Rosa and Rosita are their mother's fourth and fifth children. (Rosa and Rosita have two older brothers and one older sister.) The family came to the United States from Mexico 4 years ago, following one brother who had already settled in the area. Now another brother has just come to the United States; Mom has seven more brothers and sisters still living in Mexico.

Mom says that there were no problems with the twins' early months of life, although they only breastfed for 12 days. Because it seemed that "they didn't want to be nursed," she began to bottle-feed. Even though she had experience as a mother, she found that it was hard to care for two children at once because she tried to have them on the same schedule, so they both ate at the same time. She would hold one and put the other alongside her to feed. Her mother visited from Mexico for the first 6 months, which helped a lot.

By the time the twins were 4 months old, Mom "noticed a big difference" between them. She says that Rosa is more independent, while Rosita prefers to stay close to her mother. Rosita's temperament fits the "slow to warm up" category. Rosita sleeps with her parents, while Rosa sleeps with her brothers and sisters. Mom says, "They don't want to sleep in a separate bed yet, because we are a close family."

The twins' development was relatively similar, with both of them smiling at about 2 to 3 months, reaching for objects at about 3 months, and sitting up without support at about 5 months. However, Rosa crawled at 7 months and walked at 9 months, while Rosita didn't crawl at all and walked at 12 months. Around 10 months, both began saying "ma ma," "pa pa," and "bebe" (for "bottle"), and now they are both fluent in Spanish. They do not understand much English yet, but this is not surprising since their mother speaks only Spanish and their father and siblings are not fluent in English.

They have many abilities that can be seen when they play, and one type they enjoy is pretend, with their older sister being "Mom" and the twins being "kids." They also like to pretend to care for their dolls. Their fine motor skills are good: they stack blocks and make pictures with magic markers, but they don't know how to do puzzles because the only kind the family has are cardboard ones with many pieces, used by the older children. Mom says, "We don't have many toys at home." Other types of play they enjoy include mimicking songs they hear on TV and dancing to music. They like to ride the rocking horse when they visit their sister's Head Start class. Rosa especially likes to dance and jump, and is eager to try new activities. Rosa doesn't climb, however, because, according to Mom, that is "for boys to do." Their father doesn't play games with the twins, but he does like to "cuddle" them. When he gives them attention, Rosa comes to him right away, but Rosita stays close to her mother, so her dad especially tries to interact with her.

Their mother would like to be able to give the twins dancing and singing lessons when they are a little older. If there had been an Early Head Start program in their town, she would have liked them to attend because she wants them to learn English. Mom says that she is afraid that the twins won't be able to make friends if they don't know English, and she wishes there were a way for them to learn English before they go to Head Start. If they had been in an educare program, she would have liked the educarers to read and tell some Mexican stories because she doesn't want the twins to miss out on their Mexican storytelling heritage. She would also like educarers to carry on the values and morals of her country, such as expecting the girls to "show respect" and "do what they are told to do." She has noticed that in her older daughter's Head Start class "some of the kids are wild." She also has long-term concerns about keeping the family values that are important in her culture; for example, having young people leave their home at age 18 doesn't seem right to her, and her family would never allow behaviors such as smoking or drinking. Her main goals for an educare program would be for educarers to help Rosa and Rosita become good English speakers, and learn to get along well with other children without losing the important values of Mexican family culture.

CURRICULUM PRIORITIES

By age 3, children who are in mixed-age groups with younger toddlers present a challenge to educarers. Educarers must provide enough interesting experiences so that the "almost 3" toddler doesn't become bored or disruptive, while still maintaining activities for younger children. This may be the time for these children to visit an age 3–5 program occasionally, especially if they will be starting to attend that program soon.

Between age 2½ and 3, children show much growth. Physically, they are well coordinated, can walk and run smoothly on a variety of surfaces, and can run both slowly and quickly while maintaining balance. That is, they have achieved motor consistency. Most can pedal small tricycles, use a preferred hand for most activities, draw a closed circle by holding the crayon or marker in a tripod grasp, and zip, button, and snap clothing.

Cognitively, children remember and follow simple rules; identify almost all body parts; classify objects by shape, color, texture, and size; and solve problems that require a two-step solution. Many can count with meaning to 4 or 5; some can count to 10.

Language and general communication skills have expanded rapidly. The 3-year-old can speak in complete sentences at least three words long (some can even make 6- to-9-word sentences). They like to tell stories and are able to give the high points and sometimes quite a few details. They remember song lyrics, rhymes, and fingerplays, and initiate them spontaneously.

Socially and emotionally, they have more self-control and fewer uncontrolled emotional outbursts, although they express their emotions strongly and often articulately ("You made me mad!"). They like to help and play games with adults, and although they play mainly in parallel fashion, there are brief episodes of associative and cooperative play, which can be extended if an adult helps to sustain them. They enjoy role-playing adult actions and using imaginative speech in their pretend play. Because concept development in children who are almost 3 is more flexible and adaptive, they rely less on realistic objects when pretending; they can now substitute objects using their imaginations. For instance, a block or shoe can become a telephone, or a broom can become a horse to ride. Children this age are eager to try new experiences and seem to learn something new every day. Curriculum priorities include:

1. Having a range of opportunities available to construct physical, relational, and social knowledge in many settings, and scaffolding assistance to connect these experiences to symbols that represent knowledge, especially in mathematics and literacy
2. Providing an environment that encourages friendship development and strengthens communicative competence, within extended and more complex relationships
3. Helping children gain greater self-regulation of their behavior and emotions within the cultural contexts in which they live, and having the cognitive, social-emotional, and play skills that will enable them to make a successful transition to a preschool classroom
4. Providing culturally appropriate learning opportunities by working closely with all families

RECOMMENDED CHARACTERISTICS OF THE ENVIRONMENT

Learning/activity centers should have additional materials that hold older children's interest. Some elaborations that can be made in the environment (but certainly not all that are possible) are listed here.

- Additional props in the housekeeping area should include doll clothes with Velcro closures for ease of dressing and undressing. Brooms, dustpans, and mops can be added, as can an ironing board and play iron.
- For diversity awareness, persona dolls representing people with different abilities and disabilities can be used by children with close adult supervision. Dolls in the housekeeping corner should also reflect the racial and cultural diversity of society at large.
- More manipulative tools can be added to the water table, such as siphons, pump bottles, spray bottles, basters, and small hand pumps.
- Additions to the Play-Doh table can include rolling pins, cookie cutters, plastic knives, and a garlic press.
- Outdoors, a sandy dirt area with a nearby water source can provide an opportunity for making dams and rivers. More variety in types of shovels, scoops, and digging tools is also needed.
- In a large outdoor sandbox, a variety of small construction vehicles can be added, such as a bulldozer, steamroller, backhoe, dump truck, plow, and tractor.
- Manipulative materials can be expanded. Dressing frames for practicing lacing, snapping, buttoning, and zipping are needed. While keeping manipulatives such as table blocks and beads, you can add snap-together cubes, magnetic blocks or vehicles, lacing cards, shapes that screw together, pegs and boards, small people and vehicles, blocks that stick together, and large dominoes. Geo boards made by hammering 36 nails evenly spaced on an 8-by-8-inch board, with large rubberbands for making designs, are of interest.
- Puzzle types can be expanded. Puzzles should represent differently abled people, diverse ethnic and racial groups, people of different ages, and people in nonstereotypical occupations. Puzzles with pictures of tools, transportation vehicles, animals, nursery rhymes, and other types of puzzles that build on children's interests are recommended. The number of pieces can range up to 20. Shape sorters can also be added.
- Additions to pretend play can include sets of plastic animals (wild and farm animals, dinosaurs) and settings that represent an airport, gas station, and parking garage with appropriate vehicles. You can add tunnels and bridges to train sets.
- The woodworking center should have real tools and soft wood. Everyone, including educarers, should wear safety glasses when using tools. Children can be taught how to use a saw, hammer, and nails correctly with close adult supervision. A sturdy woodworking bench and vise are essential.
- Additions to the gross motor area can include balance beams that are narrower and a little higher than those for younger children, with two or more that connect but go off at different angles; a mini-

trampoline with a bar to hold onto while jumping; hula hoops for swinging on the hips, jumping over, or walking through while held by an adult; ring-toss games; balls of all sizes for throwing at targets or for catching and kicking; and a bowling game using commercial toy pins, empty half-gallon milk cartons, or large plastic soda bottles.

- Since many 3-year-olds emulate older siblings or parents who play sports, a T-ball set and realistic low basketball hoop can be added.
- Other active play equipment to add includes handheld traffic signs for the trike and car riding area; rocking teeter-totters that require two children to make them work; mats for tumbling; and a spin-around riding toy that requires the child to pull on the handle to make the seat turn.
- Unit blocks should be expanded to allow each child in the area to have at least 100, and space for construction without interference should be provided. Bins of toy animals, vehicles, and small figures near the blocks will encourage combining materials creatively. If possible, having the blocks next to the housekeeping area can stimulate integrative play between the two areas (building a car of blocks for taking the baby to the doctor; using blocks to be cake at a party).
- In addition to unit blocks, a small number (6–12) of mini-hollow wooden blocks allow children to build bigger "houses," "boats," and "cars." A number of commercial companies make these blocks. If space is limited inside, they can be used on an outdoor porch.
- For painting, a double easel made of clear Plexiglas is recommended. Children can paint directly onto the glass and can watch another child painting at the same time.
- More instruments should be added to the music collection. A CD player that children may use should also be added.
- The book center can have "listening and reading" areas that include a tape/CD player and headphones for at least two children, and a collection of books and tapes and CDs of stories for children to use on their own. More children's classics and new books of quality should be added to the library, as well as age-appropriate, new award-winning books. Other types of books are ones with partially hidden pictures that require children to guess what the pictures show before they turn the page, and books about shapes, colors, concepts (same-different, opposites), and simple numeracy.
- Listening lotto games, where children listen to a tape and then cover the corresponding picture on the lotto board, and concept puzzles or cards requiring children to match pieces that go together (e.g., opposites, items a baby needs), are recommended, as is a collection of familiar felt-board stories that children can use with minimal adult supervision.
- The writing center can have notebooks for each child, as well as materials for making greeting cards.

- For science, add a collection of activity boxes with various items for children to explore. Include samples of rocks and fossils; pine cones of different shapes and sizes; color paddles; magnet wands with steel or iron objects such as large paper clips, brads, nuts, and bolts; and hand lenses of different sizes. An aquarium with fish for children to care for or a mini-incubator for hatching chicks can be provided. A display table with a clear top over a 4-inch case can be purchased or made to be used for showing interesting items that children find or natural science items brought in by educarers. A felt board for dressing characters according to the weather (e.g., boots and raincoats) can also be of interest.

SAMPLE CURRICULUM ACIVITIES

Knowledge Construction

Physical/Relational Knowledge

- To enhance motor coordination, categorization, and numeracy skills, set up a fishing activity by laminating fish cutouts, placing large paper clips on them, and making a fishing pole with a dowel and string attached to a large magnet. Fish are placed in a water table or in a pretend pond on the floor, and children try to catch fish that look alike and determine how many of each type they have caught.
- A selection of "beautiful junk" can be used for collages with many colors and textures (e.g., ribbons, yarn, straws, feathers, wooden cutouts, scrap paper, sandpaper, aluminum foil) and picking out things to paste. Offer different types of glue and paste for experimenting.
- At paint easels, have a selection of colors of paint, including earth or skin tones (beige, tan, brown, and black). This can stimulate some interesting social interactions.
- You should give opportunities for cutting with blunt scissors, although children at this age typically need adult help in holding the paper while they cut. Play-Doh is easy to cut with scissors and can be an alternative to cutting paper.
- Sponge painting is enjoyed by older toddlers. If you offer it, expect that they will not be interested in making prints as much as experimenting with smearing the sponges on the paper.
- Sand collages can be made by offering play sand with grated colored chalk added to it. You can put sand in large salt shakers and have children sprinkle it over paper onto which they have squirted glue. The children can then pour off the excess sand onto another tray and observe the design they have created.
- Outdoors, you can give spray bottles filled with colored water so

children can spray on large sheets of paper hung on a fence or easel or, in winter, directly on snow.

- Indoors, balloons can be inflated and children can try to keep them in the air. (When they pop, remove them immediately.)
- Indoors or outdoors, you can make a trail of animal tracks for children to follow. There can be a surprise at the last footprint. This is especially effective after a group chant, "We're Going on a Bear Hunt," or after hearing a story about dinosaurs.
- Other science activities aid cause/effect understanding, such as sprouting grass seeds on sponges, watching a butterfly emerge from a cocoon, and planting flower seeds in a garden (a longer-range expectation). Ice cream can be made in sealable plastic bags by placing milk, sugar and vanilla extract in a small bag and then placing it in a larger sealable bag filled with ice cubes and rock salt. Children can quickly see the effects of shaking the bag as they make their own homemade ice cream.

NAEYC Accreditation Criteria 2.F.04 (Early Mathematics) Standard 2: Curriculum: "Children are provided varied opportunities and materials that encourage them to integrate mathematical terms into everyday conversation."

NAEYC Accreditation Criteria 2.J.05 (Creative Expression and Appreciation for the Arts) Standard 2: Curriculum: "Children are provided varied opportunities to develop and widen their repertoire of skills that support artistic expression (e.g., cutting, gluing, and caring for tools)."

Social Knowledge

- You can encourage children to "write" something every day. Their writings might be grocery lists or letters to friends or family members. Begin a portfolio of children's scribbles and marks to document their emerging literacy and write down children's words as they tell stories or recall special events. Children can contribute to group experience charts written after a special walk or event, and they can help write a thank-you letter to a guest who visited the educare center. Children can illustrate both their own and group stories. These are all activities related to children's development of the sense of print and word and the sense of letter and sound.
- For children with family members who live far away (as in Meiko's situation), place a bulletin board at children's level with family photos attached. Ask parents to invite distant family members

to write notes to children, which then can be posted next to their photographs.

- Show children pictures of faces reflecting a variety of emotions. Discuss with children how they think the person in each picture might be feeling. Make sure that the photos represent a mix of racial, cultural, gender, and age groups.

- Short group-time sessions (10–15 minutes) with many action songs, fingerplays, and interactive stories can be successful with children who are almost 3.

- Garden gloves can be used for fingerplays and telling stories. Character pieces can be attached to the glove fingertips by using Velcro fasteners.

- Older toddlers respond well to poems that require action on their part. The jack-in-the-box poem is a favorite: "Jack in the box, all closed up tight (children curl in a ball on knees); Not a bit of air, not a bit of light; How tired she/he must be piled in a heap; Let's open the lid and out she/he leaps! (children leap up and wave their arms over head)."

- Expand music activities in many ways. When children march to music, they can play rhythm instruments as they move. Kazoos can be made from empty paper towel rolls cut in half and colored with markers or paint; then attach a piece of slitted waxed paper over one end, and fasten with a large rubber band. Drums from empty salt, cornmeal, or oatmeal boxes can be decorated and lids glued on. Children can hit them with short dowels or with their hands. Use rhythm sticks in a variety of ways, such as singing a song or saying a chant about hitting them up high, down low, in front, behind, or beside them. Children can also play them softly, loudly, fast, or slowly, but they will need you to scaffold this experience by modeling the conditions and commenting on the qualities of sound.

- Children of this age love songs that they can move to or use hand motions with. Examples include "Sammy," "Turn Around," "Touch" (Palmer), "Going to the Zoo," "Apples and Bananas," "The Wheels on the Bus," and "Five Little Ducks" (Raffi). (See Appendix A for details.)

Integrated Knowledge

- Foot painting has a representational component as well as a social component, and adults and children can strengthen relationships during the activity. It can be challenging for you to arrange and supervise, but children have fun and experience learning. Place a chair at each end of a long sheet of butcher paper. At one end, children take off their shoes and socks and step in a tray of fingerpaint or simply paint it on their feet with a large brush. An adult helps them walk across the floor slowly, leaving their footprints on the paper. At the other end, the children sit on the chair and are helped to wash their feet in a tub of warm, soapy water. Some children will repeat these steps several times. Talking about how the prints represent their feet, looking at the footprints of other children, and helping one another (or even walking hand-in-hand) are all elaborations that foster integrated knowledge.

- Children enjoy using various tools in food preparation. They can work an eggbeater, beat with a wire whisk, crack an egg on a bowl, use a hard-boiled-egg slicer, turn the crank on an apple peeler, and turn a food mill to make applesauce or spaghetti sauce. They can mix ingredients for favorites such as pancakes, French toast, cookies, and pretzels. Many children this age will stay with you until to the end of the activity. When you discuss it afterward, they remember many of the ingredients used and the steps in the recipe. They can discuss their likes and dislikes and compare new foods to ones they know. Cooking also offers the opportunity to discuss health and safety issues with children as they use their hands as well as tools to prepare food.

- A small parachute that four or five children can use with adults can provide physical and social knowledge. You can initially give directions to lift it up high and bring it down to make a tent, sing a song and walk around holding it, or ruffle it, pretending a strong wind is blowing it. Children can later take turns giving directions.

- You can take children for short walks to observe their environment and to combine that experience with experiences they have available in the classroom (e.g., cooking after visiting a bakery or pizza parlor).

NAEYC Accreditation Criteria 2.D.04 (Language Development) Standard 2: Curriculum: "Children have varied opportunities to develop vocabulary through conversations, experiences, field trips, and books."

Social-Emotional Relationship Building

- Although independent access to stories is important, and small-group book reading is enjoyed, children this age still thrive on one-on-one reading with you alone. In addition to emerging literacy skills fostered by this individualized reading, children's relationships with you are strengthened. You may not be able to read every day with every child, but you should plan to do it systematically over a week so that all of the children get their individualized attention and meaning-building for literacy.

- By this age, almost every activity that involves educarers and peers can strengthen relationships that children have built. Interest and involvement shown by adults, and adult interaction in hearing what children have to say about their mutual experiences, make children confident and enthusiastic learners who have good self-regulation abilities. Peer involvement in activities gives children opportunities to practice social skills and develop friendships, which are an important aspect of the early years. Young children define *friends* as "the children they play with"; thus, having many opportunities to play with peers builds friendship. For shyer children, a good way to help them gain friends as well as strengthen bonds among the parents is to suggest that the shy child invite another child from educare to his home to play. Seeing a friend outside of the educare setting is the quickest way for shyer children to gain a buddy to play with at educare.

Play Development

- Children who are almost 3 enjoy much of the same materials and dramatic play themes as 2-year-olds do. However, they return to a particular play theme several times if interesting and challenging materials are added occasionally. They are adept at taking a role in pretend play with slightly older children. You should prepare prop boxes with a collection of materials that are ready to use at any time. These can be changed to reflect children's interests and abilities. Children will wrap a baby doll in a blanket, give the doll a bottle, put it in a high chair to feed it from a spoon and bowl, and take it for a walk in a stroller. Their pretend scripts have more steps in them, and they use language to label the pretend (e.g., labeling a block "cake") and narrating their script as they play (e.g., "Now the horse is going into his barn").
- Many young 3-year-olds enjoy playing with small, sturdy dollhouses. Dolls provided should represent a mix of ages, genders, and races.
- Play with persona dolls can help children identify with people who look different from themselves. When a child indicates concern or makes an insensitive comment about another's appearance or behavior, you can use an appropriate doll (e.g., a doll in wheelchair, a Native American doll) to have a dialogue and explain the feelings of that "different" person. When the dolls become "friends," it helps the children identify with those who differ from themselves, even if they are not represented in the mix of children in educare.
- Children of this age like games that use their advancing skills. For example, they enjoy a "detective" game. You say to the detective child, "I have lost my child. Can you help me find her?" Then you describe a child who is sitting in the group so that the detective can identify that child. Others will also join in, making descriptions and being detectives.

QUESTIONS FOR DISCUSSION

1. If children such as Meiko or Rosa and Rosita had come to an educare program at age 1 or age 2, how could you have helped them make the transition to a new language and social environment?

2. What are some ways in which you can support and encourage anti-bias awareness at this age? Can the values of families from other cultures be incorporated into the educare program? How would having parents involved in the program help accomplish these goals?

3. How might you help children who are just learning how to play with peers be successful, especially if they are not fluent in the dominant language? What abilities do children this age have that help them to solve conflicts more independently?

4. What are some other ways that you can foster the emerging literacy, mathematical, and spatial concepts of children at this age, and encourage the development of their sense of humor?

5. What kinds of walks or trips into the community could you plan for children to build on their understanding of the community in which they live? How could these experiences be integrated into other curricular areas (dramatic play, science, art, and so forth).

PART III

ECOLOGICAL FACTORS INFLUENCING INFANT AND TODDLER CURRICULUM

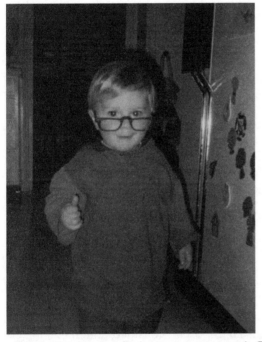

ANGUS, A SOLID, sturdy 2-year-old, is usually seen with a pacifier in his mouth. Although his mother says he was an easygoing and always hungry baby, he has become a picky eater, preferring chips and sweets to more wholesome foods. She reports that he went straight from nursing to drinking from a cup and never had a bottle.

Angus now shows strength in gross motor skills. He has climbed stairs independently since he was 14 months and he refuses to hold an adult's hand when going up or down stairs. At educare, he climbs the ladder and goes down the slide, flops on the swing seat on his stomach and swings with abandon, and pushes and pulls large toys around. Outdoors at home, he plays independently on his swing set and in his sandbox for long periods.

Indoors, he doesn't play on his own, preferring to be entertained by his mother or his 4-year-old brother. Angus has a long attention span. He enjoys listening to book reading, with animal themes being among his favorites. He watches wildlife videos at least once every day. At educare, he often observes others' play, but rarely joins in. He can be heard talking to himself as he wanders around the room.

Angus's fine motor coordination is very good. A favorite toy at home is a small set of doors with keyholes that cannot be opened except with the correctly shaped key. At educare, he will spend 8 to 10 minutes putting balls into a maze toy and watching the balls' progression until they roll out.

His vocabulary is increasing, and he has picked up slang phrases like "Oh, man" and "O-tay" (for "okay"), much to the amusement of his family. He says "please," "thank you," and "good-bye" without prompting; learns people's names quickly and uses them in context; and even remembers the names of educarers in the room he was in months ago. Angus can be helpful to other children. For example, he returned a spoon to an infant when it fell from her food tray. His social skills are amazing to his parents, but he shows no signs of interest in toilet training yet.

He has a sense of humor and tries to make others laugh, using a variety of facial expressions and responses. Although Angus is a happy, sociable child, he has quite a temper. He is persistent and demands things immediately. When he screams, his parents tell him to sit on the stairs until he is calm. If he is told to do something, he often runs away or "tunes out" and cannot be reasoned with. His mother says that redirection doesn't work well with him, and that this sometimes results in her giving him a "pop on the butt."

At educare his mother prefers a calm environment that is not over-stimulating, with caring, patient educarers. She believes consistency is essential. She doesn't want Angus getting away with socially unacceptable behavior, but she also wants his educarers to enjoy his adventurous spirit and ensure that he finds acceptable outlets.

What would you do to facilitate Angus's development in the ways his family desires (e.g., showing politeness, enjoying humor, being compliant to requests)? How would you convey to his parents your concerns about some family practices (e.g., unhealthy eating patterns, spanking, long periods of video watching) that are different from what you would recommend?

Although educarers' curriculum practices are primarily based on their knowledge of young children's development and learning, they are also influenced by the values, cultural practices, and caregiving contexts of the children's families (what Bronfenbrenner, 1993, calls the *microsystem*). The interface of family values and practices with those of educarers (part of what Bronfenbrenner calls the *mesosystem*) is an important consideration in making curriculum decisions. Family and educarer perspectives may be congruent or incongruent, especially if there are differences in cultural, racial, religious, or socioeconomic backgrounds.

Factors in the larger society also affect curriculum and how effectively educarers and families carry out their roles and responsibilities. Some of these factors are in what Bronfenbrenner (1993) calls the *exosystem*. They include values and practices promoted by schools, religious organizations, community agencies, social groups, city and county governments, and other units whose policies may have an impact on families and educarers, and thus, on young children. Other factors, which are even further removed from the day-to-day interactions of educarers and families, are related to the broader society (which Bronfenbrenner calls the *macrosystem*). Examples of these factors are economic and legal positions taken by states and nations, such as decisions about resource allocations, health and education priorities, business practices affecting employment, salary levels, family leave policies, and retirements, as well as strategic plans that governments propose. Finally, hisotorical influences (the *chronosytem,* Bronfenbrenner & Morris, 1998) may also be influential. For example, growing up in wartime, boom times, recessions, or other historical periods can affect how developmental change is perceived or valued. Part III discusses the aspects of curriculum that relate to families and the broader societal contexts in which infant and toddler curriculum is embedded. Ecological factors that are affecting and may further influence educare in the 21st century are also identified.

Chapter 12

Families and the Infant and Toddler Curriculum

Microsystem and Mesosystem Factors

As the cases in this book make explicit, families have some common concerns, but they also differ in their goals for the educare of their children. Although such differences may appear more salient when families represent nondominant cultural, racial, or religious groups, there are also differences among families who appear, on the surface, to be very similar. This is because individual children in each family differ in age, personality, and developmental status, and because families have different employment and social issues that influence what they look for in educare. For example, which family members are most involved in the child's education and care varies among families. Although children's mothers typically act as liaisons with educarers, sometimes the liaison role may be filled by a grandmother, the father, another relative, or a nonrelative (e.g., a foster parent). It is important for you to gain relevant information about every child's needs, the families' goals for their children, the concerns families may have about their children's development, and family preferences that relate to care and education. You should obtain this information as part of the intake process, and continue to update it periodically through ongoing communication with families (see Appendix D).

Families often express three major concerns when they look for nonfamily care options for infants and toddlers. Their first concern is that their child's basic needs (feeding, sleeping, safety) be well met by educarers. Their second concern is that the experiences provided in the program support the values held by the family. Their third concern is that the curriculum meets the developmental and educational goals they have for their child. Often, the second and third goals are intertwined. That is, families usually have educational goals that are congruent with their values. As society has put more emphasis on preparing for later school success, some families are asking for a more academic focus even at toddler age, and this may result in new pressures on educare programs that may or may not be developmentally appropriate.

When seeking care, families may have difficulty meeting even their first concern—good basic care—if program options in their community are lacking or too expensive. Meeting the second and third concerns may be even more difficult, especially if educarers come from different cultural or educational backgrounds from those of families. Differences may cause communication problems if families and educarers have conflicting expectations about appropriate communication or social practices, or if they use different communication styles. To complicate matters further, within a family, members may differ as to what they think constitutes good educare. For one parent, having educarers play social games might be a basic requirement, while another might see this as an optional activity. Some family members may be concerned about emerging literacy or mathematical skills, while others are more interested in having educarers follow their children's feeding and sleeping schedules carefully.

One of the first places that variation in families is evident is in how they choose the best option among the variety of options for educare. Single parents, two-parent working families, parents who have children with special needs, and parents in extended family situations may not have the same number or quality of educare options. Some families may spend much time investigating program quality before placing their children in educare, and some may ask few questions about program quality because they are desperate to find a place to send their child. The "welfare-to-work" impetus now required has made desperation likely because parents may have to start a job in only a few days, and may not have time to find a good educare setting. They may prefer care by relatives or neighbors, but this may or may not be good care. Often, "kith and kin" provide care only to help the mother, not because they want to care for the child (Porter, 1999). Families' ideas about what is good educare may vary greatly based on their cultural, socio-economic, religious, family structure, or idiosyncratic values and practices.

RECOGNIZING VARIATIONS IN FAMILY VALUES

Cultural/Ethnic/Racial Considerations

As a result of immigration and birth patterns, population predictions suggest that by 2020, the percentage of European-origin children under 18 years of age will represent only 53% of the U.S. child population. The fastest-growing population is Hispanic-origin children, who will represent 24% of the child population, followed by an increase of about 5% of children in the Asian-origin population (childstats.gov, 2004). In special education, there is a growing concern regarding the issue of ethnic and racial disproportionality among the children being served. According to one study (Hebbeler, Wagner, Spiker, Scarborough, Simeonsson, & Collier, 2001), over 44% of 5,668 families receiving services in 20 U.S. states were of non-European origin.

Traditionally, cultural differences have been viewed through the lens of a deficit model, using the mainstream, European-American culture as the norm. For children from nonmainstream groups to flourish, educarers must be sensitive not only to their individual differences but also to the cultural differences in values that these families hold, as they may differ from the educarer's own cultural background and values. Mexican American families' valuing of cooperation, politeness, respect for authority, and obedience may affect their expectations for the goals of educare (Bergen, Smith, & O'Neil, 1988). Children from Appalachian backgrounds may appear less emotionally expressive and more independent because their families value such behaviors, and African American children may respond with high emotional expressiveness and active movement because their families value those behaviors (Bergen & Mosley-Howard, 1994).

Basic child-rearing practices also differ among cultural groups. For example, co-sleeping is more commonly practiced among African-origin families than it is among European-origin families (Minde, 1998). Minde suggests obtaining a "culturally sensitive history" from families that focuses on sleep and waking patterns. Care, teaching, and play interactions between mothers and infants may differ among cultural groups, as illustrated in a study comparing Puerto Rican and European-origin mothers (Harwood, Schoelmerich, Schulze, & Gonzalez, 1999). Some of the differences noted were that European-origin mothers used more modeling strategies, encouraged autonomy in feeding, and spent more time watching their children play alone, while Puerto Rican mothers used more direct instructional strategies, directly fed their infants, and directed their children's attention more often during play. Such differences could result in Puerto Rican parents questioning some of the practices in a "responsive, child directed" educare program.

Among these varied backgrounds, there is also a wide range in "level of acculturation," which is the extent to which families are familiar with and accepting of the values and practices of the dominant culture (in the United States, this is the Eurocentric culture). Two families with the same cultural "label" may differ greatly in how their values and practices are influenced by their culture of origin and the dominant culture, and this will, in turn, have an impact on how much they differ in child-rearing practices and educational goals (Bergen & Mosley-Howard, 1994). You cannot assume that the values, goals, and communication patterns of one family from a particular culture will be the same as those of another family with that background.

Taking the time to get "culturally sensitive histories" is a useful strategy when working with families from diverse cultural backgrounds. Questions might focus on finding out which family member(s) will be the primary source of information and with whom educarers and service providers will communicate. You need to ask about the primary language spoken in the home, words the child uses to describe eating and toileting, how the family describes the child's ethnicity and whether or not the family is comfortable with visitors coming to their home. Often, families are not able to explain their cultural beliefs and values because those beliefs are so embedded in their daily lives (Phillips, 1995). By asking specific questions, educarers may be able to gain useful information to become more sensitive to families' needs and concerns.

Another practice useful for educarers is to self-reflect on their own cultural biases. You and an educarer colleague could discuss your experiences growing up in both of your cultures. When you realize how strongly your own cultural experiences have affected your attitudes, you will be more open to understanding how families from other cultures feel about their beliefs (Im, Pariakian, & Sanchez, 2007). Figure 12.1 suggests some ways educarers can work well with culturally diverse families (Phillips, 1995).

Even families immersed in the dominant American culture have value issues with implications for their satisfaction with educare. Higher valuing of "stay-at-home" mothers, which still remains a theme in certain levels of contemporary American culture, may make out-of-home working mothers feel guilty even when their children are in high-quality educare. If a child cries when left at the program or becomes ill after attending educare, those mothers may have concerns. These concerns will be even stronger if they believe educare programs are not of high quality. Also, parents who are especially concerned about their children's academic preparation need to have explicit information about how the play curriculum meets their child's educational needs and early learning standards.

Socioeconomic Considerations

Variations in families' child-rearing practices and educational goals may occur because of socioeconomic level differences, both among and within cultural groups. African Americans with high levels of education and income are more likely to be acculturated to dominant cultural values and practices than are those of lower educational and socioeconomic status (Ogbu, 1988). For example, infant-parent co-sleeping occurs more often in both low-income African American and low-income European-origin families than it does in high-income families of either group (Minde, 1998). In a study of neighborhood and family income effects on development, Klebanov, Brooks-Gunn, McCarton, and McCormick (1998) found that by age 1, the development of children from poor families is more likely to be affected by family risk factors than is that of children from nonpoor families, although the quality of the home environment mediates this finding for children from both low- and high-income families. By age 2, there is a negative associa-

FIGURE 12.1 Suggestions for Serving Culturally Diverse Families

- Learn about the cultures of children in your care and work to understand and eliminate your own biases and stereotypes regarding people whose cultures differ from your own.

- Determine how you can effectively use this knowledge in your own educare setting.

- Help families learn how to handle cultural conflict as you support the maintenance of their cultural integrity while learning to function in mainstream society.

- With the families' help, find ways to assist children you care for to function in their own culture while building competencies in the larger society.

tion of developmental level with family poverty, which is also mediated by home conditions. Neighborhood poverty level becomes a negative factor at age 3, along with family poverty and family risk factors. The researchers conclude that over the first 3 years of a child's life, family poverty, especially within a neighborhood of poverty, becomes a stronger negative influence on development, but that the quality of the home environment still makes a difference. This is important for you to remember when planning ways to engage families from low-income neighborhoods in helping their children's development.

Although in the ideal American society there is no "caste" system, in actual practice, children from families with low socioeconomic status are often out of the mainstream, especially in regard to child enrichment experiences. For example, a study by Neuman and Celano (2001) on "access to print" in different communities showed that there were great differences in literacy access (i.e., to libraries, bookstores, signs) between lower-income and higher-income neighborhoods. They suggest that this literacy deficit in the environment affects the literacy skill development of children from those neighborhoods. Low income families may also support behavioral values and practices that educarers consider socially inappropriate (e.g., encouraging physical fighting to solve problems). Poor families may also lack transportation, attending meetings with the educarer, or caring for their children's health needs problematic.

The welfare-to-work emphasis in Temporary Assistance for Needy Families (TANF) has required more low-income families to enroll their very young children into educare (Kelly & Booth, 1999). The work hours of these families may not be the typical 9 to 5 type. Thus, educarers may need to be even more sensitive to socioeconomic differences in values and practices than they have been in the past, and they need to be open to developing programs that meet the timing needs of such families.

Religious Considerations

Families often derive their child-rearing and education values from their religious views. Some of these values are obvious (e.g., neonatal circumcision; which holidays to observe), while others are more subtle (e.g., the idea that "sparing the rod spoils the child" or that a program is bad if children "just play"). Educarers do not routinely inquire about such concerns, but family members often state them strongly. As part of your intake discussion with families, you should ask whether the family has specific religious practices or concerns that could affect their child's involvement in educare. When families from different cultural groups hold strong religious beliefs about appropriate child-rearing practices, the possibility for conflict within the educare program can occur because the needs of one group may interfere with the needs of another. For example, celebrating or not celebrating various holidays can be offensive to some families. Educarers must be articulate in explaining to families why and how they can meet—or, in some cases, cannot meet—their religiously based concerns.

Family Composition Considerations

As the families in the cases throughout this book illustrate, young children live in diverse family structures (two-parent families; never married, divorced, or widowed mothers; fathers who provide primary care; teen mothers living with their parents; two-parent, same-sex families; foster parents; and families with extended family networks). Family members also may have idiosyncratic concerns, derived from their own experiences as children (e.g., "I was toilet trained by age 1"), their age (e.g., "I can't come to the conference because I'm going out with friends"), or their child's needs (e.g., "My child's disability requires a particular program"). Parents of children with disabilities want coordinated systems of care that interface educare with the other services needed by children (Kelly & Booth, 1999). Educarers also bring their own values to their role. For example, female educarers may make males (e.g., caregiving fathers, grandfathers, or male partners) feel uncomfortable in the educare setting if they act surprised to see them or make them feel unusual or out of place. Fathers often have different concerns or priorities that they want you to address, and if you ignore these, they may assume that although "participation is nice," their ideas are not needed (Flynn & Wilson, 1998). Given all of the factors that you must consider as an educarer, your ability to identify, understand, and mediate among differing values about educare is of great importance.

WORKING WITH FAMILIES WITH DIFFERING VALUES

In urban, rural, and suburban locations, the makeup of both educarer staff and families reflects the myriad of cultures and viewpoints that are present in contemporary society. As noted earlier, the one diversity exception is still the relative absence of male educarers. As this century proceeds, it is likely that educare settings will come to reflect even more cultural and gender diversity. You will need to become especially sensitive to your own attitudes, biases, and prejudices regarding families, children, and other educarers with whom you interact, all of whom may have characteristics or lifestyles that differ from yours. You must educate yourself about the values and practices that specific families bring to educare when they bring in their child. As Gonzalez-Mena (1997) points out, educarers may unknowingly treat children (and families) in a "culturally assaultive" manner when their methods of care and education conflict with those that the family prefers. You must be willing to meet these challenges with the attitude that each encounter can become a win-win experience. To do this, you must move from a place of understanding diversity differences to respecting and appreciating the diversity of cultural, socioeconomic, religious, gender, and other perspectives. If you keep an open mind and develop skills in negotiation and problem solving, you can expect that these inevitable encounters will be positive learning experiences for everyone (Gonzalez-Mena, 1997). Because diversity has implications for the infant and toddler curriculum, information about enhancing children's cultural identity development has been included in the age-level curriculum chapters of the book. There are also a number of basic strategies that educarers can use to assist in the process of relationship building with families.

Communicating About Developmentally and Educationally Appropriate Practice

Just because educarers have studied the development of young children and learned educational strategies for assisting young children's knowledge construction, social-emotional relationship building, and play development, they cannot assume that family members have the same understanding. In fact, you can probably assume that families don't understand developmentally based practices of educare. If you do not have ongoing ways to communicate with families about the reasons for particular curriculum elements in the environment, you should not be surprised when family members question why certain things occur, discount their importance, or insist on other practices. Ongoing communication about your curriculum practice should be built into the goals of the program. You should be able to show how learning standards that are now suggested for young children are being met appropriately within your play-based curriculum approach.

When their children are young, most family members are receptive to learning more about best practices, and if you have also informed yourself about cultural, religious, or other practices that the families of children in the program espouse, you should be able to explain your practices in a manner that families can understand and, hopefully, integrate with their own viewpoints. Another advantage of giving the liaison family member (probably the mother, but not always) simple but accurate words for why certain things happen in the program is that this family member can then communicate well with other family members (such as the father and grandparents). Direct communication with fathers (even noncustodial fathers) is also important, because their views may differ from those of mothers and may affect how the family seeks and accepts your suggestions. Professional practice should always be well reasoned; thus, you should know why you are doing what you are doing, and you should be able to communicate with families about those reasons. Many conflicts can be avoided if this open channel of communication about practice is maintained.

Negotiating Differences Among Conflicting Perspectives

Because there may still be conflicts between families and educarers, another skill you must practice is negotiation of differences among conflicting perspectives. Conflict-management techniques have been identified that work well with the families of young children. Most have similar recommendations. One set of techniques comes from the Ohio Commission on Dispute Resolution and Conflict Management (1999):

1. You should understand that conflict is to be expected and that conflict management does not mean trying to eliminate conflict but, rather, to learn responses that can resolve disputes without attack or avoidance of the problem.
2. You need to know that both facts and feelings are involved in conflicts and that emotions need to be acknowledged, reframed, and tamed sufficiently to see past them.
3. Communicating in conflict situations, especially when strong emotions are involved, needs to be done by

   • Using "I" statements (i.e., telling how you are affected, not blaming others)
   • Using active listening (i.e., attending to the meaning of other persons' comments)
   • Acknowledging different perceptions (i.e., letting other persons know you understand their point of view), and
   • Having a win-win goal (i.e., wishing to resolve the conflict in a way in which both parties are at least partly satisfied)

It is also important to signal through your body language that you are receptive not defensive. Miscommunication is more likely when people from different cultures are involved. The advice given to children about resolving conflict also works with educarer-family conflict:

   • Cool off
   • Take turns speaking and listening
   • Express both facts and feelings
   • Try to think of alternative solutions together
   • Agree on a solution that both can accept

Of course, already having good communication with families concerning noncontroversial issues provides the best platform for resolving controversy and conflict.

Addressing Family Values and Practices
That May Cause Harm to Young Children

Even with your use of good communication and negotiating skills, there may be some family values or practices that you must address firmly because they may cause harm to young children. For example, because of the importance of social interaction between caregiver and infant, if family members ignore the infant's needs for social interaction by rarely talking to or playing with the child while they perform routine care activities, you can express your concern that this behavior will lessen the child's ability to develop a secure attachment to the caregivers. One strategy that is sometimes helpful is to involve other family members (e.g., a grandmother) who can model social interactions with the infant so that the primary caregiver (e.g., the mother) gains an understanding of how to interact in such ways. This presupposes that you can learn who in the family can serve as a good model.

You must always make a judgment call about when you should should address concerns directly with the family. If there is evidence of extreme neglect (e.g., no diaper change from the time the child leaves the educare program until she returns the next morning), you will need to discuss this with some family member and monitor whether the situation improves. It is your legal responsibility to report evidence of physical or sexual abuse or obvious neglect for further investigation, because such behaviors are dangerous for children's physical and mental health and overall development. However, most value or practice differences can be addressed through the communication network that you have established with all the families in the educare program. Earlier efforts to get such an interactive network working well pay off when value or practice differences that might be harmful to a child need to be addressed. The intake information you collect can sometimes stave off the necessity for a confrontation about a concern you might have at a later point.

Supporting Families in High-Stress Situations

Recently, infant mental health has become a great concern, especially in stressful or traumatic situations. One issue that families have been facing over the past few years is how to deal with the effects of separation and loss caused by military deployment, injury, or death (Fraga, 2007). There are many young children in military families facing these types of stress. Fraga comments, "Even the healthiest families can become stressed. For those families who are already vulnerable and at risk, the stressor may further compromise coping mechanisms and exacerbate challenging family dynamics" (p. 5). Traumatic stressors involving relational trauma can foster depression, disconnection, attachment disorders, anxiety, and other problematic behaviors in young children. Other stressors related to separation, such as divorce, can even result in physiological "growth faltering" (Solchany, 2007). That is, they can affect the child's social-emotional and cognitive development. There are some programs to help families foster their children's mental health in traumatic situations. For military families, supportive programs have been developed to promote child and family resiliency (Yeary, 2007). However, many children are in family situations for which there is no resiliency program available.

If you notice an infant or toddler exhibiting any symptoms of mental health distress, or if you know that a family is facing very stressful situations, you should suggest community mental health resources to help them cope. Just knowing that you are aware and responsive to their situation may be helpful to them, but it is important to be knowledgeable about the services that are available in your community. If you are cognizant of severe stress factors that may be affecting a child, you will be better able to handle his mental health–related behaviors in educare. Lieberman (2006) suggests a number of strategies for dealing with situations that affect young children's mental health. They are listed in Figure 12.2.

INVOLVING FAMILIES IN THE EDUCARE PROGRAM

Among families with similar values or voiced concerns, there are still differences in their levels of involvement in educare. Because close educare-family relationships enhance infant/toddler development, most educarers have family involvement as a goal. This is a natural way to expose children meaningfully to the diversity represented in the educare group. There are different levels of meaningful involvement that families can have, based on the time they have available and their own motivation to be involved.

Some families would like to be involved in the day-to-day activities of the program, giving many suggestions, providing special materials, offering to participate as observers or facilitators of learning, and desiring detailed reports on their children's abilities, progress, and well-being. Others, who may have extensive work schedules or may be burdened with family or economic problems that distract them from care and education concerns, may wish to be only minimally involved. They may even be nonresponsive when you try to encourage their involvement in their children's experiences. With the busy schedules of most families, there are likely to be more families who want minimal involvement than families who would like high levels of involvement.

If you understand the variations in values and practices of the families and know how to communicate and negotiate within their value structures, you will be able to respect the level of involvement that they can handle at particular times. Give them opportunities that range from occasional contact to active engagement. However, because the mental health problems of young children are highly related to negative family practices, if you are concerned about a particular child's mental health, you should invite a family member to visit the program to observe. Then you can help the family member learn more about how the child's mental health issues can be seen in her behavior at educare and how more developmentally appropriate practices at home might ameliorate the child's stress.

Providing a Welcoming Environment

The message conveyed by the environment is vitally important in making family members of both genders feel that their involvement is welcome. A com-

FIGURE 12.2 Strategies for Helping Traumatized Young Children (adapted from Lieberman, 2006)

Provide a safe environment with predictable routines.

Ensure stable relationships with educarers.

Understand that difficult behaviors are triggered by similar situations of chronic stress or maltreatment.

Provide consistent reassurance about child fears and separation anxieties.

Avoid disciplinary measures that may trigger trauma.

Work with families to develop plans of action that will reassure and support children.

Use play, music, physical activity, and other means to help children express negative feelings.

Try to gain from families information about traumatic events to understand how children have been affected.

Consult with infant mental health professionals (with family) to learn helpful behavior strategies.

---

fortable, warm, and semiprivate place from which to observe the children's program and, if needed, to feed their infant is especially important for new parents. Families of toddlers also need to feel welcome, and the inviting nature of the setting can be emotionally reassuring to both children and family members. When family members feel that they can drop in when their schedule permits, that they are welcome to observe in the children's rooms or in observation spaces, and that there are special places for them to talk and interact, they will be more likely to respond favorably to suggestions for family involvement. (See Daniel, 1998, and Whitehead & Ginsberg, 1999, for additional suggestions.)

Promoting Educarer-Family Communication

A minimal level of involvement requires good communication between educarers and families. You can help families feel connected by making sure they are informed about what is happening each day, how their children have adjusted to the program, and what developmental and educational progress their children are making. If you have a consistent plan for ongoing communication, you can actively encourage a mutually supportive relationship with families. At minimum, you should keep daily charts of children's activities, record observation notes, make phone contacts, and plan regular meetings with families.

Educarer-family communication about the daily activities of children, reasons for environmental arrangements and equipment, views about important care practices, and relationships of play to early learning are all topics that interest families. By having a good communication base established, you will have more successful discussions when problems need to be addressed. Families also need to know that you will be a good listener when they explain their directions and concerns about their children's care and development. They need to feel that you really try to hear their message even when they may have some difficulty expressing it. In the busy life of educarers, taking the time to listen well may be a major challenge. Families, especially those from diverse cultures or lower socioeconomic situations, will be more likely to express their viewpoints, satisfactions, and concerns when you have established a strong, ongoing communication channel.

Individualizing Curriculum to Address Family Concerns

Because many families are pleased just to have found a quality educare program, they may not express any desires or suggestions for specific practices for individualizing the curriculum. Other families will express specific views about what they want for their children. In particular, families with children who have developmental delays may express a need for additional individualization. Some individualization may be needed just to reflect a child's personality or physical differences, however. For example, although most older toddlers nap in the afternoon, one toddler might not nap at all and another might need two naps. Often, family requests require educarers to rethink practices or to vary their practices flexibly for these children.

If your program is already responsive to individual children, you should have little problem in individualizing the curriculum to address family concerns, unless the family suggests practices with which you disagree. Such disagreements need to be negotiated and resolved, as discussed earlier. Although it is often the case that the "squeaky wheel gets the grease," you should not ignore families who do not express their concerns spontaneously. Those families are more likely to be the ones from nondominant cultures. If you value family involvement, you should be able to provide enough individualization to make families feel that your "responsive curriculum" is really responsive to the special needs of every child.

Encouraging Family Participation in the Program

Families may contribute to a program in many enriching ways. Educarers should take an "invitational," rather than a "demanding," approach, because many families already have a full load of responsibilities to meet. Invitations may encourage families with diverse cultural backgrounds to share a favorite food, their music or dances, or a simple game from their culture with older toddlers. If you make families feel welcome, they may want to observe when they have a day off from work. One of the best ways for family members to learn more about child development in general and their own child's development in particular is to observe their child in the company of other children. As they observe, you can suggest that they also watch the behaviors of another child (possibly one with skills that their child needs to learn), so that they don't focus entirely on their own child's activities. They could also be asked to take photographs of the children as they are engaged in play.

When families feel welcome, it is surprising what they will spontaneously suggest to enrich the program. They may share hobbies (helping with woodworking), educational expertise (a biologist leading a nature walk), or home practices (making bread). They may just participate in the everyday routine of the program (looking at books with children, helping with a sensory activity). When they can't actually come to the program, they might make small quilts for the doll bed, wooden cars, or a "picture book" from photos taken of the children. Even when fathers and mothers are not able to participate, grandparents, older siblings, or other relatives may enjoy an invitation to participate in some way. Another advantage of family participation is that family members gain a feeling of "ownership" toward the program, and this creates a more positive climate for children. Because young children are quick to pick up the emotional tone of their families, if family members have warm and committed attitudes toward the educare program, the children may be more comfortable and satisfied during the program day.

Involving Families in Assessment and Planning Processes

For children for whom there are concerns about possible developmental delays or who have risk factors that might result in such delays, a comprehensive assessment implemented by a transdisciplinary team of early intervention personnel (e.g., special educator, speech pathologist, occupational and physical therapists, social worker), together with family members, is required (Bergen, 1994). An Individual Family Services Plan (IFSP), which outlines the strengths and needs of the family and the developmental and educational goals for the child, is then composed by the team. Because families are regarded as experts on the needs of their own children, their involvement in identifying goals that should be the focus of intervention is an important part of the IFSP process. Many teams have parents identify their concerns through interviews or self-report surveys. Research on one of these, the Parents' Evaluation of Developmental Status (PEDS), found that parents could identify developmental problems with about the same level of accuracy (80%) as child screening instruments do (Glascoe, 1999).

Although some infants and toddlers with IFSPs may be placed in home-based early intervention programs, many will be included in educare programs with children who are developing typically. As part of the coordinated systems approach, they may be placed in both an early intervention and an educare program (Kelly & Booth, 1999). If they are in such programs, educarers from these programs are also considered members of the assessment and planning team. You will need to have good observational skills in order to observe these children within your program setting, to contribute information in the assessment and planning meetings, and to implement curriculum strategies that meet IFSP goals for each child.

While team assessment and curriculum planning is essential for children with IFSPs, all children in an educare program can benefit from this type of systematic assessment and curricular planning. You can use a modified version of the team assessment model, in which the basic team is composed of educarers and family members, with other relevant personnel added only if needed (for example, a so-cial worker or nurse who visits the family). You can involve family members (e.g., mother, father, grandparents) in observing and reporting about their children's developmental status and behaviors at home, and together with the family, you can decide on goals that will be the focus of your work with their child.

Involving families in assessment and planning can be especially helpful when they are from diverse cultural backgrounds, because you can find out what they think are important goals their children should achieve. Also, children may differ in their behavior at home and at educare. For example, a child from a bilingual family make speak extensively at home in the native language but may not speak at school in either language. The language goals for this child will be different from those for a child who does not speak at all in either setting. Involving fami-lies in assessment is an excellent way to further the educare-family partnering relationship.

If your program requires assessment of outcomes and processes related to learning standards, you can involve family members as observers of children's skill at particular tasks. You could set up a place in your room with child activi-ties for them to observe and record how the children perform. With their help, you will gain information you need while also educating them about typical child development. If family members are not available, another option is to initiate a cooperative program with high school or university students who could do such observations. This would benefit your program by giving assistance in outcome and process assessment, and also help students in education or psychology classes to gain direct experience in conducting appropriate infant and toddler assessment techniques.

Making the Most of the Home Curriculum

It is not usually the case that educarers have the time or opportunity to visit infants and toddlers in their home regularly, unless these visits are built into the program schedule, as in Early Head Start. If you are committed to building good relationships with families and providing a responsive and individualized cur-riculum for children, however, there are a number of ways that you can have an impact on the home curriculum. You can plan to make at least one visit a year to every family's home, perhaps in the evening or on the weekend, whenever the family is most likely to be there and receptive to a visit. You can learn a great deal about children's needs by having a casual home visit with their families. You can compare the children's behaviors there with their actions in the educare setting, observe family dynamics that might influence any suggestions you may make related to children's needs, and model child-adult interaction in brief play with the children at home. If home visits can be made early on by the child's primary educarer as an orientation to the educare program, the educarer can help establish immediate relationships and provide information to individualize the program for each child.

If you cannot visit the home, you can have regular telephone, newsletter, or e-mail contact to provide suggestions for enjoyable home activities that engage both family members and children in learning. This type of "homework," if included as part of the ongoing educarer-family communication system, often results in gaining family support for your curriculum goals. Families often do not think about the fact that they are providing a "home curriculum" when they select activities to engage in with their children and when they buy play materials for children to use. You can convey to families how important the choices they make for their children's home activities are in furthering development and learning, and you can give suggestions for child gifts (e.g., a toy that will help a child develop a particular skill) and activities (e.g., book reading and game playing).

SMOOTHING TRANSITIONS FROM HOME-BASED TO GROUP-BASED EDUCARE SETTINGS

For both value reasons (families may prefer home-based programs) and practical reasons (not enough available infant group-based programs), infants are more likely to be in home-based educare settings than in group-based programs, while toddlers are more often in the latter. Some families choose home-based educare for infants and select group-based educare when their children turn 3. Other families use home-based and group-based educare at the same time, depending on their work hours and family needs. Rarely are the transitions between home-based and group-based programs addressed by educarers, although these transitions are sometimes of concern to families. Although it is logical that there should be good communication between educarers in home-based and group-based settings, in actual practice there is often no communication, which makes transitions less smooth for young children. In-service training and other professional meetings for the two groups of educarers are usually separate, and their opportunities for discussing common problems and curriculum ideas are sparse. Families would benefit if educarers paid attention to facilitating child transitions between home-based and group-based educare. Educarers would benefit by broadening their knowledge of common goals, as well as differences that children encounter in the two types of educare. Families often have to manipulate such mesosystemic factors (i.e., between systems) by themselves. If they can do that with the assistance of educarers, children will benefit.

SUMMARY

Families are integral parts of the curriculum for infants and toddlers, and their values influence the types of educare they choose and their support for the curriculum of the educare programs. By understanding cultural, socioeconomic, religious, and other values that families possess, you can be more effective in working with them to provide the best curriculum for their children. There are many ways to successfully invite family involvement and to help families feel that their values and concerns are respected within the educare program.

QUESTIONS FOR DISCUSSION

1. What are some ways in which you could make families from nondominant cultures and nontraditional homes or lifestyles feel comfortable and respected in the educare program? How would you help families from more dominant/traditional backgrounds accept these differences?
2. How would you address family practices that do not fit your view of best practice (e.g., video viewing time, discipline methods) using conflict-management techniques?
3. How can you encourage families to help you provide a culturally consistent educare environment for their children?
4. How would you explain to families who want academic learning (e.g., alphabet, numbers) to be taught to their very young children what you think are appropriate methods of fostering such learning skills?

Chapter 13

Infant and Toddler Curriculum in the 21st Century

Exosystem, Macrosystem, and Chronosystem Factors

Issues related to family-educarer relationships often are discussed without consideration of exosystem, macrosystem, and chronosystem factors (Bronfenbrenner & Morris, 1998) that affect family involvement and family-educarer collaboration. However, family views regarding appropriate child care and education are often derived from the standards of cultural, racial, or religious organizations (exosystem). Their socioeconomic well-being and educare needs are affected by government health and education policies (macrosystem), and their stress levels and healthy functioning are affected by war, recession, and other historical events (chronosystem). Often, these three levels interact. For example, religious organizations may promote legislative changes and support or oppose war. Some broad systemic factors with high potential for influencing the infant and toddler curriculum, your work as an educarer, and the educare environment are:

1. Changing demographics of U. S. society
2. Technological changes affecting education
3. Advances in brain research
4. Government policies
5. Major world events

Therefore, educarers need to be knowledgeable not only about their own practice, but also about external system factors that may affect their ability to provide good educare.

DEMOGRAPHIC CHANGES

In 1999, Washington and Andrews predicted that by 2010, there would be a 2% population increase in the number of children under 18 in the United States, but a 3% decrease in the number of children under age 5. They said the greatest gains in population would come in populations over age 40, with the number of people age 45 to 64 increasing by 29%, and the number of those over 65 by 14%. Because of differential birth rates and immigration rates of cultural groups, the European origin population will be older, and the Hispanic population will be younger. Washington and Andrews predicted that by 2010, one-fifth of the school population would be children of immigrants.

Recent census data indicate that European origin children under age 15 represent 65%, Hispanic children 16%, and African American children 13%, with Asian Americans at 3% of the population (U.S. Census Bureau, 2006). Immigration and birth patterns suggest that by 2020, European-origin children under age 18 will account for 53% of the U.S. child population, with Hispanic children representing 24%. There will also be an increase in Asian children to about 5%, while the African American child population will remain relatively stable (childstats.gov, 2004). The world population—now approximately 6 billion—will increase exponentially, due both to high birth rates and lower death rates. The U.S. and world trends in population may affect the future treatment of children and families.

In this country today, over 20% of children under age 6 are part of families that live below the poverty level (the highest percentage in any NATO nation), and most live in families with at least one working parent. Income provider(s) for the family often lack health insurance themselves (although their young children may qualify for federally funded insurance, SCHIP). Many families need food supplies and this need has risen in the past few years. The need for assistance in paying the costs of educare also remains high.

The family structure in the United States has also changed, with one in eight families being made up of single mothers with children, one in four being people who live alone, one in four marriages being between people of different cultural/racial groups, and more households consisting of unrelated individuals, including some gay/lesbian families (Washington & Andrews, 1999). Older adults and single people without children may have little or no contact with children in their daily lives. These groups may be less likely to support taxes to provide services for children (a macrosystem issue).

There is growing diversity among those served by educare and among those who provide educare. In one city, 70% of home educarers were recent immigrants. There are more young children with special needs (such as health problems, disabilities, or delays), and these children come from a wider range of cultures and races. Educare directors report that parents are increasingly seeking guidance for child-rearing and management, and that more families have their children stay in educare for a greater number of hours than in the past (Cornerstones Project, 1999).

Implications of these demographic changes are presently unclear, and many policy questions remain. There may be less concern for young children's care because of increases in aging and nonparent populations, or perhaps the lower proportion of young children may make their welfare of more concern to all adults because they are a precious resource. Because more of these children will be from low-income, diverse racial/cultural, and immigrant populations, the general population may be less or more supportive of efforts to ensure high-quality educare. The fact that there is an increasing number of multicultural and nontraditional families may result in a more tolerant and caring attitude toward all families by the public, or these families may face more prejudices that negatively influence public policy efforts to improve the quality of educare programs. These are only a few of the questions resulting from changing demographics that educarers and other members of society will need to face in this century.

TECHNOLOGICAL CHANGES

Because of numerous rapid changes in technology, the concepts of "school" and "education" are undergoing major transformations. Society is already reconceptualizing where and how education occurs. For example, for older children and adults, home schooling and private schooling has increased; learning curriculum content through television, videos, CDs, and DVDs is common, and online learning sources (blogs, wikis, electronic "books," and other media) are becoming pervasive. Some technologies may create more autonomy in learners (e.g., one can quickly, directly, and independently access information), and some may involve playful, interactions (i.e., "Edutainment"). There are now videos, CDs, DVDs, and television programs for infants and toddlers. Toddlers also have computer games, often promoted to parents by marketers as early learning enhancers. Concerns have also been expressed that young children's exposure to violent media content has affected their play (Levin, 2006). Because young children learn in every setting, their education is affected by technological changes occurring in their homes (microsystem), in educare programs (mesosystem), in the larger community (exosystem), through their families' contact with the world at large (macrosystem), and through exposure to ongoing world events presented through these media (chronosystem).

Reconceptualizations of what a relevant curriculum is for postmodern society affect the curriculum of educare, because the goals that families and educarers have for young children reflect their expectations of what children will need for later success as members of their particular society (Ogbu, 1981). For example, the No Child Left Behind Act has affected learning standards for infants, not just school-age children. Adult expectations about what technological knowledge will be needed by older children and young adults may influence their views of appropriate curriculum for infants and toddlers. Technology will have an increasing influence as the century progresses, raising questions for educarers as they plan programs for young children and families. For example, deciding the role that technology-enhanced toys and other technological media will have in the educare program, and predicting how experiences with those media may affect young children's knowledge construction is an issue that all educarers are facing. Research showing positive or negative effects of technology on young children's brain development will also be a factor in such decisions, as will concerns about greater "readiness" gaps occurring between children who have access to new learning technologies and those who do not. Educarers also have concerns about how infant mental health will be affected if media interaction is substituted for responsive human interaction. These are only some of the questions resulting from technological change that educarers and families will need to face.

Biophysical and Developmental Research

In the past 20 years, there has been an explosion of knowledge about infant and toddler brain development, capabilities for learning, and the need for integrated cognitive/social-emotional experiences. Some of this research has been due to advances in brain imaging techniques (PET scans; fMRIs), methods of measuring changes in brain chemicals (e.g., levels of cortisol), and the use of attention and other physical measures (e.g., brain electrical activity, heart rate changes) to measure the responses of nonverbal children to stimuli. This information has implications for educare and for curriculum planning by educarers. For example, evidence that spurts in brain growth correspond to stages of cognitive development, that early environmental experiences play a role in determining which synaptic pathways are strengthened, and that negative influences at sensitive periods of brain development (e.g., high stress levels, poor nutrition, prenatal drug use) may impair cognitive development, social-emotional functioning, and infant mental health may make society value high-quality family care and educare even more (see Bergen & Coscia, 2001). Developmental research supports a reconsideration of the capabilities of young children, making traditional content-specific definitions of curriculum outmoded. The brain works as an interconnected network of neurons, with experiential effects on some areas of the brain (e.g., those that regulate emotions) affecting functions of other areas (e.g., language, perception, cognition). Information about how complex cognitive processes (e.g., memory) function in infancy and how the child brain organizes and constructs knowledge from stimuli gained from diverse and repeated interactions with the physical and social environment promotes integrated curriculum approaches. Content areas such as mathematics involve physical and relational knowledge components (e.g., size, sequence, pattern), social knowledge components (e.g., arbitrary mathematical symbols), and integrative components (e.g., mental organization), all of which are needed to master mathematics (Jarrell, 1998; Whitton, 1998).

Literacy also crosses physical, social, and relational knowledge domains (Bordrova & Leong, 1998). Gestural communication, oral language, written language, and reading knowledge all begin to develop before age 3. They are interrelated and contribute to young children's overall literacy (Roskos, 1999). Young children also explore the physics of motion, space, and structure and the psychology of interpersonal interactions during their earliest years.

Evidence of how the brain learns appears to be contrary to methods advocated in some curricula that have been proposed for young children. Direct teaching of factual material to prepare for testing on learning standards is not an appropriate method for helping young children's brains develop optimally. Research findings support the redefinition of the type of curriculum advocated in early childhood, which views knowledge construction, social-emotional relationships, and play development as an integrated process.

Implications drawn from brain research could result in positive or negative effects for children, families, and educarers. For example, the increased knowledge base regarding brain development can be used to support the type of curriculum that educarers have intuitively deigned as most appropriate for infants and toddlers and to give them better ways to articulate what is developmentally appropriate. On the other hand, educarers may be bombarded by "brain-based" commercial curricula that inappropriately stress accelerated and adult-directed learning goals. Research emphasis on the importance of early brain development may support the importance of social-emotional and play development and infant mental health. It may revive appreciation for play as the appropriate integrating medium for young children's development and emphasize the great importance of good educare for all young children. Hopefully, it will not result in an even greater differential in educare program quality for children of low-income and higher-income families. These and other questions regarding the curriculum implications of current and future brain development research will need to be addressed by educarers.

GOVERNMENT POLICY CHANGES

Ultimately, the future of high-quality educare and the profession of the educarer rests on policies and practices of governments and the values promoted by the larger society. Although some policies affect all working parents (e.g., income-tax deductions), many policies particularly affect families at lower socioeconomic levels. In the late 20th century, government policy initiatives such as welfare reform, Early Head Start, and No Child Left Behind resulted in changes in the lives of families who use educare. As a report from one agency dedicated to providing maternal and child health care stated, "In the past two years, welfare reform has turned the lives of MCC's [the agency's] clients upside down" (Fischer & Rozenberg, 1999, p. 17), and although the agency workers saw some positive results, they also cited many problems. On the other hand, they viewed Early Head Start initiatives as "an important resource" for families who have to find work or continue their education. Educational policies related to No Child Left Behind at the state and federal level, such as those requiring content proficiency testing in primary grades, vouchers for private school attendance, outcome assessment for Head Start, publicly funded programs for 3- and 4-year-olds, and early learning standards for infants and toddlers, are having an impact on the curriculum for infants and toddlers in every type of educare program. Policies concerning educarer training requirements, accessibility, and recommended compensation levels also are affecting the expansion and quality of educare programs, because there is a relationship between staff higher education levels (college degrees), higher salaries, and quality educare (Cost, Quality, & Outcomes Study, 1999; National Institutes of Child Health and Human Development, 1999). Values of dominant and non-dominant cultures in the United States, as expressed in the position statements of organizations, media campaigns, and lobbying groups in local, state, and federal venues, also affect the future of children and families and their educare options.

There are opportunities for those concerned about legislation and agency policies that affect young children to have a voice in promoting high-quality educare, as the Head Start experience has demonstrated. (See Washington & Andrews, 1999, for explicit strategies used by groups that have been successful in effecting social change.) The question is whether educarers will join with other groups that are concerned about high-quality educare to attempt to influence government, business, and other societal policymakers, and whether they will stay involved long enough to have an effect on policies. If there is a sufficient number of advocates and a revenue base to sustain advocacy much can be accomplished. However, positive change will also depend on whether society as a whole is committed to creating a better future for families and children. Although educarers have primary control over the immediate curriculum of the educare program, exosystem and macrosystem factors such as those discussed here can make it easier or more difficult to have developmentally and culturally appropriate curriculum for infants and toddlers.

WORLD EVENTS

In the present "flat world" society, historical events occurring in other parts of the world also have the potential to affect the educare of very young children in the United States. One example is seen in the reports of mental health difficulties infants and toddlers are facing as they experience separation and loss because of family members' deployment in war. Other world events include genocide, terrorism, disease, starvation and natural disasters that destroy families and cause suffering for young children. Although these events may seem to occur far from the U.S. educare setting, there are many potential side effects of such chronosystem events. For example, practices by countries that affect global warming may have negative results on quality of life in other parts of the world. Even events that may seem benign, such as toy production in other parts of the world, have had potentially negative effects on infants and toddlers in the United States because of toy lead content. There will be many events in this century that will have effects on the educare of children in every part of the world. Although you may not have any direct influence on these events as an educarer, it is important to be aware of how such events may affect the young children with whom you work. You may also want to become engaged in civic actions that promote worldwide healthy environments for children.

Among the issues that educarers will face is how best to support families whose involvement in world events such as war is problematic for their young children's development. Educarers may need to find additional mental health resources to assist families in coping with these problems. Societal goals focused on improving environmental quality will greatly affect young children's healthy development but there may be conflicts with those concerned about economic profits. Perhaps educarers can join forces in a global movement to affect the future of young children positively. These examples show how educare is tied to conditions in the exosystem, macrosystem, and chronosystem, and demonstrate why it is important to understand how these conditions can influence children, families, and your educare program.

SUMMARY

Curriculum for this century must prepare young children to be part of a world that will require many kinds of knowledge. Educarers can provide an environment that is rich in opportunities for all young children to develop individual talents and skills, including those from every cultural, ethnic, and racial background and from every type of home environment. Factors outside of family and educare settings, such as demographic changes, technological advances, knowledge obtained from brain research, policies of governments, and events in other parts of the world will also affect the curriculum and quality of educare. You, along with other educarers, can have a voice in reordering societal priorities to ensure that every young child has access to high-quality educare, and to empower families to join forces to address the importance of excellent educare for infants and toddlers in the years ahead.

QUESTIONS FOR DISCUSSION

1. Why have advocates for young children and their families often had difficulty influencing exosystem and macrosystem factors to achieve policies that improve the quality of educare?
2. What can you do as an advocate of quality educare to shape future exosystem, macrosystem, and chronosystem trends and enhance the quality of educare for infants and toddlers, not only in the United States, but throughout the world?

Additional Resources

CURRICULUM REFERENCES

Dodge, D. T., Rudick, S., & Berke, K-L. (2006). *The creative curriculum for infants, toddlers and twos* (2nd Ed.). Washington, D.C: Teaching Strategies.

Gonzalez-Mena, J. & Widmeyer Eyer, D. (2003). *Infants, toddlers and caregivers: A curriculum of respectful, responsive care and education* (6th ed.). New York: McGraw Hill Higher Education.

Herr, J., & Swim, T. (2002). *Creative resources for infants and toddlers* (2nd ed.). Delmar Thomson Learning.

Herr, J., & Swim, T. (2003). *Rattle time, face to face (birth to 6 months)*. Albany, NY: Delmar Thomson.

Herr, J & Swim, T. (2003). *Making sounds, making music (7 to 12 months)*. Albany, NY: Delmar Thomson.

High/Scope UK. (1999) *The High/Scope approach for under threes*. U.S. Edition (Video). High Scope Reaerch Foundation, Ypsilanti, MI.

Lansky, V. (2001).*Games babies play: From birth to twelve months* (2nd ed.). New York: MJF Books.

Miller, K. (2004). *Simple steps: Developmental activities for infants, toddlers and twos*. Beltsville, MD: Gryphon House.

Miller, K. (2002).*Things to do with toddlers and twos* (2nd ed.). Chelsea, MA: Teleshare.

Raines, S., Miller, K., Curry-Rood, L., & Dobbs, K. (2002). *Story stretchers for infants, toddlers and twos: Experiences, activities and games for popular children's books*.

Silberg, J. (2002). *Games to play with toddlers*. Beltsville, MD: Gryphon House.

Silberg, J. (2002). *Games to play with two year olds*. Beltsville, MD: Gryphon House.

Silberg, J., & D'Argo, L. (2004). *Games to play with babies*. Beltsville, MD: Gryphon House.

Warren, J., & Gnojewski, C. (2001). *Playtime props for toddlers*. Beltsville, MD: Gryphon House.

Watson, L. D., & Swim. T. (2007). *Infants and toddlers: Curriculum and teaching* (6th ed.). Albany, NY: Delmar.

SOURCES ON DEVELOPMENT AND CARE

Ages and stages of child development. PowerPoint presentation. Learning Zone Express, Owatonna, MD.

Allen, K. E., & Marotz, L. R. (2006). *Developmental profiles, pre-birth through age twelve* (7th ed.). Albany, NY: Delmar.

Gonzalez-Mena, J.(2007). *Diversity in early care and education: Honoring differences* (5th ed.). New York: McGraw-Hill.

Gonzalez-Mena, J. (2007). *50 early childhood strategies for working and communicating with diverse families.* Upper Saddle, NJ: Pearson Merrill/Prentice Hall.

Greenspan, S. I. (1999). *Building healthy minds: The six experiences that create intelligence and emotional growth in babies and young children.* Cambridge, MA: Perseus Books.

Lally, J. R., Griffin, A., Fenichel, E., Segal, M. M., Szanton, E. S., & Weissbourd, B. (2003). *Caring for infants and toddlers in groups: Developmentally appropriate practice.* Arlington, VA: Zero to Three.

Mangione, P. (Ed.). (1995). *Infant toddler caregiving: A guide to culturally sensitive care.* Sacramento, CA : California Dept. of Education and WestEd.

Post, J., & Hohmann, M. (2000). *Tender care and early learning: Supporting infants and toddlers in child care settings.* Ypsilanti, MI: High Scope Educational Research Foundation.

Reid, R. (2005). Communicating with culturally diverse infants, toddlers and their familes. *ACEI: Focus on Infants and Toddlers, 18*(2), pp.5–8.

CHILDREN'S BOOKS AND RECORDINGS

Asian Dreamland (2006). Putamayo Kids. World Music Adventures (CD).

Bailey, D. & Huszar, S. (1999) *Families* (Talk-About Books series) Annick Press.

Boynton, S. (1995). *Moo, ba, la, la, la.* New York: Little Simon.

Brown, M. W. (1990). *The runaway bunny.* New York: Harper Festival.

Brown, M. W. (1991). *Goodnight moon.* New York: HarperFestival.

Carle, E. (1984). *The very busy spider.* New York: Philomel Books.

Carle, E. (1994). *The very hungry caterpillar board book.* New York: Philomel Books.

Del Rey, M. (1999) *Universe of Song* (Spanish and English). Music for Little People (CD)

Hill, E. (1993) *Where's Spot?* New York: Putnam.

Hill, E. (1993). *Spot's noisy walk.* Lincolnwood, IL: Lewis Weber.

Martin, B., Jr. (1992). *Brown bear, brown bear, what do you see?* New York: Henry Holt and Co.

Martin, B., Jr., & Carle, E. (1997). *Polar bear, polar bear, what do you hear?* New York: Henry Holt and Co.

Meyers, S. & Frazee, M. (2001). *Everywhere babies.* San Franicisco: Harcourt.

Intrater, R. G. (2002). *Peek-a-boo you!* New York: Scholastic.

Intrater, R. G. (2002). *Hugs and kisses.* New York: Scholastic.

Intrater, R. G. (2002). *Eat!* New York: Scholastic.

Raffi. (2006). *Quiet Time.* [CD] Doylestown, PA: Homeland Publ. Troubadour Records.

Scarry, R. (1997). *Richard Scarry's cars and trucks and things that go.* New York: Golden Books.

Sweet Honey in the Rock. (2000). [CD] *Still the same me. Burlington, MA:* Rounder Kids.

Under the green corn moon: Voices of native America—lullabies. (1998). [CD] Boulder, CO: Silver Wave Records.

Criteria for Setting Up Educare Programs

The following are suggestions for setting up educare programs for infants and toddlers. They should be used as a *guide,* not as *requirements,* for best practices. The specific application of these suggestions will vary based on your program, facility, state licensing requirements, budget, and other variables.

   1. Square Footage. Please note that all figures in this section are for "usable space." The term *usable space* does not include areas dedicated to diapering, toileting, food preparation, napping, and storage. Use the guidelines in Figure 2.2 for adult:child ratios that are appropriate for each age level.

   Birth–24 months: 400 square feet usable.
   18–36 months: 500–600 square feet usable.

   Older toddlers require more space due to expanded play interests, specifically dramatic play (housekeeping/dress-up area) and construction (block area).
   Mixed-age and parent-child groups: 600 square feet usable. Mixed-age groups require both safe spaces for infants and more challenging spaces for toddlers. For example, in addition to eight children and two educarers, parent-child groups have at least eight more adults in the classroom (see Appendix C).
   2. Indoor-Outdoor Relationship. A well-designed classroom provides direct access to the play yard. This *fundamental* component should be seriously considered when choosing a site or remodeling a facility.
   3. Cribs. Porta-crib–size (24 by 38 inches to 27 by 40 inches) cribs are recommended over full-size cribs. Cribs should be consolidated in one area of the classroom (1 to 3 feet apart), instead of spread around the room. This strategy provides more functional play space. Use low wall (30–34 inches in height) partitions or toy shelves, risers, and closed storage (base cabinets) to section off the area. Note: When space is limited, parent-child groups (3-hour or less programs) should consider reducing the number of cribs in the classroom.
   4. Diapering/Toilet Area. The diapering area and children's bathroom should be located in the room, separated through half-walls (42 inches in height) or cutout window openings. This reduces the educarers' need to leave the room numerous times daily, while providing for full visual supervision of children in the room.
   5. Pods. A pod design is where one large room is divided into two rooms through a combination of half-walls and full walls. The middle area is a shared area, usually including teacher support space for diapering, food preparation,

washer/dryer, teacher workspace, and storage. A pod design is less costly than two separate rooms, which require extra plumbing and square footage. It also allows for informal visiting of children and staff between rooms and easier transitions for infants moving up into a toddler room (see Appendix C, Figure C.2).

6. *Sinks.* Each classroom should have access to a sink adjacent to the food preparation area, a sink adjacent to the diapering area, and a child-height sink in the classroom for older infants and toddlers, as follows:

Age (months)	*Sink height*
0–18	16 inches
12–24	18 inches
18–30	20 inches
24–36	22 inches

7. *Windows.* Natural light enhances the quality of the room, and children need to feel connected with the natural environment. Although some windows (or doors) may be close to ground level, it is recommended that most windows in the room be at 26-inch height. This height allows infants who are able to pull themselves to a standing up position and older children to see outside, but it also provides the ability to create an activity area against the wall. Most infant/toddler play equipment (toy shelves, housekeeping equipment, and so forth) is approximately 24 to 26 inches high. Windows of this height provide the option of having a platform area for reading or playing with blocks, and also provide enough wall space for back support for children and adults.

8. *Windowsills, Protruding Walls, and Cabinets.* To prevent serious bumps and cuts, all counters, shelves, sills, corners, lips, ledges, and edges of built-ins and equipment that are at child height must have a minimum of a 1/4-inch radius (rounded corner).

9. *Doors.* When possible, doors should swing away from the children's play area (i.e., into the hallway instead of the classroom). This increases the amount of functional space and prevents accidents from doors opening into an infant. It is also useful to have windows in doors, at adult and child height. This will increase the amount of light into the classroom, warn adults who are going into the classroom that there are children on the other side, and provide an added space for children to observe comings and goings.

10. *Flooring.* Infants and toddlers spend much of their time on the floor. For safety as well as comfort, carpet the majority of the room, except the entrance, diapering area/bathroom, eating, and messy areas (water play, painting). Use low-pile neutral-colored (earth-tone) antimicrobial carpeting (which prevents the growth of fungus and mold). Use only rubber transition strips (metal creates a tripping hazard).

11. *Creating a Landscape.* Through the use of platforms, lofts, recessed areas, low walls, and canopies placed along the periphery of the room, it is possible to sculpt your room to create a variety of age-appropriate activity areas. The walls frame the activity areas, while the center of the room remains fairly open, to allow for the circulation of children and adults as well as to provide flexible space that

can change depending on the educarer's observations of children's interest. The same principles of placement apply to family educare settings (see Appendix C, Figures C.1 and C.2).

Low wall/platform guidelines:
Reading Platform: 5 by 5 feet to 6 by 6 feet.
Block Platform: 6 by 10 feet to 7 by 11 feet (60–80 square feet).
Low Wall: 26 inches high when not connected to a platform, 30 inches
    high when connected to a platform

12. Storage. A well-designed room has an adequate amount of easily accessible storage located in the room. In addition to storage closets and base cabinet storage, wall storage should be placed adjacent to each activity area. This provides educarers access to materials without leaving the children undersupervised. In addition, storage located on the walls does not infringe on children's play space, a critical element in most rooms that are smaller than ideal.

13. Color. Bright primary colors can be overstimulating in an educare environment. Walls painted an ivory-eggshell color and furniture constructed of natural wood create a cozy, neutral background that allows children to visually discriminate toys and pictures on the wall. Splashes of color and texture can be incorporated flexibly into the room through the use of wall quilts and fabric canopies.

14. Table and Chair Height Specs

Age (mos.)	Chair height	Table height	Table size
6–18	5.5 inches	12 inches	24 x 36 inches (seats 4)
9–24	6.5 inches	14 inches	24 x 36 inches (seats 4)
18–36	8 inches	16 inches	24 x 36 inches (seats 4) or 30 x 60 inches (seats 6)

15. Toy Shelves. These should be 24 inches high by 48 inches wide by 12 inches deep. Use all-wood shelving, with wood or white laminate backing (it is more attractive and shows off materials on the shelves more clearly). To prevent tipping, secure all shelves and cubbies to the floor, wall, and/or platform.

Source: Adapted from Torelli, L., & Durrett, C. (1998). *Landscapes for learning: Designing group care environments for infants, toddlers and two-year-olds.* With permission of the copyright holder, Torelli/Durrett, Inc.

Educare Spaces

FIGURE C.1 Family Educare Setting

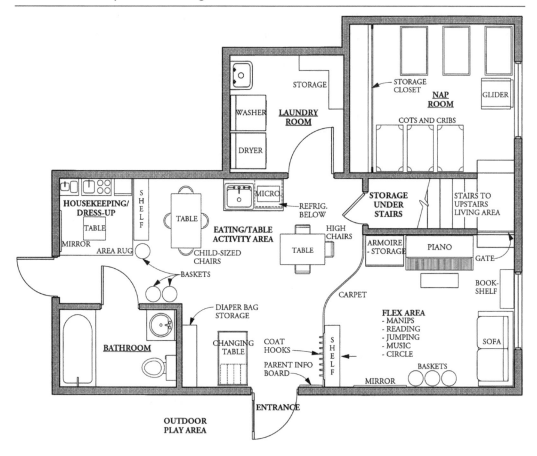

Family Educare Setting

Figure C.1 shows an infant and toddler educare setting on the ground level of a two-story home (in a one level home, this would probably be a family/living room, kitchen, and bath area). The size of space may vary as long as there are 50 square feet per child, with minimum of 350 square feet, not including bathroom or crib area. Families are welcome to observe or care for nursing needs within the setting. The layout of the space can adjust depending on the ages of the children in this multi-age setting. For example, water play and easel painting are accommodated in the table/sink area, and with the cots stacked and stored away, the nap room transforms into a block building and small vehicle area. The armoire storage unit provides an attractive way to have a large amount of storage that can be accessed easily. It can store the educare materials when children are not at educare so that the family of the educarer can use the rooms at those times. Outdoor play space into a fenced back yard is directly accessible.

Classroom

Figure C.2 (on the following page) shows an educare classroom for eight infants and toddlers (3–36 months). The entry area includes children's cubbies, parent sign-in and a cozy couch. Activity areas (reading, gross motor activity, dramatic play, construction) placed along the periphery help define the open, flexible area, which is used for "stage-set" activities and movement through the environment. The eating and wet play area (painting, water play) includes both child- and adult-height hand washing sinks. The nap room can accommodate cribs and cots. The teacher support area includes a sink, refrigerator, and stove for food preparation, along with a work station (laptop, file cabinet, shelves) for educarers. Meal preparation and note writing can be completed without leaving sight of the children. The diaper/toilet area includes a second child hand washing sink and a laundry area with a stackable washer/dryer. The lounge in this small center is used by teachers and parents. When not in use, the observation room can also be used for nursing or a private meeting.

Yard

The fenced outdoor play area shown in Figure C.3 (on page 195) is accessed directly from the educare room. Even though this yard is small (20 by 30 feet), it provides for a wide range of activity choices. Infants use the platform area around the tree for crawling and cruising. A play-kitchen is brought out for toddlers. The grass area is used for picnicking, jumping on air mattresses, using a pop-up tent for "camping," and many other types of "stage-set" experiences. Along with sand play, the yard includes a small area for dirt digging. Children love to sit up in the loft (only 28 inches high) and observe. Many of the traditional indoor activities can also occur outdoors in the porch area. The resilient, smooth area is used for eating, table activities, push and pull toys, vehicle riding, water play, painting, and chalk drawing. The yard also includes built-in benches, a storage area, and raised beds and large pots for gardening.

FIGURE C.2 Educare Pod Setting

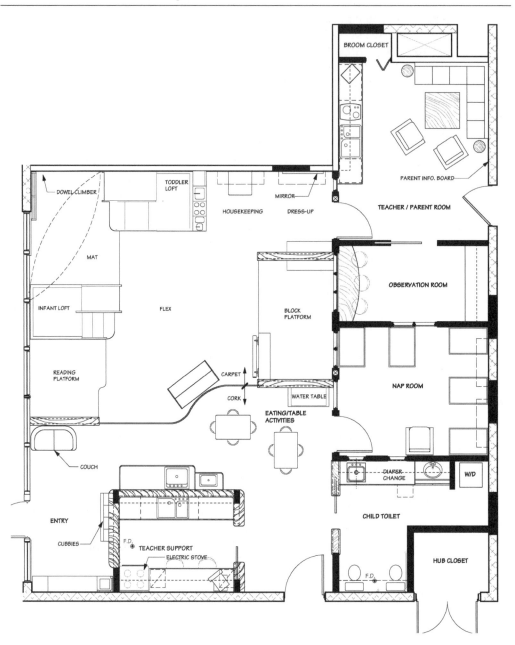

FIGURE C.3 Educare Play Yard Plan

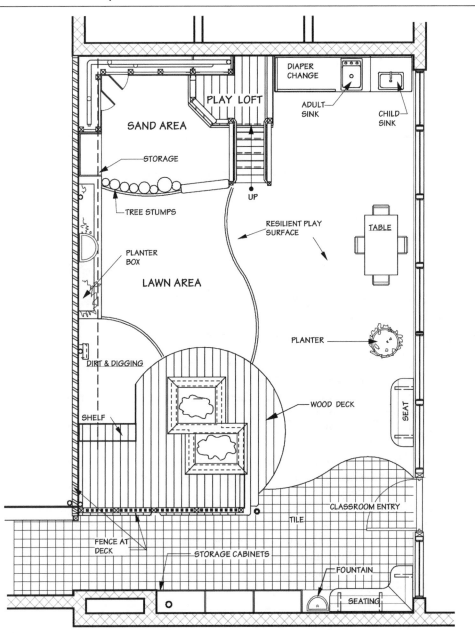

Family In-Take Questionnaire

INFANT/TODDLER CHILD-CARE ENROLLMENT FORM

Please answer the following questions to help us better serve you and your child.

Child's name: _____ Nickname(s): _____

Date of birth: _____ Location: _____

1. Names of household members; ages; relationship to child; persons primarily responsible for child care; how often?
2. What is primary language spoken at home? Other languages spoken at home; by whom?
3. How would you describe your child's ethnicity?
4. Are there special holidays your family celebrates?
5. How does your child express him/herself? Does he/she use gestures that would help us communicate with him/her?
6. What foods does your child like? Are there foods your child doesn't eat due to religious or personal beliefs?
7. If your child uses the toilet, how does he/she let you know when he/she needs to use it?
8. What are your child's napping and night time sleep patterns? Does he/she sleep alone? Does he/she use a blanket or other "lovey"? What techniques would help your child fall asleep in child care?
9. Does your child have difficulties being cared for by people other than family members?
10. What is your child's personality and emotional responsiveness like?
11. How do you discipline your child?
12. What are your goals for your child?
13. What is your reason for choosing educare?

Adapted from Mangione, P.L. (Ed.) (1995.) *Infant/toddler caregiving: A guide to culturally sensitive care* (pp. 86 – 94). San Francisco: California Department of Education and WestEd.

References

Ackerman, B.P., Abe, J.A., & Izard, C. E. (1998). Differential emotions theory and emotional development: Mindful of modularity In M.F. Mascolo and S. Griffin, (Eds.), *What develops in emotional development?* (pp. 85–106). Plenum, New York.

Adler, L. (1982). *Mother-toddler interaction: Content, style, and relations to symbolic development.* Unpublished doctoral dissertation, Rutgers University, New Brunswick, NJ.

Ainsworth, M. D. S. (1979). Infant-mother attachment. *American Psychologist, 34*, 932–937.

Allen, K. E., & Marotz, L. R. (1999). *Developmental profiles, pre-birth through eight* (3rd ed.). Albany, NY: Delmar.

American Public Health Association (APHA) and American Academy of Pediatrics (AAP). (1999). *Caring for our children: National standards, guidelines for health and safety in out-of-home child care.* Arlington, VA: National Center for Education in Maternal and Child Health.

Apple, P., Enders, S., & Wortham, S. (1998). Portfolio assessment for infants, toddlers, and preschoolers: Bridging the gap between data collection and individualized planning. In S. Wortham, A. Barbour, B. Desjean-Perrotta, P. Apple, & S. Enders (Eds.), *Portfolio assessment: A handbook for preschool and elementary educators* (pp. 31–44). Olney, MD: Association for Childhood Education International.

Bahrick, L. E., Hernandez-Reif, M., & Flom, R. (2005). The development of infant learning about specific face-voice relations. *Developmental Psychology, 41*(3), 541–552.

Bahrick, L. E., Netto, D., & Hernandez-Reif, M. (1998). Intermodal perception of adult and child faces and voices by infants. *Child Development, 69*(5), 1263–1278.

Bakerman-Kranenburg, M.J., Van Lizendoom, M. H., & Juffer, F. (2005). Disorganized infant attachment and preventive interventions: A review and meta-analysis. *Infant Mental health Journal, 26*(3), 191–216.

Baldwin, D. A., Markman, E. M., & Melartin, R. L. (1993). Infants' ability to draw inferences about nonobvious object properties: Evidence from exploratory play. *Child Development, 64*, 711–728.

Bandura, A. (1997). *Self efficacy: The exercise of control.* New York: W. H. Freeman.

Banks, M. S., & Ginsburg, A. P. (1985). Early visual preferences: A review and new theoretical treatment. In H. W. Reese (Ed.), *Advances in child development and behavior* (Vol. 19, pp. 207–246). New York: Academic Press.

Barr, R., & Hayne, H. (1999). Developmental changes in imitation from television during infancy. *Child Development, 70*(5), 1067–1081.

Barr, R., Rovee-Collier, C., & Campanella, J. (2005). Retrieval protracts deferred imitation by 6-month-olds. *Infancy, 7*(3), 263–283.

Bateson, G. (1956). The message "This is play." In B. Schaffner (Ed.), *Group process: Transactions of second conference* (pp. 145–241). New York: Josiah Macy, Jr. Foundation

Benasick, A. A. & Tallal, P. (2002). Infant discrimination of rapid auditory cures predicts later language impairment. *Behavioural Brain Research, 136*(1), 31-49.

Bennet, D. S., Bendersky, M., & Lewis, M. (2002). Facial expressivity at 4 months: A context by expression analysis. *Infancy, 3*(1), 97-113.

Bergen, D. (1994). *Assessment methods for infants and toddlers: Transdisciplinary team approaches.* New York: Teachers College Press.

Bergen, D. (Ed.). (1998). *Readings from play as a medium for learning and development.* Olney, MD: Association for Childhood Education International.

Bergen, D. (2001). Technology in the classroom: Learning in the robotic world: Active or reactive? *Childhood Education,78*(1), 249-250.

Bergen, D. (2006, July). *Laughing to learn: Parent-child play with a technology-enhanced toy.* Presented at the International Humor Conference, Copenhagen, Denmark

Bergen, D. & Coscia, J. (2001). *Brain research and childhood education; Implications for educators.* Olney, MD: Association for Childhood Education International.

Bergen, D., Gaynard, L., & Torelli, L. (1985). *The influence of the culture of an infant/toddler center on peer play behavior: Informant and observational perspectives.* Des Moines, IA: Midwest Association for the Education of Young Children. (ERIC Document Reproduction Service No. ED 257 580)

Bergen, D., & Mosley-Howard, S. (1994). Assessment perspectives for culturally diverse young children. In D. Bergen, *Assessment methods for infants and toddlers: Transdisciplinary team approaches* (pp. 190–206). New York: Teachers College Press.

Bergen, D., Smith, K., & O'Neil, S. (1988). Designing play environments for infants and toddlers. In D. Bergen (Ed.), *Play as a medium for learning and development.* Portsmouth, NH: Heinemann.

Black, M. M., Dubowitz, H., & Starr, R. (1999). African American fathers in low income, urban families: Development, behavior, and home environment of their three-year-old children. *Child Development, 70*(4), 967–978.

Bordrova, E., & Leong, D. J. (1998). Adult influences on play: The Vygotskian approach. In D. P. Fromberg & D. Bergen (Eds.), *Play from birth to twelve and beyond: Contexts, perspectives, and meanings* (pp. 277–282). New York: Garland.

Bowlby, J. (1969). *Attachment and loss: Vol. 1. Attachment.* New York: Basic Books.

Brazelton, T. B., Nugent, J. K., & Lester, B. M. (1987). Neonatal behavioral assessment scale. In J. D. Osofsky (Ed.),. *Handbook of infant development* (2nd ed., pp. 780–917). New York: John Wiley.

Bretherton, I., & Beeghly, M. (1989). Pretense: Acting "as if." In J. L. Lockman & N. L. Hazen (Eds.), *Action in social context: Perspectives on early development* (pp. 239–271). New York: Plenum.

Bronfenbrenner, U. (1993). The ecology of cognitive development: Research models and fugitive findings. In R. H. Wozniak & K. W. Fischer (Eds.), *Development in context* (pp. 3–44). Hillsdale, NJ: Erlbaum.

Bronfenbrenner, U. & Morris, P. A. (1998).The ecology of developmental process. In W. Damon (Series Ed.) & R. M. Lerner (Vol. Ed.), *Handbook of child psychology, Vol 1. Theoretical models of human development* (5th ed., pp. 993–1028). New York: Wiley.

Brown, A. M. (1990). Development of visual sensitivity to light and color vision in human infants: A critical review. *Vision Research, 30,* 1159–1188.

Bruner, J. S., & Sherwood, V. (1976). Peek-a-boo and the learning of rule structures. In J. S. Bruner, A. Jolly, & K. Sylva (Eds.), *Play: Its role in development and evolution* (pp. 277–285). New York: Basic Books.

Burtt, K. G., & Kalkstein, K. (1984). *Smart toys for babies from birth to two.* New York: Harper & Row.

Bus, A., Belsky, J., vanljzendoorn, M. H., & Crnic, K. (1997). Attachment and book-reading patterns: A study of mothers, fathers, and their toddlers. *Early Childhood Research Quarterly, 12,* 81–98.

Bushnell, E. W., & Boudreau, J. P. (1993). Motor development and the mind: The potential role of motor abilities as a determinant of aspects of perceptual development. *Child*

Development, 64, 1005–1021.

Caldwell, B. M. (1991). Educare: New product, new future. *Journal of Developmental and Behavioral Pediatrics, 12*(3), 199–205.

Carlson, E. A., & Sroufe, L. A. (1995). Contributions of attachment theory to developmental psychopathology. In D. Cicchetti & D. J. Cohen (Eds.), *Developmental psychopathology: Vol. 1: Theory and methods* (pp. 581–617). New York: Wiley.

Casasola, M. (2008). The development of infants' spatial categories. *Current Directions in Psychological Science, 17*(1), 21-30.

Catherwood, D., Crassini, B., & Freiberg, K. (1989). Infant response to stimuli of similar hue and dissimilar shape: Tracing the origins of the categorization of objects by hue. *Child Development, 60,* 752–762.

Chess, S., & Thomas, A. (1989). Temperament and its functional significance. In S. I. Greenspan & G. H. Pollock (Eds.), *The course of life* (Vol. II, pp. 163–228). Madison, CT: International Universities Press.

ChildStats.gov. (2004). Racial and ethnic composition: Percentage of U.S. children under age 18 by race and Hispanic origin, selected years. Retrieved June 27, 2005 from http:www.childstats.gov/ac2004/tables/pop3.asp.

Chomsky, N. (1976). *Reflections on language.* London: Temple Smith.

Chugani, H. T. (1995). The developing brain. In H. N. Wagner, Z. Szabo, & J. W. Buchanan (Eds.), *Principles of nuclear medicine* (pp. 483–491). Philadelphia: Saunders.

Chugani, H. T. (1997). Neuroimaging of developmental non-linearity and developmental pathologies. In R. W. Thatcher, G. R. Lyon, J. Rumsey, & N. Krasnegor (Eds.), *Developmental neuroimaging: Mapping the development of brain and behavior.* San Diego: Academic Press.

Cohen, D. H., Stern, V., & Balaban, N. (1997). *Observing and recording the behavior of young children* (4th ed.). New York: Teachers College Press.

Cornerstones Project. (1999). Change and challenge in infant/toddler child care: Perspectives from the Cornerstones Project. *Zero to Three, 19*(5), 10–15.

Cost, Quality, & Outcomes Study. (1999, March). Executive Summary. Available: www.fpq.unc.edu/~NCEDL/PAGES/cqurs.htm

Damon, W. (1988). *The moral child: Nurturing children's natural moral growth.* New York: The Free Press.

Daniel, J. E. (1998). A modern mother's place is wherever her children are: Facilitating infant and toddler mothers' transitions in child care. *Young Children, 53*(6), 4–12.

Dayus, B., Glenn, S., & Cunningham, C. (2000) Development of mastery motivation in infants with Down Syndrome. *Journal of Intellectual Disability Research, 44,* 258–259.

DeLoache, J. S., Pierroutsakos, S. L., Uttal, D. H., Rosengren, K. S., & Gottlieb, A. (1998). Grasping the nature of pictures. *Psychological Science, 9*(3), 205–210.

Derman-Sparks, L. (1988). *Anti-bias curriculum: Tools for empowering young children.* Washington, DC: National Association for the Education of Young Children.

Dodge, D. T., Rudick, S. & Berke, K-L. (2006) *The creative curriculum for infants, toddlers and twos* (2nd ed.). Washington, DC: Teaching Strategies.

Dombro, A. L., Coker, L. J., & Dodge, D. T. (1997). The creative curriculum for infants and toddlers. Washington, DC: Teaching Strategies (distributed by Gryphon House).

Dunn, J., & Dale, N. (1984). I a Daddy: 2-year-old's collaboration in joint pretend with sibling and with mother. In I. Bretherton (Ed.), *Symbolic play: The development of social understanding* (pp. 131–158). New York: Academic Press.

Elicker, J., Englund, M., & Sroufe, L. A. (1992). Predicting peer competence and peer relationships in childhood from early parent-child relationships. In R. D. Parke & G. W. Ladd (Eds.), *Family-peer relationships: Modes of linkage* (pp. 77–106). Hillsdale, NJ: Erlbaum.

Ensor, R. & Hughes, C., (2008). Content or connectedness: Mother-child talk and early social understanding. *Child Development, 70,*(1), 201–216.

Epstein, H. T. (1978). Growth spurts during brain development: Implications for educational policy and practice. In J. S. Chall & A. F. Mirsky (Eds.), *77th National Society for the Study of Education Yearbook: Education and the brain* (pp. 343–370). Chicago: University of Chicago Press.

Erikson, E. H. (1963). *Childhood and society* (2nd ed.) New York: Norton.

Farroni, T., Massaccesi, S., Menon, E., & Johnson, M. H. (2007). Direct gaze modulates face recognition in young infants. *Cognition, 102*(3), 396–404.

Farver, J. A., & Wimbarti, S. (1995). Paternal participation in toddlers' pretend play. *Social Development, 4*(1), 17–31.

Feinman, S. (1991). Bringing babies back into the social world. In M. Lewis & S. Feinman (Eds.), *Social influences and socialization in infancy* (pp. 281–326). (Genesis of Behavior, Vol. 6, Series Editors, M. Lewis & L. A. Rosenblum). New York: Plenum Press.

Feldman, R. (2007a) Parent-infant synchrony –the construction of shared timing, physiological precursors, developmental outcomes, and risk conditions. *Journal of Child Psychology & Psychiatry, 48*(3–4), 329–354.

Feldman, R. (2007b) Parent-infant synchrony: Biological foundations and developmental outcomes. *Current Directions in Psychological Science, 16*(6), 340–345.

Fenichel, E., Lurie-Hurvitz, E., & Griffin, A. (1999). Seizing the moment to build momentum for quality infant/toddler child care: Highlights of the Child Care Bureau and Head Start Bureau's National Leadership Forum on quality care for infants and toddlers. *Zero to Three, 19*(6), 3–17.

Fernald, A, Swingley, D., & Pinto, J.P. (2001). When half a word is enough: Infants can recognize spoken words using partial phonetic information. *Child Development, 2*(4), 1003–1013.

Fischer, J., & Rozenberg, C. (1999). The Maternity Care Coalition: Strategy for survival in the context of managed care and welfare reform. *Zero to Three, 19*(4), 14–19.

Floccia, C., Nazzi, T., & Bertoncini, J. (2000). Unfamiliar voice discrimination for short stimuli in newborns. *Developmental Science, 3*(2), 333-342.

Flynn, L. L., & Wilson, P. G. (1998). Partnerships with family members: What about fathers? *Young Exceptional Children, 2*(1), 21–28.

Fox, N. A., Kagan, J., & Weiskopf, F. (1979). The growth of memory during infancy. *Genetic Psychology Monographs, 99*, 91–130.

Fraga, L. (2007). Coming together around military families. *Zero to Three, 27*(6), 5–6.

Franklin, A., Pilling, M.,& Davies, I. (2004). The nature of infant color categorization: Evidence from eye movements on a target detection task. *Journal of Experimental Child Psychology, 91*(3), 227–248.

Gallagher, J. J., Rooney, R., & Campbell, S. (1999). Child care licensing regulations and child care quality in four states. *Early Childhood Research Quarterly, 14*(3), 313–333.

Garner, B P. & Bergen, D. (2006). Play development from birth to four. In D. P. Fromberg & D. Bergen, *Play from birth to twelve: Contexts, perspectives, and meanings* (2nd Ed.) (pp.13–20). New York: Routledge.

Gelman, S. A., Coley, J. D., Rosengren, K. S., Hartman, E., & Pappas, A. (1998). Beyond labeling: The role of maternal input in the acquisition of richly structured categories. *Monographs of the Society for Research in Child Development, 63* (1, Serial No. 253).

Gerber, M. (1991). *Resources for infant educarers.* Los Angeles: Resources for Infant Educarers.

Gerber, M., & Johnson, A. (1998). *Your self-confident baby: How to encourage your child's natural abilities from the very start.* New York: John Wiley.

Gilliam, W. S. (2006). *Prekindergarteners left behind: Expulsion rates in state prekindergarten systems.* New Haven: Yale University Child Study Center.

Ginsburg, K. R. (2007). The importance of play in promoting healthy child development and maintaining strong parent-child bonds. *Pediatrics, 119*(1), 182–191.

Glascoe, F. P. (1999). Communicating with parents. *Young Exceptional Children, 2*(4), 17–25.

Gonzalez-Mena, J. (1997). *Multicultural issues in child care* (2nd ed.). Mountain View, CA:

Mayfield Publishing.

Gonzalez-Mena, J. & Widmeyer Eyer, D. (2003). (6th ed.). *Infants, toddlers and caregivers: A curriculum of respectful, responsive care and education.* New York: McGraw Hill Higher Education.

Gordon, I. (1970). *Baby learning through baby play.* New York: St. Martin's Press.

Greenman, J. (2005). *Caring spaces, learning places: Children's environments that work.* Redmond, WA: Exchange Press.

Greenspan, S. (1999). *Building healthy minds: The six experiences that create intelligence and emotional growth in babies and young children.* Reading, MA: Perseus Books.

Greenspan, S., & Greenspan, N. T. (1985). *First feelings: Milestones in the emotional development of the child.* New York: Viking.

Greenspan, S. I. (1989). The development of the ego: Insights from clinical work with infants and young children. In S. I. Greenspan & G. H. Pollack (Eds.), *The course of life: Volume I Infancy* (pp. 85–164). Madison, CT: International University Press.

Gronlund, G. (2006). *Make early learning standards come alive.* St. Paul, MN: Readleaf Press

Grossmann, K., Grossmann, K. E., Fremmer-Bombik, E., Kindler, H., Scheuerer-Englisch, H., & Zimmermann, P. (2002). The uniqueness of the child-father attachment relationship: Fathers' sensitive and challenging play as a pivotal variable in a 16-year longitudinal study. *Social Development, 11*(3), 301–337.

Gunnar, M. R., & Nelson, C. A. (1994). Event-related potentials in year-old infants: Relations with emotionality and cortisol. *Child Development, 65,* 80–94.

Haight, W. L., Parke, R. D., & Black, J. E. (1997). Mothers' and fathers' beliefs about and spontaneous participation in their toddlers' pretend play. *Merrill-Palmer Quarterly, 43*(2), 271–290.

Harms, T., Cryer, D., & Clifford, R. M. (2006). *Infant/toddler environment rating scale.* New York: Teachers College Press.

Harwood, R. L., Schoelmerich, A., Schulze, P. A., & Gonzalez, Z. (1999). Cultural differences in maternal beliefs and behaviors: A study of middle-class Anglo and Puerto Rican mother-infant pairs in four everyday situations. *Child Development, 70*(4), 1005–1016.

Hebbeler, K., Wagner, M., Spiker, D., Scarborough, A., Simeonsson, R., & Collier, M. (2001). *A first look at the characteristics of children and families entering early intervention services.* Menlo Park, CA: SRI International.

Howell, K. W. (1979). *Evaluating exceptional children: A task analysis approach.* Columbus, OH: Merrill.

Hsu, H. C., Fogel, A., & Messinger, D. S. (2001). Infant non-distress vocalization during mother –infant face-to-face interaction: Factors associated with quantitative and qualitative differences. *Infant Behavior and Development, 24,* 107–128.

Im, J., Pariakian, R., & Sanchez, S. (2007). Understanding the influence of culture on caregiving practices. . . from the inside out. *Young Children, 62*(5),65–67.

International Reading Association (IRA)/National Association for the Education of Young Children (NAEYC). (1998). Learning to read and write: Developmentally appropriate practices for young children. Joint position statement. Washington, DC: National Association for the Education of Young Children.

Izard, C. (1980). The emergence of emotions and the development of consciousness in infancy. In J. M. Davidson & R. J. Davidson (Eds.), *The psychobiology of consciousness* (pp. 193–216). New York: Plenum Press.

Jarrell, R. H. (1998). Play and its influence on the development of young children's mathematical thinking. In D. P. Fromberg & D. Bergen (Eds.), *Play from birth to twelve and beyond: Contexts, perspectives, and meanings* (pp. 56–67). New York: Garland.

Jusczyk, P. W. (1995). Language acquisition: Speech sounds and phonological development. In J. L. Miller & P. D. Eimas (Eds.), *Handbook of perception and cognition: Vol. 11. Speech, language, and communication* (pp. 263–301). Orlando, FL: Academic Press.

Jusczyk, P. W., & Krumhansl, C. (1993). Pitch and rhythmic patterns affecting infants' sensitivity to musical phrase structure. *Journal of Experimental Psychology: Human Perception and Performance, 19,* 1–14.

Kamii, C., & DeVries, R. (1993). *Physical knowledge in preschool education.* New York: Teachers College Press. (Original work published 1978)

Kassow, D. A., & Dunst, C. J. (2005). Characteristics of parental sensitivity related to secure infant attachment. *Bridges, 3*(2), 1–9.

Kelley, S. A., Brownell, C. A., & Campbell, S. B. (2000). Mastery motivation and self-evaluative affect in toddlers: Longitudinal relations with maternal behavior. *Child Development, 71*(4), 1061–1071.

Kelly, J. F., & Booth, C. L. (1999). Child care for children with special needs: Issues and applications. *Infants and Young Children, 12*(1), 26–33.

Klebanov, P. K., Brooks-Gunn, J., McCarton, C., & McCormick, M. C. (1998). The contribution of neighborhood and family income to developmental test scores over the first three years of life. *Child Development, 69*(5), 1420–1436.

Kochanska, G., Tjebkes, T. L., & Forman, G. (1998). Children's emerging regulation of conduct: Restraint, compliance, and internalization from infancy to the second year. *Child Development, 69*(5), 1378–1389.

Kochanska, G., Akari, N., Prisco, T. R., & Adams, E. E. (2008). Mother-child and father-child mutually responsive orientation in the first 2 years and children's outcomes at preschool age: Mechanisms of influence. *Child Development, 79*(1), 30-44.

Lally, J. R. (1999). *Infants have their own curriculum: A responsive approach to curriculum and lesson planning for infants and toddlers. Headstart national training guide: Curriculum, a blueprint for action.* Washington, DC: Administration for Family, Children, and Youth.

Lally, J. R., Griffin, A., Fenichel, E., Segal, M. M., Szanton, E. S., & Weissbourd, B. (1995). *Caring for infants and toddlers in groups: Developmentally appropriate practice.* Arlington, VA: Zero to Three.

Lally, J.R., Mangione, P. L., & Greenwald, D. (2006). *Concepts for care; Essays on infant/toddler development and learning.* San Francisco, CA: Wested.

Levin, D. (2006). Play and violence: Understanding and responding effectively. In D. F. Fromberg & D. Bergen (Eds.) *Play from birth to twelve: Contexts, perspectives, and meanings* (2nd ed., pp.395–404). New York: Routledge.

Lewis, M., Sullivan, M. W., Stanger, C., & Weiss, M. (1989). Self development and self-conscious emotions. *Child Development, 60,* 146–156.

Lieberman, A. F. (2006). Working with traumatized young children in care and education settings. In J. R. Lally, P. L. Mangione, & D. Greenwald, *Concepts for care* (pp. 77–83). San Francisco: Wested.

Mangione, P. L. (Ed.). (1995). *In Infant-toddler caregiving: A guide to culturally sensitive care.* California Department of Education and WestEd.

Mangione, P. L. (Ed.). (1995). Appendix: Caregiver-parent information/resources forms. In Infant-toddler caregiving: A guide to culturally sensitive care. California Department of Education and WestEd.

Mangione, P.L. (2006). Creating responsive, reciprocal relationships with infants and toddlers. In J. R. Lally, P. L. Mangione, & D. Greenwald (Eds.), *Concepts for care* (pp. 25–30). San Francisco: WestEd.

McCall, R. (1974). Exploratory manipulation and play in the human infant. Monographs of the Society for Research in Child Development, 39 (2, Serial No. 155).

McElwain, N. L, & Booth-Laforce, C. (2006). Maternal sensitivity to infant distress and nondistress as predictors of infant-mother attachment security. *Journal of Family Psychology, 20*(2), 247–255.

McEwen, F., Happe, F., Bolton, P. Rijsdijk, F., Ronald, A., Dworzynski, K., & Plomin, R. (2007). Origins of individual differences in imitation: Links with language, pretend play, and socially insightful behavior in two-year-old twins. *Child Development, 78*(2), 474–492.

Mehrabian, A. (1976). *Public places and private spaces: The psychology of work, play, and living environments*. New York: Basic Books.

Meltzoff, A. N. (1988). Infant imitation and memory: Nine-month-old infants in immediate and deferred tests. *Child Development, 59*, 217–225.

Miller, P., & Garvey, C. (1984). Mother-baby role play: Its origins in social support. In I. Bretherton (Ed.), *Symbolic play: The development of social understanding* (pp. 101–130). New York: Academic Press.

Minde, K. (1998). The sleep of infants and why parents matter. *Zero to Three, 19*(2), 9–14.

National Association for the Education of Young Children. (NAEYC) (2005). Teacher-child ratios within size groups. Retrieved January 3, 2008 from http://www.naeyc.org/academy/criteria/teacher-child-rations.html

National Association for the Education of Young Children (NAEYC) Early Childhood Program Standards and Accreditation Criteria: The Mark of Quality in Early Childhood Education (2007). Washington, DC: National Association for the Education of Young Children. Retrieved December 2007 from http://www.naeyc.org/academy/NAEYCAccreditationCriteria.

National Child Care Information Center (2007). Selected State Early Learning Guidelines on the Web. Retrieved Dember 2007 from http://www.nccic.org/pubs/goodstart/elgwebsites.html.

National Institutes of Child Health and Human Development. (1999). NICHD Study of Early Child Care. Retrieved March 1999 from http://www.nichd.nih.gov/research/supported/setcyd/cfm

Nelson, K. (1973). Structure and strategy in learning to talk. *Monographs of the Society for Research in Child Development, 38*(1–2), 1–35.

Neuman, S. B. & Celano, D. (2001). Access to print in low-income and middle-income communities: An ecological study of four neighborhoods. *Reading Research Quarterly, 36*(1), 3–26.

Ogbu, J. (1981). The origins of human competence: A cultural-ecological perspective. *Child Development, 52*, 413–429.

Ogbu, J. (1988). Black education: A cultural-ecological perspective. In H. P. McAdoo (Ed.), *Black families* (pp. 169–184). Newbury Park, CA: Sage.

Ohio Commission on Dispute Resolution and Conflict Management. (1999). *Teaching skills of peace through children's literature*. Cleveland: Ursuline Academy.

Olds, A. R. (1998). Places of beauty. In D. Bergen (Ed.), *Readings from play as a medium for learning and development* (pp. 123–127). Olney, MD: Association for Childhood Education International.

O'Neill, M., Bard, K. A., Linnell, M., & Fluck, M. (2005). Maternal gestures with 20-month-old infants in two contexts. *Developmental Science, 8*(4), 352–359.

Outz, J. H. (1993). A changing population's call to action. *National Voter, 42*(4), 5–6.

Pawl, J. (2006). Infant mental health. In J. R. Lally, P. L. Mangione, & D. Greenwald, *Concepts for care*, (pp. 71–76) San Francisco: WestEd.

Pearson, B. Z. & Mangione, P. L. (2006). Nurturing very young children who experience more than one language. In J. R. Lally, P. L. Mangione, & D. Greenwald, *Concepts for care* (pp.31–40) San Francisco: WestEd.

Perry, B. D. (1994). Neurobiological sequelae of childhood trauma: PTSD in children. In M. M. Murburg (Ed.), *Catecholamine function in posttraumatic stress disorder: Emerging concepts* (pp. 233–256). Washington, DC: American Psychiatric Press.

Perry, B. D., Pollard, R. A., Blakley, T. L., Baker, W. L., & Vigilante, D. (1995). Childhood trauma, the neurobiology of adaptation, and "use-dependent" development of the brain: How "states" become "traits." *Infant Mental Health Journal, 259*(4), 271–291.

Perry, D. F., Dunne, M. C., McFadden, L., & Campbell, D. (2008). Reducing the risk for preschool expulsion: Mental health consultation for young children's challenging behaviors. *Journal of Child and Family Studies, 17*(1), 44–54.

Petitio, L. A., Molowka, S., Sergio, L. E., Levy, B., & Ostry, D. J.(2003). Baby hands that move to the rhythm of language: Hearing babies acquiring sign languages babble silently on the hands. *Cognition, 93*(1), 43–73.

Phillips, C. B. (1995). Culture: a process that empowers. In P. I. Mangione (Ed.), *In Infant-toddler caregiving: A guide to culturally sensitive care* (pp. 2–10). San Francisco: California Department of Education and WestEd.

Piaget, J. (1952). *The origins of intelligence in children.* New York: Free Press.

Piaget, J. (1962). *Play, dreams and imitation in childhood.* New York: Norton.

Porter, T. (1999). Infants and toddlers in kith and kin care: Findings from the informal care project. *Zero to Three, 19*(6), 27–35.

Random House Living Dictionary. (2000). Simon & Schuster New Millennium Encyclopedia and Home Reference Library [CD/On-line]. New York: Simon & Schuster. Retrieved from www.randomhouse.com

Rakoczy, H., Tomasello, M., & Striano, T. (2005). On tools and toys: How children learn to act on and pretend with "virgin objects." *Developmental Science, 8*(1), 57–73.

Reisland, N., & Snow, C. (1997). Maternal pitch height in ordinary and play situations. *Journal of Child Language, 23*(2), 269–278.

Roskos, K. (1999, October). *Reading, writing, research, and reality.* Presentation at Miami University, Oxford, OH.

Rovee-Collier, C. (1997). The development of infant memory. *Current Directions in Psychological Science, 8*(3), 80–85.

Rusher, A. S., Cross, D. R., & Ware, A. M. (2005). Infant and toddler play: Assessmetn of exploratory style and developmental level. *Early Childhood Research Quarterly, 10*(3), 297–315.

Ryalls, B. O., Gul, R. E., & Ryalls, K. R. (2000). Infant imitation of peer and adult models: Evidence for a peer model advantage. *Merrill-Palmer Quarterly, 46*(1),188–202.

Sahoo, S. K. (1998). Novelty and complexity in human infants' exploratory behavior. *Perceptual & Motor Skills, 86*(2), 698.

Schmuckler, M. A., & Fairhall, J. L. (2001). Visual-proprioceptive intermodal perceptionusing point light displays. *Child Development, 72*(4), 949–962.

Schore, A. N. (2001). The effects of early relational trauma on right brain development, affect regulation, and infant mental health. *Infant Mental Health Journal, 22*(1v2), 201–269

Sexton, D., Snyder, P., Sharpton, W. R., & Stricklin, S. (1993). Infants and toddlers with special needs and their families. Olney, MD: Association for Childhood Education International.

Shore, R. (1996). *Rethinking the brain: New insights into early development.* New York: Families and Work Institute.

Skouteris, H., McKenzie, B. E., & Day, R. H. (1992). Integration of sequential information for shape perception by infants: A developmental study. *Child Development, 63,* 1164–1176.

Solchany, J. (2007). Consequences of divorce in infancy: Three case studies of growth faltering. *Zero to Three, 27*(6), 34–41.

Spelke, E. S., Breinlinger, K., Macomber, J., & Jacobson, K. (1992). Origins of knowledge. *Psychological Review, 99,* 605–632.

Spence, M. J., & DeCasper, Q. J. (1987). Prenatal experience with low-frequency maternal voice sounds influences neonatal perception of maternal voice samples. *Infant Behavior and Development, 10,* 133–142.

Surbeck, E., & Kelley, M. (1991). Personalizing care with infants, toddlers, and families. Olney, MD: Association for Childhood Education.

Susedek, J. S. (1983). Fun and happiness in learning to read: A step by step method for teaching infants, toddlers, and preschoolers. Cambridge, OH: The Susedik Method.

Sutton-Smith, B. (1979). Epilogue: Play as performance. In B. Sutton-Smith (Ed.), *Play and learning* (pp. 295–322). New York: Gardner Press.

Swingley, D., & Aslin, R. N. (2000). Spoken word recognition and lexical representation in very young children. *Cognition, 76,* 147–166.

Tamis-LeMonda, C. S., Shannon, J. D., Cabrera, N. J., & Lamb, M. E. (2004). Fathers and mothers at play with their 2- and 3-year-olds: Contributions to language and cognitive development. *Child Development, 75*(6), 1806–1820.

Task Force on Education. (1990). *Education America: State strategies for achieving the national education goals.* Washington, DC: National Governors' Association.

Thomas, A., Chess, S., & Birch, H. G. (1997). The origin of personality. In R. Diessner (Ed.), *Sources: Notable selections in human development.* Guilford, CT: Dushkin/ McGraw-Hill. (Reprinted from Scientific American, 223, 102, 104–109)

Thomas, J. M. & Clark, R. (1998). Disruptive behavior in the very young child: Diagnostic classification: 0-3 guides identification of risk factors and relational interventions. *Infant Mental Health Journal, 19*(2), 229–244.

Thompson, R. (2007). Mothers' violence victimization and children's behavior problems: Examining the link. *American Journal of Orthopsychiatry, 77*(2), 306–315.

Thompson, R. A. (2006). Nurturing developing brains, minds, and hearts, In J. R. Lally, P. L. Mangione, & D. Greenwald, *Concepts for care* (pp. 47–54). San Francisco: WestEd.

Torelli, L., & Durrett, C. (1998). Landscapes for learning: Designing group care environments for infants, toddlers, and two-year-olds. Berkeley, CA: Spaces for Children.

United States Census Bureau, (2006). Population 2006. Retrieved, Jan. 3, 2008 from http://www.census.gov/prod/www/statistical-abstract-2001-2005/html

Uzguris, I., & Hunt, J. McV. (1974). *Assessment in infancy.* Urbana: University of Illinois Press.

Vygotsky, L. (1962). *Thought and language.* Cambridge, MA: MIT Press.

Wachs, T. A. (1985). Home stimulation and cognitive development. In C. C. Brown & W. Gottfried (Eds.), *Play interactions: The role of toys and parental involvement in children's development* (pp. 142–152). Skillman, NJ: Johnson & Johnson.

Wachs, T. A. (1993). Multidimensional correlates of individual variability in play and exploration. In M. H. Bornstein & A. W. O'Reilly (Eds.), *The role of play in the development of thought* (New Directions for Child Development series, Vol. 59, pp. 43–53). San Francisco: Jossey-Bass.

Washington, V., & Andrews, J. D. (Eds.). (1999). *Children of 2010.* Washington, DC: National Association for the Education of Young Children.

Whitehead, L. C., & Ginsberg, S. I. (1999). Creating a family-like atmosphere in child care settings: All the more difficult in large child care centers. *Young Children, 54*(2), 4–10.

Whitton, S. (1998). The playful ways of mathematicians' work. In D. P. Fromberg & D. Bergen (Eds.), *Play from birth to twelve and beyond: Contexts, perspectives, and meanings* (pp. 473–481). New York: Garland.

Widerstrom, A. H., Mowder, B. A., & Sandall, S. R. (1991). *At-risk and handicapped newborns and infants: Development, assessment, and intervention.* Englewood Cliffs, NJ: Prentice Hall.

Wolf, D., & Grollman, S. (1982). Style and sequence in early symbolic play. In M. Franklin & N. Smith (Eds.), *New directions in child development: Early symbolization* (No. 3, pp. 117–138). Hillsdale, NJ: Erlbaum.

Wood, B., Bruner, J. S., & Ross, G. (1976). The role of tutoring in problem solving. *Journal of Child Psychology and Psychiatry, 17,* 89–100.

Yeary, J. (2007). Operation parenting edge: Promoting resiliency through prevention. *Zero to Three, 27*(6), 7–12

Youngblade, L. M., & Dunn, J. (1996). Individual differences in young children's pretend play with mother and siblings: Links to relationships and understanding of other people's feelings and beliefs. *Child Development, 66*(5), 1472–1492.

Wolverton, B. C. (1997). *How to grow fresh air.* New York: Penguin.

Index

About the Authors

Doris Bergen, Ph.D., is a Distinguished Professor in the Department of Educational Psychology at Miami University, where she teaches human development, play development, assessment of young children, early intervention, and research methods. Her university scholarship and teaching span more than 30 years and have made her prominent internationally, as well as a designated university Distinguished Scholar. She is the author or editor of eight books, two of which have also been published in Chinese, and numerous refereed journal articles and book chapters. She has also served as the editor of the *Journal of Research in Childhood Education,* has been a preschool and elementary teacher, designed an infant and toddler university program, and served as president of the National Association of Early Childhood Teacher Educators. Her bachelor's degree is from Ohio State University, and her master's and doctoral degrees are from Michigan State University in educational psychology and child development.

Rebecca Reid, M.A.T., is a professor in the Early Childhood Division at the State University of New York, College of Agriculture and Technology at Cobleskill, where she has taught for the past 25 years. She has supervised practicum students in the college child care center and the campus laboratory nursery school. She also teaches a course on infants and toddlers. Her previous work experience includes serving as a co-director/head teacher in a toddler program, teaching elementary school, and working as a master teacher in the nursery school at the University of California at Davis. She has a Bachelor of Science degree in child development from San Diego State University and a Master of Arts in Teaching from Oakland University.

Louis Torelli, M.S. Ed., is a nationally recognized leader in infant/toddler child care design. Working in the early childhood field since the late 1970s, he began his career as an infant/toddler caregiver. Currently, he is a partner with architect Charles Durrett in the hcild care facility design firm Spaces for Children. A frequent speaker at conferences throughout the country, he consults regularly for child care centers and Early Head Start programs. He is on the faculty of the WestEd Program for Infant and Toddler Caregivers Training of Trainers Institute. He holds an undergraduate degree in early childhood education from Queens College and a graduate degree in infant and toddler development and behavior from Wheelock College.